SCORERS
VERSUS
GOALIES

SCORERS
VERSUS
GOALIES

FIREFLY BOOKS

A FIREFLY BOOK

Published by Firefly Books Ltd. 2020
Copyright © 2020 Firefly Books Ltd.
Text copyright © 2020 Hockey Hall of Fame
Photographs copyright © as listed on page 256

First printing

Publisher Cataloging-in-Publication Data (U.S.): 2020939889

A CIP record for this title is available from Library and Archives Canada

Published in the United States by
Firefly Books (U.S.) Inc.
P.O. Box 1338, Ellicott Station
Buffalo, New York 14205

Published in Canada by
Firefly Books Ltd.
50 Staples Avenue, Unit 1
Richmond Hill, Ontario L4B 0A7

Cover Design: Stacey Cho
Interior design: Sam Tse and Hartley Millson
Contributing Writers: Chris McDonell, Steve Milton, Mike Ryan, and Eric Zweig.
Statistical Research: Daniel Doyon

Printed in Canada

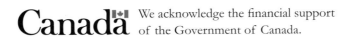

Canada We acknowledge the financial support of the Government of Canada.

CONTENTS

INTRODUCTION

BEST VS. BEST VS. BEST

WELCOME TO THE SHOWDOWN LIKE NO OTHER!
In the following pages, you'll find fascinating profiles and eye-opening statistics on the best scorers and goalies to ever play in the NHL. These athletes are the best-of-the-best as established by the Hockey Hall of Fame.

However, the Hall of Famers who made the cut in *Scorers Versus Goalies* are an exclusive group: the players who notched 500-or-more goals and the goalies in the Hall whose job it was to thwart them. Who was the first NHLer to score 500-or-more goals? None other than the imitable Maurice Richard. So, that's where our statistical comparison begins. (For good measure — and especially for those fans of pioneer hockey — we've also provided essays on the early-era scorers and goalies who forged the game but could never have imagined such a thing as a 500-goal scorer. (See pages 10 and 128, respectively.)

To see how the elite group of 59 modern-era NHLers (37 scorers and 22 goalies) stack up against each other, turn to page 216. It's a true best-vs-best-vs-best, as we uncover not only how each scorer and goalie fared against each other, but also how scorers fared against other scorers, and more. For a larger conversation on each star, enjoy the profiles on the scorers (page 18) and the goalies (page 128).

Let the debate over the best goal scorer and puck stopper begin!

Glenn Hall thwarts Frank Mahovlich in the 1960s.

PART 1

THE SCORERS

Early-Era Goal Scorers 10

18 MAURICE **RICHARD**	22 GORDIE **HOWE**	26 JEAN **BELIVEAU**	30 JOHNNY **BUCYK**	33 FRANK **MAHOVLICH**
36 BOBBY **HULL**	40 STAN **MIKITA**	44 PHIL **ESPOSITO**	48 GILBERT **PERREAULT**	50 MARCEL **DIONNE**
52 GUY **LAFLEUR**	55 LANNY **MCDONALD**	58 BRYAN **TROTTIER**	61 MIKE **BOSSY**	64 MIKE **GARTNER**

| 66 MICHEL GOULET | 68 WAYNE GRETZKY | 72 MARK MESSIER | 77 JARI KURRI | 79 DINO CICCARELLI |

| 80 RON FRANCIS | 82 DALE HAWERCHUK | 85 JOE MULLEN | 87 DAVE ANDREYCHUK | 89 STEVE YZERMAN |

| 92 MARIO LEMIEUX | 96 BRETT HULL | 100 JOE NIEUWENDYK | 103 LUC ROBITAILLE | 105 BRENDAN SHANAHAN | 108 MARK RECCHI |

| 110 JOE SAKIC | 114 MIKE MODANO | 117 MATS SUNDIN | 119 TEEMU SELANNE | 122 JAROME IGINLA | 124 MARIAN HOSSA |

EARLY-ERA GOAL SCORERS

by Eric Zweig

FROM THE BEGINNING, HOCKEY HAS ALWAYS BEEN ABOUT SCORING GOALS.

The Spalding *Ice Hockey and Ice Polo Guide* of 1898 may well be the earliest book written about the sport. Edited and compiled by J.A. Tuthill of the Montclair Athletic Club in Montclair, New Jersey, the book notes that the object of the game is simply "to drive the 'puck' between and through the opponent's goal posts."

One year later, future Hockey Hall of Famer Arthur Farrell wrote the first book on hockey published in Canada. He doesn't state them until chapter four, but Farrell's thoughts are exactly the same: "What is the objective point, the central idea, in the game of hockey? To score — to lift, slide, push or knock the puck through your opponent's goal."

Obviously, hockey's early-era stars played a different-looking game than the one we are familiar with today. With their equipment and training techniques, they couldn't skate like today's players or shoot like them either. It's just as hard to imagine early goaltenders lunging from post to post or sprawling to make saves — of course in the beginning, they couldn't, because the rules back then required them to remain on their feet at all times. Even as the rules loosened, acrobatic play was frowned upon. That was certainly an advantage for early-era scorers. Then again, the sticks they carried bore little resemblance to

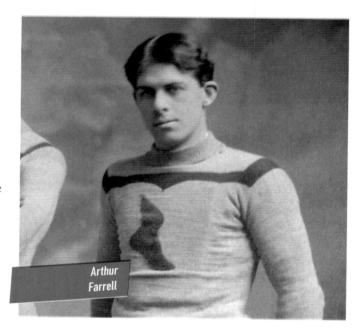

Arthur Farrell

the rocket-launching composite sticks of today. And of course at the start, there was no forward passing.

Still, there were plenty of goals being scored — and the fans loved it.

The 1890s and Early 1900s

This is Arthur Farrell's era. The game in those days was played with seven players on the ice, and yet teams from this time had very small rosters. Players were expected to play for a full 60 minutes. Substitutions were allowed only in the case of severe injury — and not always then. Being on the ice for the duration of the game certainly gave the top players more opportunities to score, as did the style of play.

The need to pace themselves meant players tended to stick to their positions. Imagine the rink as a table hockey game, with slots that allow players to go only so far. Defensemen usually confined their activities to trying to stop goals in their own end. Forwards didn't do much back-checking. As a result, they got most of the goals, with the center — because he played in the middle — usually getting the most of all. The extra player (the seventh), known as the rover, was generally free to roam the ice, helping out on defense and on offense too. The rover was often a team's most talented player and so would also score a lot of goals. And everyone agreed that scoring goals, not preventing them, was the whole point.

In his book, Farrell turns to some of the greats of the game (circa 1899) to discuss how each position is properly played. The section on forwards is written by Farrell's teammate Harry Trihey, captain of the Montreal Shamrocks, who had just concluded their first of two consecutive seasons as Stanley Cup champions.

"The essentials of a forward," writes Trihey, "are science, speed, coolness, endurance and stickhandling, which embraces shooting … Science and speed are exercised at all times during the game; coolness is essential, especially when a forward is near his opponent's goal; endurance is taxed in the second half of the match, and stickhandling is a necessary quality whenever the player has the puck."

When it came specifically to scoring, Trihey believed, "most goals are scored on a rush, not from a scrimmage, and for this reason it is advisable not to lose too much energy in tussling for the puck behind the goal line." He also felt "it is a mistake to attempt to score when too far removed from the goal or at too great an angle to the side." His key piece of advice was that "the most successful shot for the goal is a lift that raises the puck only as high as the goal-minder's knee." Clearly, not all of Trihey's advice holds true anymore.

He is, however, one of hockey's first great scoring stars. Trihey made his debut at the highest level of the game, playing a single contest with the Shamrocks in the Amateur Hockey Association of Canada in 1896–97. A year later he played the full eight-game season and scored 3 goals. In 1898–99, Trihey

Notable Early-Era Scorers

DAN BAIN

Led the Manitoba and Northwest Hockey Association in scoring for five straight seasons with the Winnipeg Victorias, from 1894–95 through 1898–99, and became the first player in hockey history to score a Stanley Cup–winning goal in overtime, in 1901.

TOMMY PHILLIPS

Led the Manitoba Hockey League in scoring for three straight seasons, from 1904–05 to 1906–07, and had all four goals in a 4–2 victory and three more in an 8–6 win as the Kenora Thistles swept the Montreal Wanderers to win the Stanley Cup in January 1907.

ERNIE RUSSELL

Led the Eastern Canada Amateur Hockey Association with 42 goals in just nine games for the Montreal Wanderers in the 10-game 1906–07 season and added 12 goals in five Stanley Cup games, likely making him hockey's first 50-goal scorer at the game's highest level.

MARTY WALSH

Ottawa Senators star led the Eastern Canada Hockey Association in scoring, with 42 goals in 12 games, in 1908–09. He also led the National Hockey Association in scoring, with either 35 or 37 goals in 16 games in 1910–11 and added 10 goals in a Stanley Cup game against Port Arthur on March 16, 1911.

DIDIER PITRE

Known as Cannonball for his powerful shot, he played hockey at the highest level from 1903–04 through 1922–23. Pitre led the International Hockey League with 41 goals in 22 games in 1905–06 and had 30 goals in 20 games for the Montreal Canadiens in the National Hockey Association in 1914–15.

CYCLONE TAYLOR

A high-scoring defenseman with the Ottawa Senators and Renfrew Millionaires in the east, he moved west and led the Pacific Coast Hockey Association in goals three times and points five times with the Vancouver Millionaires between 1912 and 1919, while playing as a center and rover.

broke out as hockey's best player, and the Shamrocks became the greatest team of the time. Trihey led the newly organized Canadian Amateur Hockey League (CAHL) with 19 goals in just seven games played that season. On February 4, 1899, he scored 10 goals in the Shamrocks' 13–4 victory over Quebec. No other player in hockey history has ever scored more goals in a regular season game in a league that competed for the Stanley Cup.

A year later Trihey led the CAHL in scoring again, and the Shamrocks repeated as Stanley Cup champions. In six Stanley Cup challenge games over those two seasons, Trihey had 15 goals. Even so, his biggest contributions to hockey can't be counted among his statistics. Trihey and his linemates (Farrell and another future Hall of Famer, Fred Scanlan) are said to have introduced new strategies to the game by passing the puck among themselves rather than relying on individual rushes. This so-called scientific approach or combination game was a revelation — even though at the time the Shamrocks could make only drop passes and cross-ice maneuvers, as forward passing hadn't yet been introduced. Before his final season as a player in 1900–01, Trihey also served on the committee that recommended the CAHL adopt goal nets rather than continue to use posts with no

mesh, as was the tradition at the time.

The CAHL also gave rise to scoring stars Russell "Dubbie" Bowie and Frank McGee. Bowie topped the CAHL in goals in four of five seasons from 1900–01 through 1904–05 and added another goal-scoring crown in the Eastern Canada Amateur Hockey Association in 1907–08. All told, Bowie scored 239 goals in just 80 games played with the Montreal Victorias in his 10 seasons at hockey's highest level. That's an average of nearly 3 goals per game! Many fans from his generation considered Bowie to be the greatest player they ever saw, and yet (perhaps because he won only one Stanley Cup series, in his rookie season of 1898–99) he is mostly forgotten today. But not every name from this early era is beyond recognition.

Like Bowie, Frank McGee averaged 3 goals per game in his career, although he played just four seasons at hockey's highest level. From 1902–03 through 1905–06, McGee played only 23 regular-season games but scored at least 68 goals (some sources say 71). In addition, his Ottawa Hockey Club — commonly referred to as the Silver Seven — held the Stanley Cup for nearly all of those four seasons, allowing McGee to take part in 22 playoff games, in which he recorded more than 60 goals (63 or 64

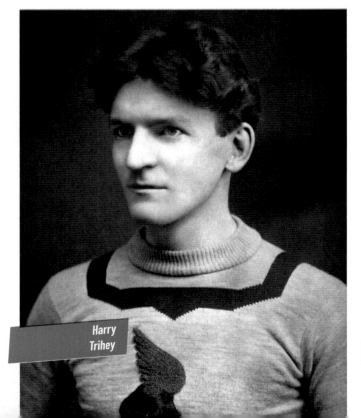

Harry Trihey

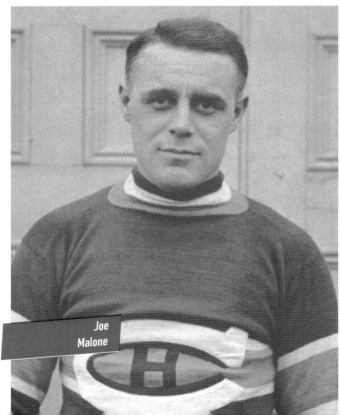

Joe Malone

depending on the source). Fourteen of McGee's goals came in a single game on January 16, 1905, when he led Ottawa to a 23–2 victory over Dawson City in a Stanley Cup challenge. His exploits are all the more amazing considering he'd suffered a severe loss of vision after taking a puck in the face during a game in 1900. One hundred years after losing his life in 1916 as a soldier in World War I, "One-Eyed Frank McGee" remains a hockey legend.

The NHL's First Scoring Star

Many fans have heard of Joe Malone. He's the player whose single-season NHL goal-scoring record was surpassed by Maurice "Rocket" Richard when the Rocket potted 50 goals in 50 games in 1944–45. Malone's record — 44 goals in just 20 games played with the Montreal Canadiens in 1917–18 — propelled him to mythical status, but Malone's reputation as a scorer was already well established.

Many early-era rules had already changed when Malone tore up the NHL in its debut season. The National Hockey Association (NHA, forerunner of the NHL) moved to three 20-minute periods instead of two 30-minute halves for its second season in 1910–11, and then dropped the rover in 1911–12. The rival Pacific Coast Hockey Association introduced forward passing in 1913–14 and allowed goalies to drop to the ice beginning in 1916–17. The NHL didn't follow through on that rule until midway through its inaugural season of 1917–18, and didn't introduce forward passing until 1918–19.

Malone's 44-goal season meant he scored at a clip of 2.20 goals per game, giving him the oldest unequaled mark in the *NHL Official Guide & Record Book* — and it's one that's not likely to be broken. The feat, however, was nothing out of the ordinary for the player known as Phantom Joe. Five years before the formation of the NHL, Malone led the NHA with 43 goals in 20 games for the Quebec Bulldogs in 1912–13. In that league's final season of 1916–17, he topped the circuit again, although Malone's 41 goals in 19 games actually tied him with Frank Nighbor of the Ottawa Senators. Returning to Quebec from Montreal in 1919–20, Malone led the NHL with 39 goals in 24 games, including 7 against the Toronto St. Pats on January 31, 1920,

Notable Early-Era Scorers

GORDON ROBERTS
Set a single-season record in the Pacific Coast Hockey Association with 43 goals in 23 games for the Stanley Cup–champion Seattle Metropolitans in 1916–17.

CY DENNENY
His 36 goals in 20 games in 1917–18 ranked second during the NHL's first season. He finished second in scoring four more times in the next eight years and led the league in 1922–23. His 248 goals were the most in NHL history when he retired in 1929.

HARRY "PUNCH" BROADBENT
Led the NHL with 32 goals and 46 points in 24 games in 1921–22 and set a record that still stands by scoring at least one goal in 16 consecutive games from December 21, 1921, to February 15, 1922.

BABE DYE
Led the NHL with 35 goals in 24 games in 1920–21, with 26 goals in 22 games in 1922–23 and with 38 goals in 29 games in 1924–25. His 9 goals in five games for the Toronto St. Pats in the 1922 Stanley Cup Final are the most ever by an NHL player in a Stanley Cup series.

BILL COOK
Led the Western Canadian Hockey League in scoring twice and later won two NHL scoring titles and three NHL goal-scoring crowns. He remains the NHL's oldest scoring leader with his victory in 1932–33 when he was 37 years, 5 months old.

CHARLIE CONACHER
Star of the Toronto Maple Leafs' Kid line with center Joe Primeau and left-winger Busher Jackson during the 1930s, he led or shared the NHL lead in goal scoring five times — a mark equaled or bested by only Maurice Richard, Gordie Howe, Bobby Hull, Phil Esposito and Alex Ovechkin.

and 6 against the Ottawa Senators on March 10. The seven-goal game is another of Malone's solo records that may never be broken, and yet he'd had better nights on two occasions earlier in his career. Malone scored nine times in a Stanley Cup game for Quebec on March 8, 1913, and had 8 goals against the Montreal Wanderers in the NHA on February 28, 1917.

In all, Malone scored a league-record 179 goals in 123 games in the NHA, 143 goals in 126 NHL games, and another 23 goals in leagues that predated both, giving him a total of 345 goals for his career (which, depending on sources, was either 276 or 280 regular-season games).

Montreal's Other Game Breaker

Joe Malone shared the ice with another goal-scoring maestro in the fierce Newsy Lalonde — the two were teammates for the NHL's first two seasons.

Suiting up in no fewer than nine leagues that were eligible (or attempted to challenge) for the Stanley Cup in the 23 years from 1904 to 1927, Lalonde played in 341 pro-league games and scored an amazing 449 goals. He won scoring titles (either goals or points or both) in the Ontario Professional Hockey League, the NHA (twice), the Pacific Coast Hockey Association, the NHL (twice) and the Western Canada Hockey League. He played for literally a dozen teams in his career, but Lalonde is most closely associated with the Montreal Canadiens, for whom he scored the first goal in franchise history on January 5, 1910. He remained with Montreal for all but one season through 1921–22.

Lalonde came from Cornwall, Ontario, and it's debatable how much French he actually spoke, but it was his speed and skill — along with teammates Jack Laviolette and Didier Pitre — that earned the Canadiens their Flying Frenchmen moniker back in the NHA.

In the words of Charles Coleman, whose three-volume set *The Trail of the Stanley Cup* in the 1960s was the first great work on early hockey, Lalonde was not just a great scorer but "a great fighter with a fiery temper [who] went after opponents, spectators and even teammates on occasion … A born leader, he was almost always the captain or playing manager of his team. There were no

Howie Morenz

desultory performances without incurring the whiplash of his tongue."

As would Maurice Richard a generation later, Lalonde drew a crowd. Coleman writes, "His followers turned out to cheer him, and others bought their way in to scream, 'Get Lalonde.'"

Newsy scored 9 goals in a game for the Renfrew Millionaires of the NHA on March 11, 1910, and had 8 for Toronto in the Ontario pro league on February 29, 1908. His three career six-goal games include the first one in NHL history on January 10, 1920. His mark of 5 goals in an NHL playoff game in Montreal's 6–3 win over Ottawa on March 1, 1919, has been tied by Maurice Richard, Darryl Sittler, Reggie Leach and Mario Lemieux but is yet to be broken.

The Torch Is Passed

Montreal's line of scoring stars was continued when Howie Morenz, the "Stratford Streak," joined the Canadiens in 1923–24, two seasons after Lalonde traveled west to play in the Western pro leagues.

It was around this time that changes were coming for the NHL. When the league first introduced forward passing in 1918–19, it was allowed only in

Nels
Stewart

signed his first contract during the summer of 1923, but under pressure to stay at home and continue his amateur career, he fretted about becoming a professional and losing his amateur status if he failed to make a good impression in the NHL.

He needn't have worried.

Known as the Stratford Streak for his skating skill (as well as the hometown in Ontario he'd been afraid to leave behind), Morenz combined blazing speed and tremendous agility to become the NHL's biggest offensive star. Playing center alongside left-winger Aurèle Joliat (who would be his linemate for most of his career), the rookie Morenz helped the Canadiens win the Stanley Cup in 1924. They won it again in 1930 and 1931. Morenz led the league in goals and points in 1927–28 and won a second scoring title in 1930–31, while also winning the Hart Trophy as MVP in both seasons. The following season he became the first player to win the Hart three times.

Though Morenz came from English-speaking Ontario, he was the darling of Montreal and the very epitome of the Flying Frenchmen. On March 17, 1932, Morenz picked up his 334th career point to become the NHL's all-time leader in points. His 249th career goal on December 23, 1933, made him the leading goal-scorer as well. However, injuries were beginning to slow him down, and after the 1933–34 season, Morenz was dealt to Chicago. He split the 1935–36 season between the Black Hawks and the New York Rangers but returned to Montreal the following year. Tragically, his career ended when he suffered a badly broken leg during a game on January 28, 1937. He died a few weeks later, on March 8, of a pulmonary embolism while still in hospital. Morenz's funeral was held on March 11, 1937, at center ice in the Montreal Forum. About twelve thousand people attended. Almost as many stood outside the building to pay tribute. Thousands more lined the streets en route to the cemetery in order to pay their last respects.

Morenz had scored 271 goals in his career, but during his final season of 1936–37, his NHL record was surpassed by Nels Stewart. Stewart had been born in Montreal but was raised in Toronto. He later played hockey in Cleveland for five seasons between 1920 and 1925, leading the U.S. Amateur Hockey Association in goals four times. He returned to the

the neutral zone. As the league grew — from a low of three teams playing just 18 games that year to ten teams playing 44 games in 1926–27 — rosters began to expand as well. Some star players (mostly defensemen, but a few forwards) were still playing close to 60 minutes a night, but many teams now rotated two forward lines. By the end of the decade, some clubs utilized three. Bigger rosters and better-rested players meant stronger defensive hockey, and offense began to decline. In 1928–29, Toronto's Ace Bailey led the NHL with just 22 goals in 44 games, while George Hainsworth of the Canadiens posted 22 shutouts and a 0.92 goals-against average. The NHL finally permitted forward passing everywhere on the ice the following season, and scoring predictably skyrocketed.

No one had scored 40 goals since Joe Malone's 44 in 1917–18. But in 1929–30, Boston's Cooney Weiland (43 goals), his teammate Dit Clapper (41 goals) and Montreal's Morenz (40 goals) hit the mark. All three were future members of the Hockey Hall of Fame, but only Morenz enjoys the mythic status of Frank McGee, Joe Malone and Newsy Lalonde.

Morenz initially had cold feet about the NHL. He

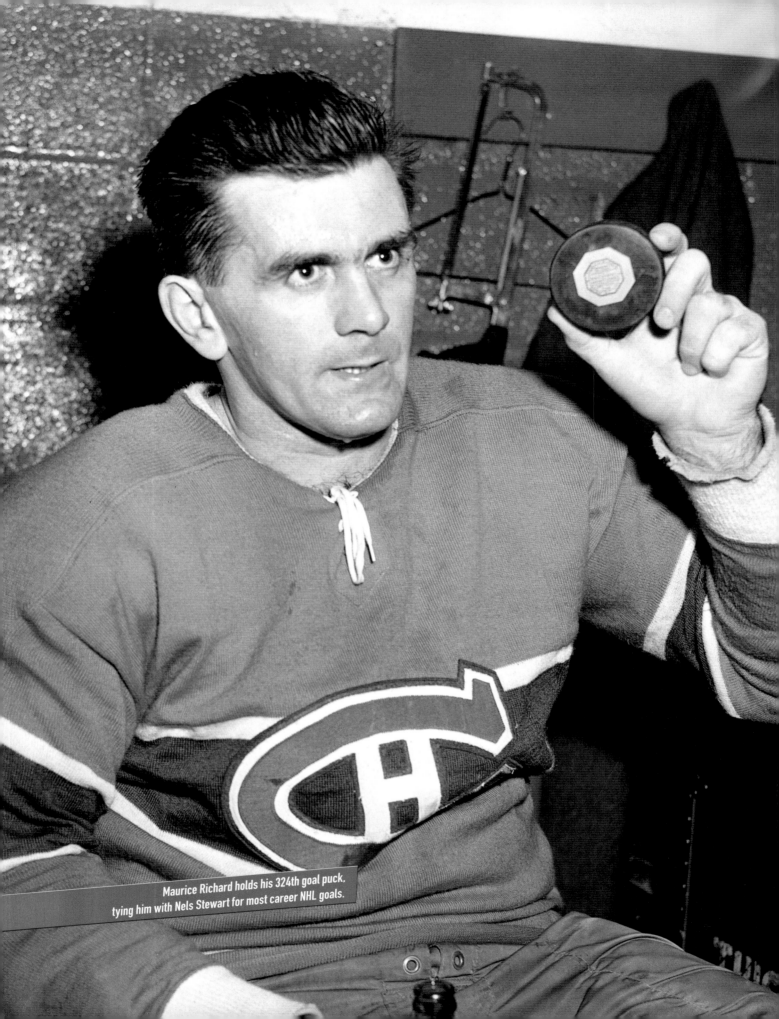

Maurice Richard holds his 324th goal puck, tying him with Nels Stewart for most career NHL goals.

city of his birth to play for the Montreal Maroons as an NHL rookie in 1925–26. Stewart led the league with 34 goals and 42 points during the 36-game season, earning the Hart Trophy as MVP and leading the Maroons to a Stanley Cup championship in just their second season in the league.

Stewart was nowhere near the speedy skater that Howie Morenz was, but the deadly accuracy of his shot earned him the nickname Old Poison. He played in the NHL until 1939–40, scoring a career-best 39 goals in the high-scoring season of 1929–30 and leading the league for a second time with 23 goals in 1936–37. In his 16 NHL seasons, Stewart finished among the top 10 in goals 13 times and ended his career with 324. He remained the league's career goal-scoring leader until being surpassed by Maurice Richard on November 8, 1952.

*   *   *

Maurice Richard had many admirers, but none so credible as the great Newsy Lalonde. The former Montreal goal-scorer remained a lifelong Canadiens fan. When, in 1942, he got his first look at the man who would one day pass him as hockey's goal-scoring champion, he could see the greatness in the player who would be called Rocket.

"He's the best rookie to show in a long time," Lalonde told Dink Carroll of the *Montreal Gazette* about Richard. "He's got hockey instinct and does everything right. Even when he falls down, he looks good … The boy's a natural. [His] timing is perfect."

Harry Trihey — who died in December 1942 — hadn't said anything about timing to Art Farrell in 1899. If he'd ever seen the Rocket in action, he might have.

Richard's timing, though, wasn't limited to his relentless pursuit of goals; he had timing in a theatrical sense too. His 325th NHL goal, the one that broke Nels Stewart's career NHL record, came exactly ten years to the day that Richard had scored his first NHL goal. From then on, every goal Richard scored set a new NHL record. His 400th came on December 18, 1954, against Chicago's Al Rollins — the same man he had beaten for goal number 325.

Entering the 1957–58 season, Richard was the oldest man in the NHL. By then he'd scored 493 career goals (sailing well past Lalonde's career professional goal tally of 449), and he notched 6 more in Montreal's first five games to reach 499. His 500th goal — again against Chicago — on October 19, 1957, set off a huge celebration at the Montreal Forum.

Though he'd play until 1960 and help Montreal win the Stanley Cup three more times, Maurice Richard's 500th goal was the last great moment of his career. Wayne Gretzky has pushed the NHL record to 894 goals, but the milestone Richard reached nearly 60 years ago — like his 50 goals in a single season — remains the benchmark against which all great scorers are measured.

MAURICE RICHARD

1943–1960

Setting the Gold Standard

THE PEOPLE OF MONTREAL HAVE LONG MEMORIES, ESPECIALLY WHEN IT COMES TO THEIR BELOVED CANADIENS, AND THE city and team are intertwined as in no other place. Maurice Richard is a pillar of the franchise's rich history, a working-class hero from the Bordeaux neighborhood in Montreal, who grew up playing in the local system. He registered under aliases so he could play on multiple teams at once, and on one he scored 133 of the team's 144 goals.

Richard joined the Canadiens in 1942 out of the Montreal Royals junior team but played only 16 games before breaking his leg. After wrist and ankle fractures in junior, which kept him from enlisting in the armed forces despite multiple attempts, some thought he might not be able to handle the physicality of the NHL.

But the league was decimated by World War II, and Richard earned a regular spot on the team. His fortitude would become a defining part of his legend.

In 1943, Richard was teamed with Toe Blake and Elmer Lach on the Punch line, and he scored 32 goals in 46 games — tops on the team and just behind the league leader. He had 12 more in nine playoff games, including 5 in a 5–1 win over the Toronto Maple Leafs, in which he was named first, second and third star, and the Canadiens ended a 13-year drought with the 1944 Stanley Cup. The legend of the Rocket was starting to form.

The following season on December 28, Richard skipped the morning skate because he was moving his family into a new apartment. Although most of the city would've been honored to lend a hand, Richard's blue-collar roots and work ethic, along with NHL wages at the time, meant he did the job himself.

Exhausted, he asked to be excused from the game, and he was not originally in the lineup. But play he did, and two minutes into the match against the Detroit Red Wings, Richard had his 1st goal. After a respite during the first intermission, he scored 2 more goals 8 seconds apart early in the second period, before adding another goal and his 2nd assist of the night before the end of the frame. It was 7–1 after two periods, and Richard had 6 points.

Halfway through the third, Richard scored his 5th goal of the night to tie a team and NHL record with 7 points in the game, and with just 13 seconds remaining, Lach redirected a Richard pass to make the score 9–2 and give Richard the new record of 8 points in one game. And Richard did it with a teammate's stick after breaking his own early in the game.

Richard had started slowly that season, with 9 goals in his first 28 games, but caught fire and surged past Joe Malone's NHL record of 44 goals in a single season. It was a record that had stood for 27 years.

In the second-last game of the season, referee King Clancy disallowed what would have been Richard's 50th of the season. So, in the 50th and final game of the 1944–45 season, Richard entered with 49 goals.

He stayed on 49 against the Boston Bruins for nearly the entire game. With 2:15 to play and the Bruins nursing a 2–1 lead, Richard finally broke free of the Bruins checking and beat goalie Harvey Bennett to become the first man with 50 goals in an NHL season.

Richard's feat instantly established the threshold for NHL scoring greatness and the magical number for goals in a season. It remains the gold standard for goal-scorers even now, when teams play 32 more games in a season.

According to Hall of Fame goalie Glenn Hall, who faced Richard as a member of the Red Wings and Black Hawks: "When he came flying towards you with the puck on his stick, his eyes were all lit up, flashing and gleaming like a pinball machine. It was terrifying."

Once the puck was in the net, however, Richard was the humble kid from Bordeaux, just doing the job he was paid to do — score goals.

"While the referee waits for the clamor to subside, Richard cruises solemnly in slow circles, somewhat embarrassed by the ovation, his normally expressive dark eyes fixed on the ice," said an article in *Sports Illustrated* in 1954. "The slow circles add up to a brief moment of uncoiling, one of the few he ever allows himself. He is a terribly intense man, forever driving

himself to come up to the almost impossible high standard of performance he sets."

The second 50-goal NHL season wouldn't happen for another 16 years. Former teammate Bernie Geoffrion did it in 70 games in 1961 — the year Richard was inducted into the Hall of Fame.

His record 8 points in a game stood for more than three decades, and it took 36 years until the next player had 50 goals in 50 games. Mike Bossy did it in 1980–81, the season before Wayne Gretzky scored 50 in 39 games to set the mark that still stands. Still only four players have averaged a goal per game in a season since Richard first did it in 1944–45.

Richard's records — and there were many, including most goals in a season, in the playoffs and in a career — would be broken, but no one would

represent a culture like Richard did, and no one would play the game with such flair.

"There are goals, and then there are Richard goals," said coach Irvin. "He doesn't get lucky goals. He can get to the puck and do things to it quicker than any man I've ever seen — even if he has to lug two defensemen with him. And his shots! They go in with such velocity that all of the net bulges."

Sports Illustrated, which rarely cast its eyes north of the border in Richard's day, called him the "Babe Ruth of hockey."

The article continues: "Because of his courage, his skill, and that magical uncultivatable quality, true magnetism, Richard has reigned in Montreal and throughout the province of Quebec as a hero whose hold on the public has no parallel in sport

today, unless it be the countrywide adoration that the people of Spain have from time to time heaped on their rare master matadors."

Richard was there to say goodbye when the Forum closed in 1996, one of his last public appearances before his death in 2000. The crowd stood and gave him an 11-minute ovation before he was even introduced. He brought them to their feet as he had in the same building half a century ago. They remembered his 544 career goals and the way he played in the post-season, when the stakes were highest — the 82 goals, seven hat tricks, 18 game-winners (six of them in overtime) and the eight Stanley Cups he brought home to Montreal, including five in a row to end his career.

And they hadn't forgotten the defining moments. Nights like December 28, 1944, and the 8 points, or the series-winning goal in Game 7 against the Bruins in 1952, as blood ran down his face after he was knocked unconscious.

Or March 17, 1955, when fans revolted after NHL commissioner Clarence Campbell suspended Richard for the remainder of the season and the duration of the playoffs for punching an official. The "Richard Riot" is seen as a catalyst in the Quiet Revolution — a surging of Quebec pride and nationalism in the 1950s and '60s.

The fans stopped only when he raised his hand to quiet them, tears welling in those dark eyes as he stood on Montreal ice one last time.

GORDIE HOWE

1947–1980

Breaking the Rocket's Record

MR. HOCKEY WAS MR. EVERYTHING FOR THE DETROIT RED WINGS, SO IT'S NO SURPRISE HE WAS KILLING A penalty when he became the NHL's all-time leading goal-scorer.

On October 27, 1963, Gordie Howe scored the 544th goal of his career, against Gump Worsley in a 6–4 loss to the Canadiens. In doing so, he tied the record set by Maurice "Rocket" Richard — the man Howe knocked out with one punch the first time he played the Canadiens in Montreal — who had retired three years earlier.

But then Howe went cold, going five games without a goal.

"Looking back at the chase for number 545, I know now that I was far too deep into my own head," wrote Howe in his autobiography *Mr. Hockey.* "As the slump went on, I started thinking about all the things I knew about putting the puck in the net. I even thought back to playing goalie as a kid."

Howe was the sixth of nine children growing up on a farm in Saskatchewan. He started his hockey career in net before moving up to defense and finally to forward. At 15 he tried out for the New York Rangers but left camp early because he was homesick.

A year later he made an impression on Detroit coach and general manager Jack Adams in a tryout with the Red Wings in Windsor, Ontario. Impressed with Howe's ambidexterity — he scored a goal

shooting left and another from the right side — Adams signed him, and two years later in 1946, Howe made his NHL debut.

After his first NHL game, the *Detroit News* wrote: "Gordon Howe is the squad's baby, 18 years old. But he was one of Detroit's most valuable men last night. In his first major league game, he scored a goal, skated tirelessly and had perfect poise. The goal came when he literally powered his way through the players from the blue line to the goalmouth."

That power was a sign of things to come — Howe elbowed his way to the top as one of the toughest players of his era — but the goal wasn't. He scored

just seven times in his first season and had only 35 goals in his first three years in the league.

In his first All-Star Game, in 1948, Howe got a five-minute penalty for fighting. Once he learned to stay out of the penalty box, however, he managed at least 20 goals every season for the next three decades.

In 1949–50, the Production line of Howe, Sid Abel and Ted Lindsay claimed the top three spots in the NHL scoring race. Against the Toronto Maple Leafs in the first game of the playoffs that year, Howe missed a check on Ted Kennedy and crashed head-first into the boards. Unconscious with a

fractured skull, he was rushed to the hospital, where a doctor drilled into his skull to relieve the pressure.

He was in critical condition and was told he'd never play again, but the following season, with a soft spot on his head and a facial tic, Howe led the NHL with 86 points — 20 more than runner-up Richard. His 43 goals were one more than Richard's and earned him the first of five goal-scoring titles.

By 1963 — in his 18th season — Howe had more points (1,220) and assists (676) than anyone in NHL history, and he was bearing down on Richard's goal-scoring record when he started to overthink and lose sight of his game.

"What I wasn't doing at the time, though, was remembering to see what the puck sees," said Howe. "Doing that allows you to simply take what's given to you. That's how I got number 545."

On November 10 the Red Wings were playing the Canadiens again, and at 15:06 of the second period, Howe took a pass from Billy McNeill and beat goalie Charlie Hodge low between the post and his right pad for a shorthanded goal.

"All I remember is the puck going plunk," said Howe after the 3–0 win. "Now I can start enjoying life again."

The biggest crowd of the year at the Olympia — 15,027, with 3,000 more turned away at the gate — gave Howe an ovation that lasted more than 10 minutes.

"I don't know what felt better: the outpouring of appreciation from thousands of fans or the relief of getting the monkey off my back. Either way it was a moment I'll never forget. With the big goal out of the way, I also knew my teammates would stop walking on eggshells around me. They'd been treating me like I was a starting pitcher going for a no-hitter."

Howe wasn't close to finished. In 1969 he scored his 715th goal, which was newsworthy in the United States because he had surpassed Babe Ruth's home run total. When he retired for the first time in 1971, after 25 seasons in Detroit, the runners-up on the all-time scoring list were far behind in his rearview mirror. His 786 goals were 232 more than Bobby Hull, his 1,023 assists were 300 ahead of Alex Delvecchio, and with 1,809 points, he had a whopping 590 more than Jean Béliveau.

Writer Mordecai Richler called Howe "the man for whom time had stopped," and the ageless wonder returned with the Houston Aeros of the World Hockey Association (WHA) in 1973 so he could play with sons Mark and Marty. In 1974 at the age of 46, he led the WHA in scoring, with 100 points, and was named league MVP.

After the WHA merged with the NHL in 1979, the 51-year-old Howe played all 80 games for the Hartford Whalers before retiring for good in 1980. "This man could run up Mount Everest," the team cardiologist said before the right-winger's final season.

Howe was in the top 5 in NHL scoring in 20 straight seasons (1949–50 through 1968–69), was named to the first All-Star Team 12 times and to the Second Team nine more, and he won six Art Ross Trophies, six Hart Trophies and four Stanley Cups.

Howe's final NHL tally was 1,767 games played, 801 goals scored and 1,850 points — not to mention 1,685 penalty minutes — in a career that started the year after World War II ended.

Named to the 1980 All-Star Game in Detroit by coach Scotty Bowman, 32 years after his first All-Star Game, Howe played against 19-year-old rookie Wayne Gretzky. The kid who grew up idolizing Howe would eventually break his record for goals.

"As much as I enjoyed holding down the top spot, I knew it wouldn't last forever," wrote Howe in *Mr. Hockey*.

"You don't get called 'the Great One' unless you're something special, and Wayne, it goes without saying, was a once-in-a-generation talent. Watching his artistry on the ice was a treat for everyone who loves the game of hockey. If anyone had to bump me down the ladder, I'm happy that it was him. As I've always said since then, the way I see it, the record is in good hands."

The NHL record, at least. With their WHA tallies included, Howe had 975 goals to Gretzky's 931.

It's a record that may last forever — just as the career of the tireless skater, who on some nights played 45 minutes, seemed to do.

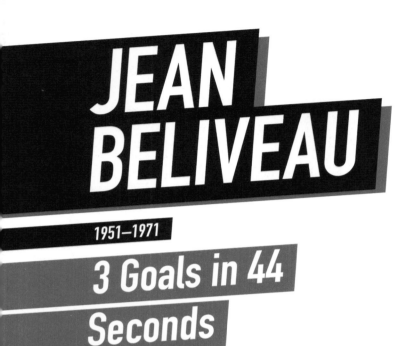

JEAN BÉLIVEAU

1951–1971

3 Goals in 44 Seconds

L EGEND HAS IT THAT THE MONTREAL CANADIENS WERE SO EN- AMORED WITH JEAN BÉLIVEAU THAT THEY BOUGHT THE ENTIRE Quebec Senior Hockey League (QSHL) to get him into the team's famed sainte-flanelle.

Béliveau was playing for the Quebec Aces, and he was fiercely loyal to his team. And although the QSHL was officially an amateur league, between playing hockey and doing promotional work for local businesses, Béliveau was earning more than anyone in the NHL. But in May of 1953, the Quebec league voted to turn pro. The question of Montreal's pur- chasing the league is the debate of hockey scholars, as is the Canadiens' influence on the QSHL's vote; however, what isn't disputed is that Montreal owned Béliveau's professional rights. Playing for the Aces was no longer an option, and in October he signed a five-year contract with Montreal. Béliveau's arrival altered the course of the franchise, and three years later it would change the rules of the NHL.

The elegant Béliveau, who scored his first NHL hat trick in 1952 while on a three-game tryout, was a contrast and complement to the fury and fire of Canadiens star Maurice "Rocket" Richard.

"He is a perfect coach's hockey player because he studies and learns," said Canadiens general manager Frank Selke of Béliveau. "He's moving and planning all the time, thinking out the play required for each situation. A perfectionist."

That meticulousness explains why Béliveau wasn't happy in November 1955, even though the Cana- diens were in first place and he had 14 points in the team's first 12 games.

"I don't think I was ever so discouraged as I was at the start of the 1955–56 season," said Béliveau in Andy O'Brien's book *Fire-Wagon Hockey.* "I must have hit fifteen goal posts before Toe Blake told me to start shooting at the net, rather than at a particular spot, until I broke my slump. Sure enough, a couple did, and I did all right."

Playing the Boston Bruins on a Saturday night at the Montreal Forum, Béliveau was more than all right. His second career hat trick was historic and game changing.

The Bruins were up 2–0 on goals by Leo Boivin and Doug Mohns when Boston's Cal Gardner was penalized with 10 seconds left in the first period. Just 16 seconds into the second period, Hal Laycoe joined Gardner in the penalty box to put the Canadiens up two men.

First-year coach Blake wisely sent out defensemen Doug Harvey and Tom Johnson with his all-world forward line of Béliveau, Richard and Bert Olmstead.

At 42 seconds of the second period, Béliveau redirected a pass from Olmstead behind goalie Terry Sawchuk to make it 2–1. Just 26 seconds later the two combined for Béliveau's 2nd to tie the game, and

moments after that he had his 3rd goal of the power play, and the Habs had a 3–2 lead.

At 44 seconds it was the fastest hat trick in Canadiens history and second fastest in NHL history, after the Chicago Black Hawks' Bill Mosienko, who scored 3 in 21 seconds in 1952.

Olmstead had 3 assists on the power play and added another as Béliveau scored his 4th goal of the night — at even strength — in the third period as Montreal went on to win, 4–2. It was the first of Béliveau's three career four-goal games.

Playing the Bruins again a day later, Béliveau scored a 5th goal in a 3–3 tie. The weekend tear put him on top of the league with 19 points.

By season's end, Béliveau had 47 goals and 88 points in 70 games to win the Art Ross and Hart Trophies. He added 12 goals in 10 playoff games as Montreal lifted the first of five straight Stanley Cups in 1956.

Less heralded were Béliveau's 143 penalty minutes in 1955–56, good for third in the NHL. Though he was known to play with class and respect, when opponents took liberties with the 6-foot-3, 205-pound superstar, he knew how to take care of himself and earn his space.

"He had size, strength, reach. He could really shoot the puck, and he was tougher than you might remember. If you got close to him, you got a cross-check," recalled teammate Dick Duff after Béliveau died in 2014. "It was a treat to play with him, a treat to watch him play. And he had time for everybody. No matter who it was. No matter what the situation was.

Jean Béliveau receives the Hart Trophy from Gordie Howe.

"He was a statesman for us. If there was some-one to meet, he met them. If the prime minister came into our room, it was Jean who spoke to him. He could handle any situation. He could have been governor general and turned that down. I think he would have been perfect for that job."

On February 11, 1971, at the Forum, 39-year-old Béliveau had the 18th and last hat trick of his career, also becoming the fourth player in NHL history to reach 500 goals, after Richard, Gordie Howe and Bobby Hull.

His milestone goal was scored against rookie goaltender Gilles Gilbert of the Minnesota North Stars. After the game he sought out Gilbert, who was standing with his parents in the Forum concourse.

"He came up to me and, almost apologetically, told me that, it didn't matter who would have been in net tonight, it was a night where everything went his way," remembered Gilbert. "He told me that I would have a long and successful career in the NHL, gave me his hand and left. It's special. I don't think anybody else would have done that."

At the end of the 1970–71 season, Béliveau had 507 career goals, and he capped his final season with the 10th Stanley Cup of his career and fifth as captain of the Canadiens. After receiving the Cup in Chicago, he lifted it over his head and took it for a victory lap, knowing it was his last as a player. That sort of celebration is now a tradition.

"I am not merely celebrating the Canadiens' triumph," said Béliveau of his trip around the ice. "I am celebrating the superb game of ice hockey and what it means to all of us."

Béliveau was part of seven more titles as a member of the Canadiens' front office. His name is engraved on the Cup a record 17 times.

Béliveau also had a lasting impact on the NHL rulebook. Back in 1955–56, the Canadiens scored multiple goals on a single power play eight times, including Béliveau's 44-second power-play hat trick on November 5.

In January 1956 at the urging of rival general managers, NHL president Clarence Campbell discussed allowing penalized players to return to the ice after a power-play goal instead of serving the entire two minutes regardless of how many goals were scored. At the 39th annual board of governors meeting in June, he officially introduced Rule 26(c), known colloquially as "the Canadiens Rule." It stated: "If while a team is 'shorthanded' by one or more minor or bench minor penalties, the opposing team scores a goal, the first of such penalties shall automatically terminate."

The six teams voted 5–1 in favor of the rule change. The lone dissenting vote came from Montreal. When it was suggested to NHL GMs that the Montreal power play was the impetus for the change, Boston's Lynn Patrick responded, "That's nonsense."

Montreal's Selke, though, wasn't so sure. "You might outvote me on that one. But you'll never convince me of its justice. In all the years of Detroit's dominance and their almighty power play, there was no suggestion of such a change. Now Canadiens have finally built one, and you want to introduce a rule to weaken it …

"Go get a power play of your own."

JOHNNY BUCYK

1956–1978

Clearing the Runway for Orr to Take Flight

I T'S ONE OF THE MOST ENDURING IMAGES IN HOCKEY HISTORY: BOBBY ORR, THE MAN WHO ALTERED THE COURSE OF THE Boston Bruins and the game of hockey itself, flying through the air after being tripped by St. Louis Blues defenseman Noel Picard. Just moments before he took flight, Orr had scored the overtime goal that gave the Bruins their first Stanley Cup championship in 29 years.

But the game had gone into overtime only because the vastly underrated Johnny Bucyk tipped in John McKenzie's shot at 13:28 of the third period to tie the score at 3.

When Orr arrived in the fall of 1966, the Bruins' prospects changed immediately, although they would finish last in his rookie season. For Bucyk, 1966–67 was the eighth straight season in which he'd missed the playoffs with the Bruins. For many of those years, the large left-winger with the reputation for clean play was one of the only reasons to watch the moribund Bruins.

It was a symbol of continuity and hard work that the second-most important Bruins goal in four decades would come from the man who had been the heart of the franchise for 13 years. Bucyk had set up his more famous teammates for goals and scored more than anyone cared to notice, all while playing third fiddle among NHL left-wingers to Bobby Hull and Frank Mahovlich.

He had been to the Stanley Cup Final only twice before; the most recent was a six-game loss to the dynastic Montreal Canadiens in the spring of 1958, his first year in Boston.

"I had waited a dozen years for that moment, and I was going to enjoy it," Bucyk recalled of hoisting the Stanley Cup for the first time. The Bruins didn't have an official captain in 1969–70, but Bucyk's teammates made sure he was the one to lift the Cup before anyone else, because of what he'd meant to the franchise and the horrible years he'd endured with class and humility before the Bruins finally reached the top.

Bucyk had been captain in Orr's rookie season, succeeding Leo Boivin, but he and coach Harry Sinden thought it might be better to spread the

leadership chores around. So for six years he shared the duties with the likes of Phil Esposito, Ted Green and Ed Westfall.

"We worked together, and whatever had to be done, we did it," he explained.

When Sinden became GM, he reinstated Bucyk as captain for four more seasons, and since his retirement as a player in 1978, Bucyk has worked in a number of roles for the Bruins. With the exception of Milt Schmidt, no Bruin has been as closely tied to the franchise for as long as Bucyk.

Fittingly, Schmidt, whose playing career in Boston stretched from 1937 to 1955, was Bucyk's coach for seven years in Boston. And on December 2, 1967,

when Bucyk scored his 229th and 230th goals as a Bruin, it was Schmidt's team record that he broke. Schmidt, by now the club's rookie GM, was in attendance. To illustrate how quickly the team's fortunes were changing, that game was the Bruins' 10th home win of the season, equaling their total for all of 1966–67.

Bucyk was almost always overshadowed: by Red Wings stars when he began his career in Detroit; by Terry Sawchuk, for whom he was traded; by Vic Stasiuk and Bronco Horvath, his one-time teammates on the Uke line; and by Phil Esposito, Bobby Orr and Gerry Cheevers when the Bruins finally caught and surpassed the Canadiens. Bucyk nevertheless put up Hall of Fame numbers, and when he retired, he was the highest-scoring left-winger of all time and the fourth leading scorer in NHL history. He was the

left wing on the Bruins' prolific power play — one of the best in history — firing and redirecting shots from his office about four feet in front of the crease.

Until Orr made hockey — and photographic — history, Bucyk was among the favorites for the Conn Smythe Trophy as most valuable performer of the 1970 playoffs. He scored a hat trick in Game 1, including the first goal of the final, and the penultimate goal of the series gave him at least one in each game of the sweep.

"I've thought of myself as a spear carrier, not a star," he has said. "It has added up. I'm not a glamor guy and I've just gone along, getting what I could out of every game."

And he never got more out of any game than the one he sent into overtime for Bobby Orr to immortalize.

FRANK MAHOVLICH

Mid-Career Resurgence Fuels Unlikely Championship

For Montreal Canadiens fans, the spring of 1971 was marked by Jean Béliveau's last hurrah, Ken Dryden's astounding goaltending debut, Henri Richard's bitter public criticism of coach Al MacNeil and a dramatic postseason run. Almost always over-looked, however, is Frank Mahovlich's spectacular scoring — and timing — during that spring's playoffs.

The Big M, traded to Montreal from Detroit just three months earlier, had found comfort and inspiration playing with the Canadiens and his younger brother Peter, and he helped the Habs win what was arguably the most unexpected Cup in franchise history.

Mahovlich set a postseason scoring record with 27 points and led all playoff scorers, with 14 goals. Those goals were vitally important as the underdog Canadiens upset the heavily favored Boston Bruins — the defending Stanley Cup champions — in seven games in the quarterfinals. The Canadiens went on to defeat Minnesota in six games and then edged Chicago to become just the second team in NHL history to clinch the Cup in a Game 7 on the road.

"While Ken Dryden was getting it done defensively, Mahovlich was unstoppable on offense," Montreal's iconic hockey columnist Red Fisher recalled years later. "It's unlikely the Canadiens would have won the Cup without him."

In the arc of Canadiens history, Mahovlich's three years in bleu, blanc et rouge represent the

Mahovlich during his days in Toronto, where he often felt like a misunderstood star.

goal-scoring bridge between Béliveau's waning years and the ascendance of Guy Lafleur. But in the spring of 1971, he was the overwhelmingly dominant offensive force.

"For the first time in his career, Frank does not have big pressure on him," Béliveau said at the time. "He always used to be a tense man. Now look at him; he is so relaxed."

The uncommonly tranquil Mahovlich did not register his first point of the playoffs until the last 80 seconds in the second game of the Boston series: he potted an insurance goal that put an exclamation point on one of the greatest single-game playoff recoveries in franchise history. The Habs, behind 5–1 in the second period, scored six unanswered goals to win the game 7–5 and tie the series.

"It was a helluva comeback," recalled Mahovlich, whose father, Pete Sr., was in the audience to watch his sons play. "But I think the next game was the big one."

After that Game 2 insurance marker, Mahovlich scored three of the Canadiens' next four, including the winning and insurance goals as Montreal beat Boston 3–1 in Game 3.

The Habs dropped the fourth and fifth games — as expected — but Mahovlich had 2 assists in Game 6 to extend the series, scored in the first period of Game 7 to tie the score at 1 and fired an insurance marker early in the third to give him 10 points in the series.

After he contributed 9 points to the elimination of the North Stars in the semifinal Mahovlich scored his first goal of the final in a losing cause to Chicago in Game 2. He then got the tying goal and the insurance marker as Montreal closed the gap with a 4–2 victory in Game 3 and recorded a key assist as the Canadiens knotted the series in Game 4.

With Montreal needing to win after the Black Hawks had taken a 3-2 series lead in Game 5, Mahovlich was in on three Montreal goals in

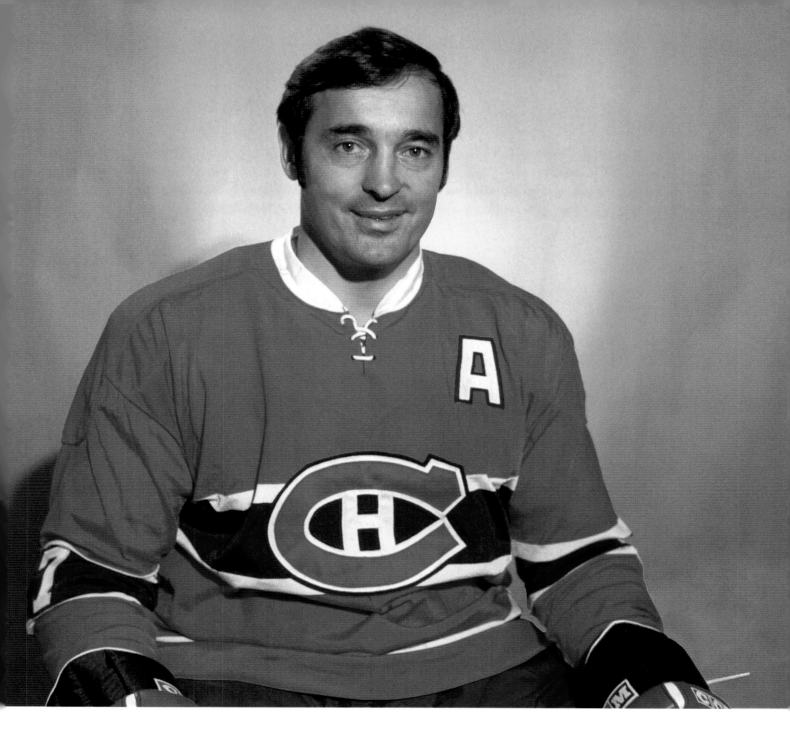

Game 6, almost single-handedly forcing a seventh game. He assisted on a tying goal in the first period and tied the score at 2 with a goal early in the third period, before setting up Pete Mahovlich's short-handed game-winner in the third period. He also missed a penalty shot against Tony Esposito.

Montreal won Game 7 with a pair of goals from Henri Richard, who always said 1971 was the greatest of his 11 Cup triumphs because of the ongoing friction with coach MacNeil.

With 4 goals and 8 points against the Black Hawks, Mahovlich outscored Bobby Hull in the first final series in nine years to match the two swash-buckling left-wingers against each other. He also outshone his brother Pete, who had 5 goals and 7 points in the series.

And while Dryden won the Conn Smythe Trophy as best playoff performer, it could just as well have been Frank Mahovlich, whose acquisition from the Red Wings has been described as the best midseason pickup in league history.

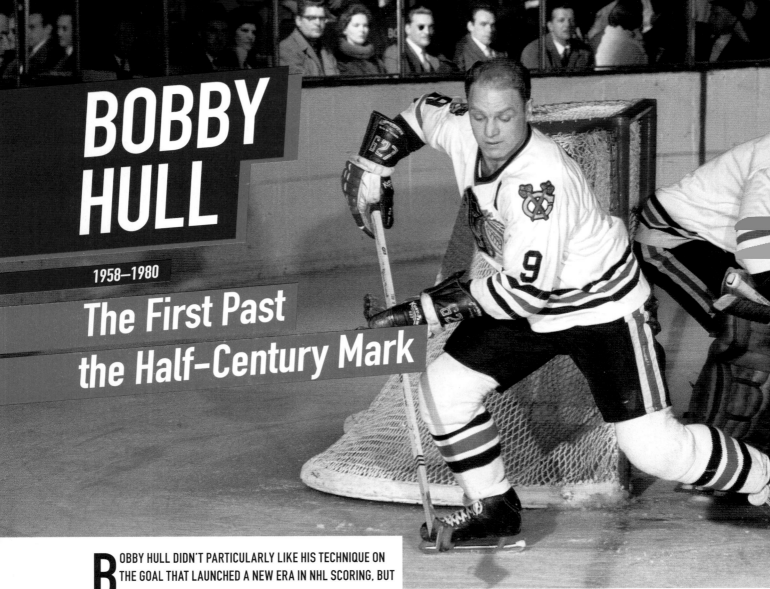

BOBBY HULL

1958–1980

The First Past the Half-Century Mark

BOBBY HULL DIDN'T PARTICULARLY LIKE HIS TECHNIQUE ON THE GOAL THAT LAUNCHED A NEW ERA IN NHL SCORING, BUT he loved the result.

"I moved the puck out front for the slap shot. I got it out too far and almost topped it — didn't get real good wood on the thing, and it skidded away, skimming the ice," Hull recalled of his 51st goal of the 1965–66 season, when he became the first player to surpass the 50-goal single-season mark he'd shared with Rocket Richard and Bernie "Boom-Boom" Geoffrion. "I watched it all the way into the corner of the net. I'll never forget the ovation. I haven't heard anything like it in my life, and I don't think I ever will again."

The power-play goal, scored at 5:38 of the third period on March 12, 1966, eluded New York Rangers goalie Cesare Maniago from about 40 feet away. The goal initiated a seven-minute standing ovation for the Golden Jet, who, since arriving in the Windy City as a swashbuckling 18-year-old in 1957, had been the catalyst for the once moribund Chicago Black Hawks

regaining the hearts — and raucous vocal support — of then dwindling Chicago Stadium crowds.

After he scored the goal that put him alone among NHL shooters, Hull skated around the edge of the ice grabbing the hands of delirious fans who were leaning over the glass to share the moment they had known would come.

Like the four-minute mile — the once unthinkable barrier that now stands as a benchmark for runners looking to make the leap to elite-level competition — the 50-goal season in the NHL had become a reachable but spectacularly rare standard. Hull first hit the mark in 1961–62, a year after Geoffrion had become only the second player to reach the milestone. But Hull's repeated assault on the total (five times in 10 seasons), combined with a massive NHL expansion in 1967, helped pop the cork. In the 10 years after Hull beat Maniago for his 51st goal, there were 24 50-goal seasons recorded in the NHL. Every Original Six team outside Toronto had registered at least one 50-goal season by 1973, and even an expansion team could boast one — Philadelphia's Rick MacLeish potted an even 50 goals and 50 assists that year.

Hull's ascension to hockey royalty had been expected since he and, to a similar degree, Frank Mahovlich arrived in the NHL as teenagers with lethal shots and speed down the wing. Mahovlich nearly beat Hull to the 50-goal mark, coming two twine busters shy of the total in 1960–61, the year before Hull would notch his first 50. Then, as Hull perfected the severely curved blade of his stick — an innovation credited to teammate Stan Mikita — and his shot became faster and harder with a less predictable flight path, Hull's name was carved among the most feared shooters of all time. His slapper was once timed at 118.3 miles per hour.

His arrival in Chicago coincided with the emergence of many young stars in the Black Hawks' system who helped the team rebuild after a stretch of 12 seasons from 1946–47 to 1957–58 with only one playoff appearance. By the summer of 1961, Hull's third season with the club, the Black Hawks were Stanley Cup champions.

With hockey alive and well in Chicago, Hull became the face of the league. He won his first Art Ross Trophy the year before the Black Hawks won the Cup, and he won back-to-back Hart Trophies in 1964–65 and 1965–66.

That 1965–66 Chicago club had the most prolific offense in the league, edging the Montreal Canadiens by a single goal. But on Hull's march to surpassing 50, Chicago went completely dry. With Hull sitting on 50 goals, the Black Hawks were shut out in the next three straight games, 5–0 by Toronto, 1–0 by Montreal and 1–0 by the same Rangers they would face three days later. The Hawks and Habs were locked in a tight battle for first place, and the 1–0 loss to Montreal and netminder Gump Worsley — who in earlier years had allowed both Gordie Howe's 600th goal and Hull's first-time 50th — was particularly concerning for Chicago.

"We're thinking about the playoffs," insisted coach Billy Reay. "There are a lot of games to play, and

Bobby is going to get the record along the way."

Hull wouldn't get it until the third period of the second game of back-to-back appointments with the Rangers. When New York's future Hall of Famer Harry Howell took a penalty late in the third, anticipation began to bubble in the Madhouse on Madison. After taking the puck from the Rangers' Reggie Fleming (a former Chicago teammate with Hull), the speedy left-winger stormed over the New York blue line and released the famous drive.

"Their defense and wingers were backing in," Hull

recalled. "I stopped 10 feet inside the blue line and saw they were still backing up." And as teammate Eric Nesterenko passed in front of the net, temporarily screening Maniago, Hull let the low slapper go.

"Nesterenko lifted the blade of my stick," Maniago said matter-of-factly after the game, "and the puck went under it."

It was not the only benchmark goal Maniago surrendered in his NHL career. Geoffrion scored his 50th against him in 1961, and when Mikita registered his 500th career goal in 1977, Maniago was in net.

Perhaps because of an overfocus on Hull's breaking the record, the Black Hawks' strong season lost some steam at the end. They finished 8 points back of the Canadiens and were upset by the Red Wings in the first round of the playoffs. But Hull had a record 97 points and won the Art Ross Trophy by a whopping 19 points over Mikita. It was the last time a left-winger would lead the NHL in scoring until Alexander Ovechkin topped the column in 2008.

Hull never did win another Cup with the Hawks, but they were always in the mix, and until he made the head-turning decision to join the World Hockey Association, Chicago fans could always count on the hard-shooting star to lift them from their seats. Chicago Stadium fans had established a reputation unmatched around the league for their thunderous and raucous support.

"It was the crowd," Hull said. "When I played in that great building — Chicago Stadium — and I picked up the puck, I could feel every voice. It was like the fans were coming up the ice right behind me."

STAN MIKITA

1959–1980

Slaying the Montreal Dragon

WHEN THE CHICAGO BLACK HAWKS WON THEIR UNLIKELY STANLEY CUP OVER THE DETROIT RED WINGS IN 1961, Stan Mikita actually thought the bigger test had been Chicago's semifinal series against the dynastic Montreal Canadiens.

Mikita, just 20 and in only his second full NHL season, led the Stanley Cup playoffs with 6 goals, including the winning goal in Game 5 of the final at the raucous Chicago Stadium, which put the Black Hawks one win away from the Cup. But it was the Montreal series he savored most.

"We considered the Detroit series a bit anticlimactic," Mikita said years later. "They had some great hockey players, but we didn't think it was as big a deal as beating the Montreal Canadiens."

Montreal, who'd finished 17 points ahead of Chicago, was favored to easily advance to the final over the young Black Hawks. The Canadiens had won the last five Stanley Cups, and adding a sixth seemed likely.

"We decided, 'Let's play it together as a team and as friends and everything else,'" Mikita recalled of

Chicago's late-season attitude adjustment that saw the team hit its stride as the playoffs approached.

"And you take the blame for everything that's not given to somebody. So that's what brought us together. And the attitude is what carried us through."

After splitting the first two games of the series, the best-of-seven contest swung on Murray Balfour's

triple-overtime goal for Chicago in Game 3.

Montreal's Henri Richard had tied the score with only 30 seconds left in regulation time, and the Habs would have won the game if referee Dalton McArthur had not disallowed two Montreal goals in extra time. Then, midway through the third overtime period, McArthur gave Montreal's Dickie Moore a penalty. On the ensuing Chicago power play, the puck came back to the left side of the blue line, where, Mikita recalled, "I was so excited, I was off balance, and I kind of fanned on the shot, but it bounced through, and Murray Balfour put it through Jacques Plante's legs.

"That was the confidence builder we needed. We

knew we could beat Montreal, but we had to show them we could do it. Surviving a marathon like that broke their spirit and bolstered ours."

The Habs won Game 4, but Chicago dominated the fifth and sixth games of the series (both 3–0 shutouts) to face the Wings in the final.

Mikita's ascendance to scoring star started during the 1960–61 season. As a rookie in 1959–60, Mikita had only 8 goals and 26 points in 67 games, and he spent far too much time in the penalty box (his 119 minutes ranked fourth in the NHL). He didn't lose any of his truculence in the Cup year (still racking up 100

minutes), but he showed the scoring touch he'd displayed in junior hockey, more than doubling his output to 53 points — including 19 goals — in 66 games.

After scoring the game-winner in Game 5 of the final against Detroit, two nights later in Game 6, he assisted on the game and Cup winner by linemate Ab McDonald to give the Black Hawks their first championship since 1938.

Mikita would go on to reach great personal heights in the years following the Hawks' 1961 Cup win.

His most astounding transformation was from an ornery, aggressive player who averaged 114 penalty

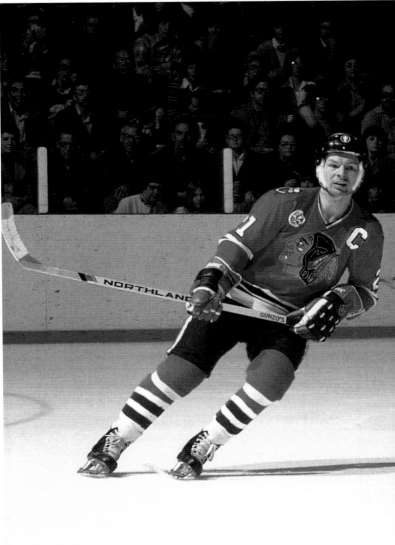

minutes per season (over his first six seasons) into a multiple Lady Byng Trophy–winner as the league's most gentlemanly player. In 1966–67, Mikita's eighth season, he cut his penalty minutes to 12 and was awarded the Lady Byng for the first time. Moreover, that season he also became the first player to be awarded three major trophies in a single season, snagging the Art Ross Trophy (most points) and the Hart Trophy (NHL MVP) in addition to the Lady Byng. Just to show it wasn't a fluke, he repeated the trifecta the next season.

Hawks coach Billy Reay, Chicago's bench boss from 1963–64 to 1976–77, said of Mikita's offensive awakening, "[He was] about the brightest hockey player I've ever seen. He plans every move three jumps ahead, like a good pool player. I have to say that I have never seen a better center. Maybe some could do one thing better than Stan, like skating faster or shooting harder, but none of them could do all the things that a center has to do as well as Stan does."

Mikita retired with 541 big league markers and was proof positive that a change in attitude is sometimes all it takes to make a difference.

PHIL ESPOSITO

1964–1981

Taking Scoring to a New Level

I N 1967 WHEN PHIL ESPOSITO WAS TOLD HE'D BEEN TRADED TO THE BOSTON BRUINS FROM THE CHICAGO BLACK HAWKS — going from first to worst in the NHL — he considered calling it quits. He was only 25, but the steel plant in his hometown of Sault Ste. Marie, Ontario, where he worked during the NHL off-season, paid as well and offered a more secure future.

Growing up, Esposito acquired a reputation that stuck with him in Chicago: he was too mouthy, too slow, too fat and having too much fun away from the rink. That reputation cost him a spot on midget and junior teams and led to his trade to Boston. But whenever he was on the ice, he put up points and put the puck in the net.

Once he decided to report to the Bruins' training camp, coaches parked Esposito in the slot, where his wingers could feed him the puck. His 6-foot-1, 205-pound body would absorb punishment while he deflected shots or scored on rebounds. He became "the highest paid garbage collector in the United States," as hockey writer Stan Fischler put it.

"Scoring is easy," Esposito later said. "You simply stand in the slot, take your beating and shoot the puck into the net."

Despite Fischler's quip, Esposito was making only $8,000 a year when he went to the Bruins. They refused his contract demand of $12,000 but agreed to pay him bonuses for hitting a series of scoring targets.

It was a wise negotiation by Esposito. In his second game as a Bruin, he scored 4 goals — 3 on the power play — and in his first year in Boston, he led the NHL in assists.

In 1968–69, Esposito became the first NHL player with more than 100 points. He had 126 points, including 49 goals, shattering the record of 97 points shared by Chicago teammates Stan Mikita and Bobby Hull — his old playing and drinking partner.

The following year Esposito had 99 points, and he scored 13 goals and 27 points in 14 playoff games as the Bruins ended a 29-year Stanley Cup drought in May 1970. The Bruins had gone from the NHL basement to the penthouse, with a swagger that started with their leading scorer.

And in 1970–71, with the help of wingers Ken Hodge and Wayne Cashman, Esposito took scoring to heights previously unimaginable.

On March 10 he tied Hull's single-season record of 58 goals, in an 8–1 win over the California Golden Seals. The next night the Bruins were in Los Angeles to play the Kings.

Hockey hadn't captured the imagination of the Golden State, and "there was relatively nobody in the building for the game," according to Esposito, despite the attractions of the NHL's resident powerhouse team and a record on the verge of being broken.

On a rebound, Esposito beat Kings goalie Denis DeJordy — a former Chicago teammate — to become the NHL's greatest goal-scorer.

"I saw Green take the shot, and I know Teddy shoots low," described Esposito after the game. "I knew I could score if I could get my stick on it. I've played with DeJordy, and I thought I could beat him."

There was little fanfare, however. "I celebrated the goal the same as I did any other goal," said Esposito years later.

Esposito also scored his 60th goal that night, surpassing the total of 59 that Montreal Canadiens legend Jean Béliveau had scored in the regular season and playoffs in 1955–56. The two goals gave him 128 points on the season, breaking his own record set just two years earlier.

"I'm glad it's over," said Esposito after the Bruins won 7–2, making them the first team in NHL history to win 50 games in a season.

"With 11 games after this one, I knew sooner or

later I'd get it. But I've been fortunate against Los Angeles, and I like playing here. I'm just glad the pressure's off."

Esposito went on to score 16 goals in those 11 games, finishing the 78-game season with 76 goals and 76 assists for 152 points. He also set a record with 550 shots in the season — only one player has since come within 100 shots of that number.

With the bonuses he earned by scoring 76 goals, Esposito finally quit Algoma Steel for good.

The Bruins had the top-4 scorers in the NHL in 1970–71, led by Esposito, who credits his teammates for his success that year.

"I could never have broken the record without my teammates," says Esposito. "From Bobby Orr to [John] McKenzie, from Hodge to Cashman, from [Johnny] Bucyk to [Gerry] Cheevers. Without them, I couldn't have done it in a million years."

The group was incredibly close. "Was this really a team," asked the Boston Globe's Kevin Paul Dupont, "or some sort of brotherhood that had come together years after signing a blood oath in the backwoods of Canada?"

One of the legends of Beantown is that teammates — led by Orr in hospital scrubs — wheeled Esposito's gurney out of Massachusetts General and through the snowy streets of Boston after he had knee surgery in 1973. They ended up at Orr's bar, the Branding Iron.

"Doc, don't worry, we are handling Phil just like a baby," said Orr over the phone when the surgeon tracked him down. "He's having a beer, and we will have him back in 15 minutes."

After his record-setting campaign, Esposito had three more years with more than 60 goals before the rebuilding Bruins dealt him to the New York Rangers early in the 1975–76 season.

As a Bruin, Esposito had won five scoring titles, led the NHL in goals for six straight seasons, won the Hart Trophy twice, won the Lester Pearson Trophy for league MVP as chosen by the players and won the Lester Patrick Trophy for his contribution to hockey in the United States.

Esposito finished his career on Broadway in January 1981, halfway through his 18th season. "I started losing my enthusiasm," he admitted.

"Seven goals in 40 games — that's not Phil Esposito," said Carol Vadnais, who had been traded to the Rangers with Esposito. "The defense was checking him as hard; they were checking him as if he were 28 years old. But he was 38."

With 717 career goals and 1,590 points, Esposito trailed only Gordie Howe in both categories when he walked away.

The season Esposito retired, Wayne Gretzky broke his single-season points record, with 164, and in 1981–82 he set the new mark for goals, with 92. Esposito was in Buffalo to present Gretzky with the puck he used to score his 77th goal.

Afterwards, a relieved Gretzky said, "It took the pressure off me. Now Phil can stop following me around and get back to his business."

Esposito entered the Hall of Fame in 1984, but his heart was still in Boston: "I don't care [about being inducted into] the Hall of Fame, to tell you the truth. My biggest thrill was having my number retired at Boston Garden. That to me is where it's at."

Esposito, who quit Catholic school in Grade 12 to pursue his hockey dream, inspired the bumper sticker popular in Boston in the 1970s: "Jesus saves — and Esposito puts in the rebound."

GILBERT PERREAULT

1971–1987
Making Connections

THE 1970 NHL DRAFT WAS SET TO BE ONE TO REMEMBER. WITH THE ADDITION OF THE BUFFALO SABRES AND VANCOUVER Canucks for the 1970–71 season, it was decided that the two expansion franchises would be given the first two selections in the draft. The spin of a numbered wheel would determine which club got the first overall pick — and the chance to select scoring sensation Gilbert Perreault.

A star on the Montreal Junior Canadiens (a team in the Ontario major junior circuit despite its geographic location), Perreault was Ontario league MVP in 1970, as the young Canadiens became just the third team in major junior history to win back-to-back Memorial Cups.

Perreault, from Victoriaville, Quebec, was raised on the smoothness of Montreal Canadiens stars Jean Béliveau and Dickie Moore. He emulated his heroes with skating and puckhandling skills rarely seen together.

On draft day, NHL president Clarence Campbell was given the honor of spinning the wheel. The Canucks had numbers one to 10; the Buffalo Sabres had 11 to 20. Sabres general manager Punch Imlach's lucky number was 11, and that's where the wheel landed. Legend has it the Canucks thought they had won after Campbell initially misread 11 as "1" and announced it as such. But Imlach rightfully challenged the call, and Perreault was on his way to

Western New York as the new face of the expansion franchise. As a tribute to the wheel of fortune, he chose to wear No. 11, and he'd be the only player in team history to do so.

Perreault scored his first NHL goal in the Sabres' first ever game, notching the winner in a 2–1 victory over Pittsburgh on October 10, 1970. He'd collect 511 more.

That game-winner was the first of a rookie-record 38 goals that season, which earned Perreault the Calder Trophy and kicked off one of the most successful marriages between player and franchise in NHL history.

"In my first seasons, Imlach told me to go for goals and not worry about checking," recalls Perreault of advice that would not be given in today's NHL.

"That really helped me get my confidence. The first few years I was there, it was loose. I was rushing the puck a lot. We had style."

The following year the Sabres drafted Perreault's junior teammate Richard Martin as their first pick, and after acquiring René Robert in the spring of 1972, the famed French Connection line was formed.

In 1972–73 the linemates finished the season as the Sabres' top-3 scorers and led the team to the playoffs for the first time.

The three Quebec-born players inspired the song "Look Out Here Comes the French Connection" in 1975, the year the Sabres reached the Stanley Cup Final against the Philadelphia Flyers. The series included the infamous fog game, won on a goal by Robert from Perreault in overtime. In the end the Broad Street Bullies' tough tactics nullified the Sabres' skill, and the Flyers won in six games. It was the closest Perreault got to the NHL title.

"After eight or nine years in Buffalo, I thought about asking for a trade. I wondered if a change would help my career. I was also curious to see how things were done elsewhere," says Perreault. "Even the thought of going to the Canadiens crept into my head. We had a lot of good years in Buffalo, but every hockey player wants to win the Stanley Cup.

"In the end I was glad to finish with the Sabres."

When Perreault retired in November 1986, he had 512 goals and 814 assists for 1,326 points in 1,191 regular-season games. He still holds Buffalo franchise records for goals, assists, points and games played, and he's immortalized in bronze with his French Connection linemates outside the First Niagara Center in Buffalo.

The soft-spoken star announced himself with a game-winning goal that October night in 1970, and 20 years later the Sabres retired his No. 11.

"Having a chance to play for the same team for 17 years was a highlight. In my first year I set a record in the NHL for scoring 38 goals. That was a highlight. Scoring 500 goals was a highlight. I had a lot of fun. Hockey has to be fun to be good. If the sport isn't enjoyable, then you can't be successful."

MARCEL DIONNE

1972–1989

The Last Scoring Champion Before Gretzky's Remarkable Run

I N 1980, MARCEL DIONNE ENDED UP IN A TIE FOR THE NHL LEAD IN TOTAL POINTS. BUT HE WAS DECLARED THE WINNER OF THE Art Ross Trophy because he had scored two more goals than the other guy. He admits to experiencing mixed emotions about it all.

"In the back of my mind I was thinking, 'I consider that it's a tie because I believe assists are just as important,'" Dionne recalls. "'But I guess that's the rule, so I won it. But geez, it's going to be 10 years before anyone else wins it again, so I'm glad I won it now.'"

Dionne's mental calculation was not far off. It would take eight seasons before Mario Lemieux wrestled the NHL scoring crown from the head of Wayne Gretzky, who had tied Dionne in 1979–80 with 137 points. Gretzky went on to win the scoring race in 10 of the next 14 seasons.

"But as far as I'm concerned, we tied for the scoring title," Dionne insists. "Sometimes making an assist meant a lot more than scoring itself. I remember many times breaking out 2-on-none, and I always had the greatest satisfaction in giving the other guy the puck for a chance to score.

"You teach kids a passing play is as good as scoring goals."

So it was fitting that, when Dionne actually won his only scoring title, he did it by racking up 2 assists in the final game of the regular season.

Dionne, whose 731 career regular-season goals

trail only those of Gretzky, Gordie Howe, Brett Hull and Jaromir Jagr on the all-time list, scored 53 goals and had 84 assists. Gretzky, making his NHL debut a year after turning pro in the World Hockey Association, which merged with the NHL in the summer of 1979, had 51 goals and 86 assists.

It was Dionne's second 50-goal season and kicked off a string of five straight years in which he went 50 or higher.

The goal that gave Dionne the Art Ross came at 4:15 of the first period of a 4–1 win over Quebec in the seventh-to-last game of the schedule. The insurance marker came two nights later against the Colorado Rockies.

Dionne's pursuit of the title was ably assisted by his mates on the Los Angeles Kings' Triple Crown line. Over the 1979–80 and 1980–81 seasons, Dionne and his wingers, Charlie Simmer and Dave Taylor, averaged 112 points each, and in 1980–81 they became the first forward unit to each record 100 or more points.

Dionne still appreciates the fact that he played on a three-man line, compared to the modern practice of two simpatico players teamed with a rotating third man.

"That was really significant in the '50s and '60s and early '70s," Dionne recalled to NHL.com. "You had a unit that played [together] a lot. As a unit, I look at the Islanders, like [Mike] Bossy, [Bryan] Trottier

and Clark Gillies. You look at the French Connection with René Robert, [Gilbert] Perreault and [Rick] Martin. People love that.

"To have a successful line, you've got to get along together and respond together. That's what we had. We had a lot of chemistry.

"The rest was just poetry on the ice; it was unbelievable: tremendous effort, a lot of goals, a lot of points, a lot of puck control, which you don't have today — it's puck-chasing."

Despite the exploits of the Triple Crown line, the Kings were defeated in the opening round of the playoffs four straight years. In 1980 it was a 3–1 loss to the Cup-bound New York Islanders, who had finished 17 points ahead of them in the standings.

Because the Kings didn't win a league or conference championship in his time, Dionne is sometimes overlooked when fans list the top players of all time, even though he ranks fifth in career goals and sixth in points.

"My idea was simple. Put it on net, anywhere, any time. Most of the time, I tried to do the screen shot and use the defenseman. Our defensemen stood up more than they do today.

"And you have to be patient, move the puck to get the shot."

While he considered the assist just as important, Dionne enjoyed every one of his 700-plus goals.

"I never thought it was boring to score a goal," he says, adding with a laugh, "but it was not like today, when guys act like they've never scored before. But I guess they don't score as often now."

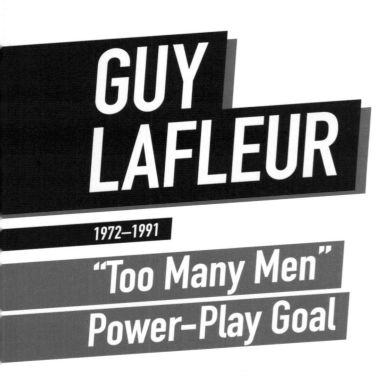

GUY LAFLEUR

1972–1991

"Too Many Men" Power-Play Goal

NEW ENGLANDERS SIMPLY CALL IT "TOO MANY MEN," USUAL-
LY UNDER THEIR BREATH, ACCOMPANIED BY A STRING OF
colorful, unprintable adjectives.

Michael Farber of *Sports Illustrated* called it "the most significant penalty in the history of major sports in North America."

Canadians remember legendary CBC announcer Danny Gallivan's call: "Lafleur, coming out rather gingerly on the right side …" The words and images are now part of Montreal Canadiens lore.

On May 10, 1979, the Montreal Canadiens hosted the Boston Bruins in Game 7 of their Stanley Cup semifinal series. Conditions seemed to favor the Habs: the home team had won each of the first six games, and while Boston had Bobby Orr and a big, tough, skilled team, Montreal had nine future Hall of Famers in its lineup. The Canadiens were also three-time defending Stanley Cup champions, having won the last two against the Bruins.

Don Cherry, winner of the Jack Adams Award in 1976 and still some years away from becoming Canada's most famous and notorious hockey commentator, was the Bruins' coach. The image of Cherry sarcastically acknowledging the Forum faithful while standing on the boards was seen weekly during the introduction of his Coach's Corner segment on *Hockey Night in Canada*.

Many think the gesture was a response to the history-altering penalty for having too many men on the ice, but it was in fact prompted by a hooking penalty on Bruins defenseman Dick Redmond earlier in the wild third period.

According to then-Bruins general manager Harry Sinden, the only sure things in life were "death, taxes and the first penalty in the Forum."

The questionable hooking call wasn't the first penalty in Game 7, and it wasn't even the most significant of the period. With the Habs trailing 3–1 after two, Montreal's Mark Napier scored before Guy Lapointe tied it on the power play while Redmond was in the penalty box.

But the Bruins shocked the Forum faithful when Rick Middleton bounced a backhander off goalie Ken Dryden from a bad angle. Less than four minutes stood between a Bruins upset and the end of a Montreal dynasty.

"We were all overhyped," remembers the Bruins' Mike Milbury. "In the emotion of the moment, we displayed a lack of awareness, a lack of restraint, a lack of discipline."

With 2:34 left to play and the Bruins clinging to a one-goal lead and Stanley Cup dreams, they were whistled for having too many men on the ice. Whether it was the handiwork of the ghosts of the Forum or of Cherry trying to keep Don Marcotte on the ice to shadow Lafleur while he double-shifted,

linesman John D'Amico and referee Bob Myers had no choice. The Bruins had violated Rule 18 (now Rule 74.1), and everyone could see it.

"I can see D'Amico — hand in the air — look up with sad eyes, like, 'Sorry, Grapes, I gotta call this,'" said Cherry.

On the ensuing power play, Montreal coach Scotty Bowman put out Larry Robinson, Serge Savard, Steve Shutt, Jacques Lemaire and Guy Lafleur. All five players are now in the Hall of Fame.

Even among such stars, Lafleur's aura stood out. He was a living legend in French Canada, heir to Maurice Richard and Jean Béliveau as the king of the team, sport and province.

Béliveau retired in 1971, the same year the Canadiens secured the first overall pick from the California Golden Seals to select Lafleur, who had just led the Quebec Remparts to the Memorial Cup title.

"When I was a kid, all we saw on TV was the Canadiens, and all I wanted to be was Béliveau," said Lafleur. "We had one bleu, blanc et rouge Canadiens sweater, and I fought the others for the right to wear it. I dreaded to be drafted by any other team but the Canadiens, and when they took me I was so happy."

Entering the 1978–79 season, Lafleur was the two-time reigning Hart Trophy winner, and his 52 goals and 129 points that campaign were part of a run of six straight seasons of 50 goals and 100 points — an NHL first. He was the quickest in history to 1,000 points and simply the best player on one of the best teams ever assembled, so on the Too Many Men power play, the puck was going to go through him.

"Any time you've got Lafleur in the lineup," said Robinson, "you've got a chance."

Lafleur started the play in his own end, passing the puck up to Lemaire at the Bruins blue line. Lemaire took the zone and dropped the puck back for Lafleur, who then skated "gingerly" — as Gallivan put it — down the boards, in contrast to his usual blazing speed. He retrieved Lemaire's drop pass behind the faceoff circle and hammered it past Gilbert. With 74 seconds left to play, the game was tied.

It was a "one-in-a-hundred shot," recounted Bowman.

It wasn't luck, according to Montreal defenseman Brian Engblom: "Guy had such a pure shot. He'd go out early for practice, and he'd take eight or 10 pucks to the top of the right circle. Then he'd start

shooting. It was like a click off a golf club. Click, bang — post and in. Click, bang — crossbar and in. His sense of the net, his sense of the corners, was beyond normal human comprehension. That was a great goal because it was Flower."

Yvon Lambert scored at 9:33 of overtime to win the game and the series, and the Canadiens went on to take their fourth consecutive Stanley Cup by defeating the New York Rangers in five games. Lafleur had 10 goals and 23 points in 16 playoff games.

That was the end of an era. In the off-season, Bowman went to Buffalo, Lemaire left to play and coach in Switzerland, and Dryden and captain Yvan Cournoyer retired. The outcome of the series also helped spell the end of Cherry's time in Boston.

"Not to be disrespectful, but for a lot of people, Too Many Men was a little bit like when Kennedy was shot," says Cherry. "People come up to me all the time and tell me where they were when it happened. They tell me stuff like they were watching it with their dad in the basement, and it seems like yesterday. Bruins fans'll say, 'You don't know how I felt.' I tell 'em, 'Yes, I do.'"

The goal remains a defining moment in the NHL's most passionate rivalry and in the Hall of Fame career of its scorer. "It's who Lafleur was. It marked his greatness," said Milbury.

"What could be more appropriate?" asked Gallivan on the broadcast, after letting the mayhem in the stands and the image of a dejected Gilbert sitting on the ice speak for itself.

"Has there been a more exciting right-winger than Guy Lafleur?" wrote legendary Montreal hockey writer Red Fisher, who covered Richard and Gordie Howe. "Sure, Howe was stronger, scored more goals and lasted much longer, but was there anyone more exciting than a Lafleur, golden mane flying, skipping and dancing beyond one man and then another and then, in one motion, releasing that wonderfully accurate shot of his?

"At his best — in 961 regular-season and 124 playoff games with the Canadiens — Lafleur was not merely hockey's finest and most exciting player. He was its artist, its sculptor. With his speed and hissing shot, which produced 518 Canadiens regular-season goals, he could turn games into things of beauty."

LANNY McDONALD

1974–1989

Making His Last Goal Count

LANNY McDONALD COULD BE EXCUSED IF HE THOUGHT HE'D NEVER SCORE A BIGGER GOAL THAN HIS OVERTIME WINNER for the Toronto Maple Leafs in Game 7 of the 1978 quarterfinal against the New York Islanders.

Playing with a broken wrist and a broken nose, McDonald took a pass from defenseman Ian Turnbull and flung it past Islander goalie Chico Resch, giving Toronto an upset victory in the series and its first trip to the Stanley Cup semifinal in 11 years.

Put simply, it was going to take an extraordinary moment to overshadow that feat.

That moment arrived at 4:24 in the second period of Game 6 of the 1989 Stanley Cup Final, when McDonald converted an extraordinarily accurate pass from 22-year-old Joe Nieuwendyk to put the Flames up 2–1. It would turn out to be the final goal of his career, and McDonald scored it at the Montreal Forum, the rink where he had scored his first NHL goal 16 years earlier.

Although teammate Doug Gilmour would score a third-period power-play goal that was officially the Cup winner and later add an empty-netter to seal the Calgary Flames' 4–2 victory over the Montreal Canadiens, it was the McDonald goal that put the Flames ahead for good on their way to their only Stanley Cup title.

"It was the highlight, no question," McDonald says of the 1989 Cup win and the goal that came

in the last game of his admirable career. "First of all, you always dream of scoring a goal that would help win the Stanley Cup, so in Game 6 you score the go-ahead goal. It doesn't get much better than that — especially in the Forum, against Montreal and against Patrick Roy."

McDonald, raised in Hanna, Alberta, was the team captain for that game, but he had been left out of the lineup for the series' previous three games, making the championship even sweeter.

"The Islander goal when no one gave us a chance to win one game — let alone four — was special … Both goals stand up, and up until then, the Islander goal was the highlight. But to help win the Stanley Cup — I'd have to say that's the best. For a guy from the West, to be [part of] the only team ever to win the Stanley Cup on Canadiens ice … There was no way we wanted to go to Game 7 … "

McDonald, now the chair of the Hockey Hall of Fame board of directors, wore two of hockey's most historically prestigious numbers during his career with Toronto, Colorado and Calgary. He beat the Islanders with No. 7 on his back in 1978 and was No. 9 when he and three teammates broke in on the Montreal defense in Game 6 of the '89 final.

"I had been in the penalty box," McDonald recalls. "I had missed a great opportunity then hooked Bobby Smith, trying to get the puck back. I came out of the penalty box and jumped right in on a 3-on-2. Jamie Macoun fed up to Hakan Loob, up through center. We get over the far blue line, and now it's a true 3-on-2. Loob over to Nieuwendyk, who was on the left side, and in one motion he threw it all the way across to the right side. I don't think a lot of people realize what a great pass it was. It went between Chris Chelios' skates and his stick — a very hard pass and right on the stick.

"We knew that when it went side to side, Patrick Roy goes down and tries to cover as much net as possible. And the only place was top shelf [glove side]. And when that puck went in, I was like, 'Oh my God, let's stop the game right now and get out of here.' But we had a period and a half left to play."

McDonald, who had recorded his 500th regular-season goal, 500th assist and 1,000th point earlier in the year, was the first Flame to hoist the Cup. Watching that game, his best friend and former teammate, Darryl Sittler, says he had a tear in his eye. For his part, McDonald described the victory as the "most peaceful" feeling he'd ever had in hockey.

Lanny McDonald hoists the Stanley Cup
following the 1989 final.

BRYAN TROTTIER

1976–1994

From Personal Best to Team Success

I T'S THE STUFF OF HOCKEY LEGEND AND CANADIAN HERITAGE MOMENTS: A YOUNG BOY HONES HIS SKILLS ON FROZEN Frenchman Creek in Val Marie, Saskatchewan, and grows up to set records and lift Stanley Cups in the bright lights of New York.

"There was a beaver dam next to our house," recalls Bryan Trottier of his childhood just north of the Montana border. "Dad figured it out — chopped that beaver dam and it was like a Zamboni. We'd have fresh ice in the morning. We were spoiled rotten; we didn't know what it was like not to have good ice all winter long."

Trottier was a gentle soul, but in a more violent era of hockey, making hard fists of soft hands was considered a necessary part of the game. Dave "Tiger" Williams — who became the NHL's all-time leader in penalty minutes — was a teammate with Trottier on the Swift Current Broncos of the Western Hockey League, and he taught the talented center to fight and to survive. That apprenticeship added the grit and dogged defense to Trottier's game that would be his signature, even as he lit up NHL scoreboards.

Drafted by the New York Islanders 22nd overall in 1974 at the age of 17, Trottier joined the team in 1975 and won the Calder Trophy as Rookie of the Year after setting a then-rookie record with 95 points.

Two days before Christmas 1978, Trottier set another record, which still stands.

The Islanders' hated New York rival, the Rangers, were visiting Nassau Coliseum, but vacation might've been on everyone's minds in the pedestrian first period. Trottier opened the scoring, and the game was tied 1–1 after one. Nothing suggested history was about to be made.

At 1:08 of the second period, the Rangers' Ron Duguay took a penalty, and just three seconds into the power play, Trottier set up Mike Bossy for a goal. Less than three minutes later, Trottier scored his 2nd of the night, followed even more quickly with an assist on a Garry Howatt goal. With only 5:08 gone, he had 3 points on 3 Islander goals in the period.

Trottier then assisted on Bossy's 2nd goal of the night at 11:21 and scored twice himself in the final 90 seconds of the period. The Islanders went into the second intermission with an 7–2 lead thanks to Trottier's record–setting second period of 3 goals and 3 assists for 6 points.

Trottier added his 5th goal and 8th point in the third as the Islanders finished what started as a snoozer with a dominant 9–4 win. The victory pushed their record to 21-4-7 and extended their undefeated streak at home to 16 games (12-0-4).

To this day there have been only 16 eight-point games in NHL history (accomplished by only 13 players). However, just two players since World War II — and eight in history — have scored more goals in a game than Trottier's 5.

In the season that would see the last of the Montreal Canadiens' four straight Stanley Cups, this regular season game signaled a changing of the guard. Mike Bossy would go on to set an Islanders record with 69 goals, most of which were assisted by Trottier, who set his own high-water mark in points, with 134 (47 goals, 87 assists). Those totals earned Trottier both the Art Ross Trophy as the league's leading scorer and the Hart Trophy as NHL MVP.

The Islanders were the top seed in the playoffs in 1979 but lost in six games to the Rangers in the semi-final. It was the last time they'd lose a playoff round

journalist Stan Fischler, who's covered the game since 1954, maintained that 19 was better than 99: "Trottier has ripened into the most effective total forward since Gordie Howe."

Just as age eventually caught up with Howe, Trottier's scoring pace slowed, and he was bought out by the Islanders in 1990 after 15 years with the team. Offered a front office job, the gritty center felt he had more hockey in him, and he signed with the ascending Pittsburgh Penguins.

Trottier learned to be a professional as a callow rookie with the Islanders by watching and learning from teammates and leaders Denis Potvin and Clark Gillies. His arrival in Pittsburgh was primarily to provide the ultra-talented but young Penguins — a club that included Mario Lemieux and Jaromir Jagr — with mentoring of their own. It was a winning combination: Trottier won two more Cups with the Penguins in 1991 and 1992 before retiring. Restless without the game, he returned for half the 1993–94 season before he called it a career.

In 1,279 NHL games, Trottier had 524 goals, including 68 game-winners, and 1,425 points. He had more than 100 points in six seasons and finished his career with a plus/minus record of plus-470. He also played in eight All-Star games and two Canada Cups, once for Canada and once for the U.S. As a North American Indian, he holds dual citizenship.

"I'm very proud of my heritage," says Trottier. "My mom's Irish, my dad's Cree-Métis-French. My bloodlines are strong. There's some bullheadedness and determination built into the bloodlines, and I love it. I love my parents for it; I'm proud of it — proud of my Canadian roots, but I'm North American."

Trottier was inducted into the Hall of Fame in 1997 and was the inspiration for the next generation of complete players with 19 on their jerseys — from Steve Yzerman to Joe Sakic to Shane Doan — who could score but weren't afraid to do the dirty work that's crucial for success in the NHL.

In "Letter to My Younger Self" in the *Players' Tribune*, Trottier wrote, "It's never going to be pretty. It's never going to happen the way you plan it. Sometimes you just have to go out to the beaver dam with a machete and start chopping wood."

for quite some time. In 1980 the Islanders won the first of four straight Stanley Cups, and Trottier took home the Conn Smythe Trophy as playoff MVP. With a chance to win a record-tying fifth straight championship in 1984, the Islanders lost in the final to the Edmonton Oilers, the NHL's new superpower led by Wayne Gretzky.

Trottier and Gretzky were two of the best players in the game in the early 1980s, but Islanders Hall of Fame coach Al Arbour said he wouldn't have traded Trottier for Gretzky, who was rewriting the record books but never had a 6-point period.

While Arbour might've had a New York bias,

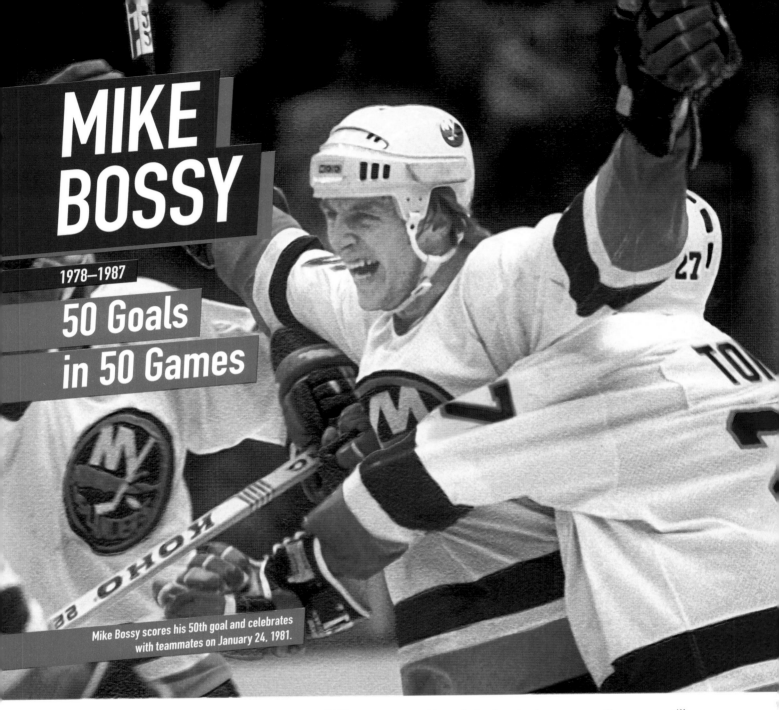

MIKE BOSSY

1978–1987

50 Goals in 50 Games

Mike Bossy scores his 50th goal and celebrates with teammates on January 24, 1981.

"I TOLD THE CANADIENS TO DRAFT HIM IN 1977, BUT THEY WOULDN'T LISTEN TO ME," SAID MONTREAL LEGEND Maurice Richard of Mike Bossy, the wiry local star with the quick release.

"They said he wasn't good enough defensively. What the Canadiens didn't understand is when you can score goals like he can, you don't watch your man. He watches you."

Bossy grew up in Ahuntsic, a borough of Montreal, where Richard spent much of his life. The kid who once scored 23 goals in a game and 170 in a season joined the major junior Laval National at 14.

After 309 goals in four junior seasons, Bossy was still passed over by 12 teams, including the New York Rangers and the Toronto Maple Leafs twice each.

The New York Islanders picked Bossy 15th overall, and in his first training camp, coach Al Arbour put him on a line with Bryan Trottier and Clark Gillies. The trio would become one of the most potent and productive in NHL history.

In 1977–78, Bossy proved Richard's prescience: he became one of 23 players in NHL history to score 50 goals in a season, as he set a rookie record with 53 and was named rookie of the year.

After scoring more than 50 in each of the next two seasons, including a career-high 69 in 1978–79, Bossy quietly set a goal for himself in 1980–81: to score 50 goals in 50 games. Only Richard had done that, 36 years earlier in 1944–45.

Bossy had 25 goals in his first 23 games, but it wasn't until after he scored his 36th goal — with six hat tricks to that point — and the normally reticent Bossy admitted to a reporter that he wanted to break Phil Esposito's record of 76 goals, that it became a story.

Other teams also took note and did their best to prevent Bossy from matching the Rocket's milestone against them. He still managed 48 goals through 47 games, and in Game 48 the Calgary Flames were focused more on thwarting Bossy than winning.

"I was very disappointed in the way Calgary played," said Islanders captain Denis Potvin. "All they did was check. They were down, 2–0, and they didn't seem the least bit interested in playing offensively. All they wanted to do, it seemed, was protect their net and stop Bossy from scoring."

Bossy was also held goalless in Game 49 against the Detroit Red Wings, despite some gilt-edged chances, but at least the defending Stanley Cup–champion Islanders were winning.

"I should have given Bossy my glasses," said Arbour. "Two chances at an empty net. But if they won't go in, they won't go in. You know Bossy. He can still explode at any time. I can't complain, though, with back-to-back shutouts."

Bossy wasn't the only one chasing history. Charlie Simmer of the Los Angeles Kings was also on a torrid goal-scoring pace. He had 46 goals in 49 games, and in his 50th, a matinee on January 24, 1981, he had 3 goals, leaving him one shy of Richard's achievement.

A few hours after the Kings game, Bossy and the Islanders were playing at home against the Quebec Nordiques in their 50th game of the season. He was still sitting on 48 goals, and when he was held without a shot after two periods, it looked as though he'd join Simmer in coming tantalizingly close.

Bossy spent the second intermission in a bathroom stall, smoking cigarettes and pondering what he'd say to the media after the game.

But with just over five minutes left and the game tied, 4–4, Bossy scored his 49th on a backhand, and at 18:31 he took a cross-ice pass from Trottier at the left faceoff circle and scored his 50th on goalie Ron Grahame.

"It was not an easy journey," remembered Bossy years later. "I began our 48th game with 48 goals. No goals in two straight games left me with having to score two in Game 50. I cut it even closer by waiting until the last two minutes, precisely 1:29, to score number 50. I was dancing on the ice, there was bedlam in the crowd and one of my personal hockey career objectives was accomplished."

His memorable and exuberant goal jig was an expression of pure joy and relief.

"The hardest part was never being able to be satisfied with what I had accomplished in any one game. I always had another game to go on to. There were times when I had a couple of three-goal games, but I didn't have time to savor them because you had to go out the next night and stay on pace. It was a constant whirlwind."

According to broadcaster Dick Irvin: "It was a great television shot of him doing a tap dance after that goal. He told me once he was embarrassed by it now, the way he celebrated."

When Bossy got back to the dressing room after the 7–4 win, he got a phone call from Richard, congratulating him on matching his accomplishment.

Richard, who received a letter from Joe Malone when he broke his record of 44 goals set in 1917–18, also sent Bossy a telegram that read in part: "I knew one day my record would be surpassed or tied, but I had always hoped that it would be by the player from Ahuntsic that I have admired from the start. We are proud of you here in Quebec."

Bossy went on to score 68 goals, and he had another 17 and a record 35 points in 18 playoff games to lead the Islanders to their second straight Stanley Cup.

Only one season after Bossy's 50 in 50, Wayne Gretzky scored 50 goals in 39 games. The Great One managed to pot 50 goals in fewer than 50 games twice more, and since then only Mario Lemieux and Brett Hull have done it.

Bossy is tied with Gretzky for a record nine

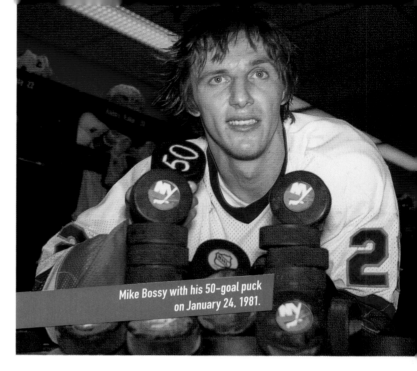

Mike Bossy with his 50-goal puck on January 24, 1981.

seasons with more than 50 goals, and only Bossy did it in consecutive seasons. The only year when he didn't hit the 50-goal plateau was 1986–87, his 10th and final season, when back problems limited him to 63 games.

Bossy retired in 1987 at the age of just 30, with five seasons of 60 or more goals, four Stanley Cups, three Lady Byng Trophies and countless goals left in his hands.

In a career cut short by injury, Bossy might have been the purest goal-scorer in NHL history. With 573 goals in 752 regular-season games, he's the all-time leader in goals per game, at 0.762. That puts him ahead of Cy Denneny and Babe Dye in the early 20th century, and Gretzky, Lemieux and Hull in the modern era.

Bossy was inducted into the Hall of Fame in 1991, and 24 years later he was reunited with the puck that he used to score his 50th goal in 50 games. His daughter had actually given it to her swim coach as a thank-you gift, and after Bossy refused to take it back, it was sold on eBay.

Gavin Maloof, who owns the Palms hotel in Las Vegas and is a minority owner of the city's NHL franchise, bought the puck and gave it back to Bossy.

"We need to get this puck," he said. "It means a lot to Mr. Bossy. Fifty goals in 50 games. Only a handful of people have ever done that. I needed to buy this puck. I don't care how much it costs."

MIKE GARTNER SAYS HE WAS ABLE TO SCORE GOALS SO CONSISTENTLY IN THE NHL BECAUSE "MY HANDS HAD finally caught up to my feet."

And what feet. Gartner set a long-standing record for the fastest time in the NHL skills competition and was acclaimed throughout his career for constantly outracing his check down the right side of the ice. When he retired in 1998, he held the records for most seasons with 30 goals (17 of them, a record that still stands) and most consecutive 30-goal seasons (15, a mark since tied by Jaromir Jagr). From his first NHL season with the Washington Capitals to his 18th and penultimate season with the Phoenix Coyotes, the only time he did not hit 30 goals was in the lockout-shortened 1994–95 season, when each team played only 48 games, of which he played just 38.

Another key to his offensive consistency was a knack for staying off the injured list. "I stayed relatively healthy throughout my career, and before you know it, I was in my 9th, 10th, 11th season, and somebody said, 'That's your 10th year in a row in which you've scored 30 goals. Do you know the record is 13?'" he told the Hockey Hall of Fame. "I didn't know it at the time. I was given a certain amount of talent, and I wanted to do the best I could every time I stepped onto the ice. I really strived for that consistency, and as a result, I was able to have it."

After playing for Cincinnati in the World Hockey Association's final year, during which he scored "only" 27 times as a 19-year-old playing on a line with fellow teenager Mark Messier, Gartner was drafted fourth overall by Washington. He soon developed an improved scoring touch, notching 84 goals in his first two NHL seasons. He credits the scoring surge to the opportunities provided by the Capitals.

Gartner reached the 30-goal plateau for the 17th and final time on March 6, 1997, in the Coyotes' 5–0 road victory over the Tampa Bay Lightning. He scored the 30th against Rick Tabaracci and his 31st against Corey Schwab — one on a power play, the other at even strength.

His marker against Tabaracci, at 9:46 of the second period, cinched his 17th 30-goal season in 17 full-schedule years, and then he hit the 1,300-point mark of his career with his goal against Schwab early in the third period. The night before he had netted number 29 by redirecting Craig Janney's power-play shot in a 3–0 win over goalie John Vanbiesbrouck and the Florida Panthers. The back-to-back victories in the state of Florida moved Phoenix a game over .500 in their first season out of Winnipeg and helped ensure they would make the playoffs.

Gartner, traded to Phoenix from Toronto in the off-season, was no stranger to landmark lamplighters. He scored the first goal for the new franchise in

the team's second game as the Coyotes, recording Phoenix's first-ever hat track in the same game. He also scored the last goal in the Chicago Stadium and was the first NHLer to record his 500th goal, 500th assist and 1,000th point in the same season.

Gartner's inclusion in the Hockey Hall of Fame has been questioned in some quarters, but not among those who really know the game. He retired as the second-highest goal-scoring right-winger and fifth overall goal-scorer in NHL history, with 708 goals. He is fourth all time in right-wing scoring, more than balancing out the fact that he scored 50 goals in a season only once and didn't play in a Stanley Cup Final, make an all-star team or win an individual league award. But few players have shown his propensity for regularly delivering a goal total that still holds cachet: 30 in a season.

"Thirty goals is something I've always looked at as a real minimum for a goal-scorer," he said right after he put his 17th such campaign to bed.

He set that high bar early in his career and kept clearing it year after year.

MICHEL GOULET

Right Place, Right Time

IT IS A RECORD THAT, UNTIL THE SPRING OF 2016, MICHEL GOULET DIDN'T KNOW HE SHARED.

"Really?" the Hall of Fame leftwinger said when told that he and Phil Esposito, who did it twice, are the only players in NHL history to score 16 game-winning goals in a single season. "It's something I've never thought too much about. The stats were nothing back then like they are today."

"Back then" was the 1983–84 season, the Quebec Nordiques' fifth in the NHL after the league expanded in 1979 to absorb Quebec, Edmonton, Winnipeg and Hartford, the four surviving World Hockey Association franchises. Goulet, who had played in Quebec City as a junior and in Birmingham as an underage 18-year-old in the WHA, was one of the centerpieces of the entertaining, puck-moving Nordiques. Quebec considered him a must-get in the 1979 amateur draft— a draft that, because of the abundance of young WHA talent, is regularly acknowledged as the strongest and deepest in NHL history.

Although the Nordiques drafted late, at 20th overall, they were able to land Goulet because of a clause in his Birmingham contract that stipulated if the team folded, Quebec had to be offered his rights ahead of any other NHL team. Goulet's agent obtained a court order to enforce the clause, and that scared off the teams selecting earlier in the first round.

One of the reasons Goulet didn't know he shares the record for game-winning goals is that he placed every one of his 548 regular-season goals in high regard.

"I don't really have a favorite," he explains. "To me, goals are special. I didn't win the Cup, but there were still goals that could make a difference. I remember having 4 against Montreal one time, and that was special because of the intense rivalry.

"There is no question that playing on the top two lines, you wanted to be a guy who made a difference, and I tried to play as a player who could make an impact.

"I'm no Wayne Gretzky, I'm no Mario Lemieux. The thing I tried to do as much as score goals was to be consistent year after year. I didn't try to just score goals; I wanted to be a playmaker too."

With that many game-winners, it would be natural to assume that Goulet was being set up by Peter Stastny, which was certainly true in some power-play situations.

"But Dale Hunter was my regular center," he points out. "We played together for seven years. As we all know, we didn't have too many right-handed shots playing center in those days [Hunter shot left], so the left wing was always the back-checker."

Which makes Goulet's scoring prowess all the more impressive. Goulet ranked second in goals in 1983–84, with 56, and more than a quarter of them were game-winners. He made the NHL First All-Star Team while helping the Nordiques to a franchise-record 34 wins, although Quebec could not get past their bitter archrival, Montreal, in the second round of the playoffs, which the Canadiens won in six games. It was one of four consecutive 50-goal seasons for Goulet, who at 23 became the second-youngest player (behind 20-year-old Gretzky) among the top-10 leading scorers of game-winning goals in a season.

There is a running debate as to whether a game-winning goal should be the one that puts a team ahead to stay (as in soccer) or, as the NHL defines the term, the goal that in hindsight gives the winning team one more goal than the losing team's total. The latter is, properly, the goal that ensures victory.

"Sometimes it's the goal that made the difference, and sometimes it's the third goal in a 6–2 game," Goulet shrugs.

In his 15 other NHL and WHA seasons, Goulet was never credited with more than six game-winners.

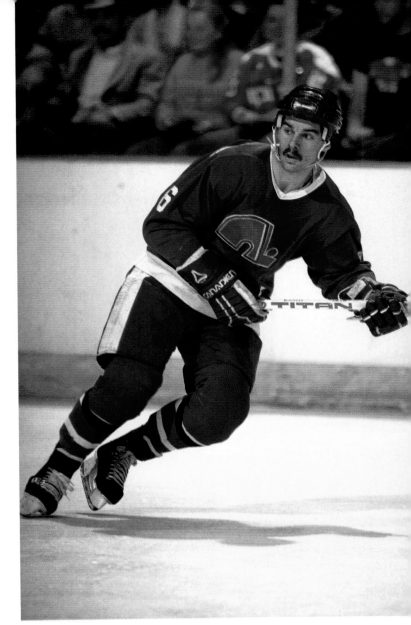

"Sometimes I think these things just happen," he said. "It's a lot about being in the right place at the right time."

Goulet has said, only half-jokingly, that he might have scored 100 goals in a season if he had played on Gretzky's line. Gretzky was his center in the 1984 Canada Cup, and three years later Goulet was often overlooked as a rotating third member of a line that also boasted Gretzky and Mario Lemieux in the fabulously entertaining 1987 Canada Cup.

"My biggest goals were the 2 against Sweden in the '84 Canada Cup. But to me, goals are special, all goals.

"A goal is a goal."

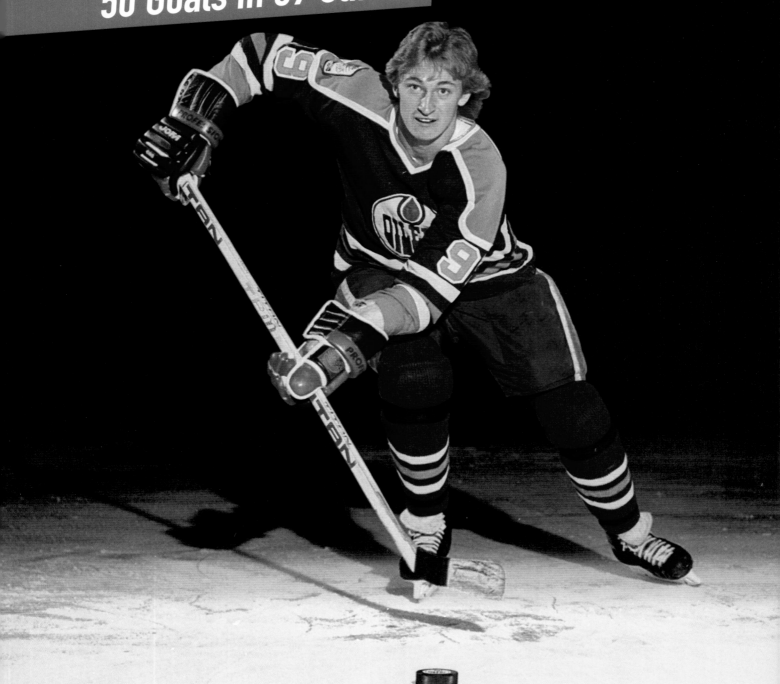

WAYNE GRETZKY

1979–1999

50 Goals in 39 Games

WITH HIS SLIGHT PHYSIQUE AND FEATHERED HAIR, 18-YEAR-OLD WAYNE GRETZKY LOOKED AT LEAST AS much like a kid hanging around in front of the corner store bumming smokes, in his hometown of Brantford, as a prospect on the cusp of stepping into the NHL in 1979. Yet two years later, he set one of the most unbreakable records in NHL history.

The transition to the big stage turned out to be an easy one for the scoring sensation, who had been in the public eye since before puberty. Gretzky tied for the NHL scoring lead in his rookie year, but the Art Ross Trophy was awarded to Marcel Dionne because he had 53 goals to Gretzky's 51. That went against Walter Gretzky's early lesson that an assist is just as good as a goal — advice his son took to heart, developing extrasensory passing skills.

"Everyone will tell you, 'Oh yeah, I saw it right away. He was a genius on the ice.' They're lying," says Tom McVie, who coached against the Edmonton Oilers in the World Hockey Association and NHL, of the young Gretzky. "To me, he looked like somebody's little brother. It looked like he was going to get killed. But he made one pass that season that made me stop and think. He was behind the net with two guys, and he made this back pass to Blair MacDonald. I remember thinking, 'How did he know he was there?'"

Gretzky won the Hart Trophy as league MVP in his first NHL season and kept it in his sophomore year, in which he scored 55 goals and won the Art Ross outright. NHL defensemen had made a Faustian bargain by then, letting him shoot because his distribution of the puck was so deadly.

Ever-evolving, in his third season Gretzky took what his opponents gave him.

"I don't think anyone had to tell him to shoot more," says former teammate Kevin Lowe. "I think that teams may have started to pay more attention to covering his wings and left him alone. And one thing about Wayne: he always made the right play."

Living his own mantra that you miss 100 percent of the shots you don't take, Gretzky was on pace to reach the gold standard — or should that be "goal standard"? — set by the Montreal Canadiens' Maurice Richard in 1944–45: the symmetrical feat of 50 goals in 50 games. The Rocket's pace went unmatched for 36 years, until Mike Bossy of the New York Islanders scored his 50th goal in the Islanders' 50th game on January 24, 1981.

On Halloween 1981, Gretzky scored 4 goals in the Oilers' 13th game, a night he credits with igniting his momentous season. It was the first of four games that season in which he scored at least 4 goals — a modern NHL record, matched only once: by Gretzky himself, two seasons later.

In late November he scored his 31st goal early in game 26. It was his 7th goal in seven periods, but then he went cold. Over the next four games, he was goal-less.

Gretzky scored a single goal in each of the following four games to give him 35 goals in 34 contests. With Gretzky still on pace to match Richard and Bossy, fans were starting to think about getting tickets for game 50 in late January.

Then the Oilers headed home for a five-game engagement around Christmastime, and what a wonderful gift Gretzky had for Edmonton. On December 19, he had 3 goals and 7 points in a win over the Minnesota North Stars. The next night, he scored twice in a loss to the Calgary Flames. On December 23, he added a goal as the Oilers beat the Vancouver Canucks, putting him at 41 goals in 37 games.

Then came the Oilers whopping 10–5 win over the Los Angeles Kings on December 27, in which Gretzky had another 4-goal game. In four games at the Northlands Coliseum, he had 10 goals and 19 points, and with 45 goals in 38 games, the Richard-Bossy milestone seemed inevitable, if a few games away.

"I thought to myself, 'You can't choke now,'" said Gretzky.

The fifth game of the homestand was on December 30 against a strong Philadelphia Flyers team backed by goalie Pete Peeters. Gretzky, though, started early, with a little luck.

"Charlie Huddy took a shot from the left point that bounced off the boards and right to me at the corner of the net, and I put it in. I thought to myself, 'How fortunate.'"

It was that kind of night. Later in the first period, he finished a 4-on-2, surprising Peeters with a shot from 20 feet out. In the second, he earned his hat trick by splitting the Flyers defense and firing home a slap shot. In the third, he hit goal 49 after cutting to the middle and slapping another over Peeters's shoulder.

History and highlights show Peeters as the victim, but he also robbed the red-hot scorer on several occasions. "I had eight or nine good chances," remembers Gretzky. "Their goalie made some terrific saves."

With the Oilers leading 6–5, Peeters went off for an extra attacker. Gretzky sealed the 7–5 win and a place in history with three seconds left in the game. The empty-netter was assisted by goalie Grant Fuhr and Glenn Anderson, as Bill Barber dove to block it.

"Bill Barber said that if I were going in alone on an empty net for the 50th goal, he'd throw his stick [which results in an automatic goal]," says Gretzky. "That would have made a great trivia question: how I scored my 50th goal without putting the puck into the net."

Gretzky had scored 9 goals in two games — the only time in modern NHL history a player has had back-to-back games with at least four goals — to reach 50 in only 39 games.

After witnessing Gretzky's historic game up close, Flyer great and fellow Hall of Famer Bobby Clarke said, "I know everything that's been written about you. I think none of it is adequate."

Gretzky was held off the score sheet in his next game but had 11 goals in the next 11 games to hit 61 in 50 games, which also remains a record. On February 24, 1982, he broke Phil Esposito's single-season goal record of 76, scoring goals 77, 78 and 79 in the last seven minutes of the game. The natural hat trick continued a streak of four consecutive 5-point games, as he surpassed Esposito with six weeks still left in the season.

Gretzky finished the year with 92, but, even with a record that still stands and seems ironclad, it didn't quite meet his standards.

"It was a thrill to get 92 goals, but in some ways, I thought I let myself down by not getting 100," reminisced Gretzky 30 years later. "Maybe I should have pushed myself more."

Gretzky had 10 hat tricks in 1981–82, and, living up to his father Walter's wise words, in each of those games he added enough assists to give him at least 5 points. With 120 assists, his 212 total points obliterated the record of 164 he had set the year before, which in turn had broken Esposito's old mark of 152, set in 1970–71. It was the first of four seasons in which Gretzky had at least 200 points. No other player has ever done that.

The scrawny kid who grew up to be the greatest scorer in hockey history would retire with more than 60 official NHL records to his name, along with a host of accomplishments that don't appear in the league's *Official Guide & Record Book*. The one that matters most to him is the one least likely to be equaled.

"People ask me all the time about my records, but to me, that's my favorite," says Gretzky about his 50 goals in 39 games. "They're all made to be broken; that's what sports is.

"That's what's so great about sports, but that's my favorite because I think that will be the hardest to break."

MARK MESSIER

1979–2004

The Guaranteed Win

BABE RUTH'S CALLED SHOT IN 1932. JOE NAMATH'S SUPER BOWL GUARANTEE IN 1969. WHEN IT COMES TO LEGENDARY New York sports moments, they don't get much bigger. But there's debate that the Babe didn't actually call his shot, and Namath's guarantee was hardly the boisterous proclamation historical revisionists claim. There's no debate, however, about what Mark Messier said to reporters when his New York Rangers were facing elimination in Game 6 of the Eastern Conference final against the hated New Jersey Devils.

"We're going to go in there and win Game 6."

Messier was already a star when he arrived on Broadway. He could have retired after his Edmonton days as one of the all-time greats, but he had another chapter to write.

In Edmonton, Wayne Gretzky was an artist, and Messier, the 48th overall pick in 1979, was "the Moose." He was the prototype of the ideal hockey player — equally able to bull his way through opponents, elbows and fists high, or fire the puck inside the post with his signature leg kick. Often both on the same shift.

The Oilers were swept in their first Stanley Cup Final by the New York Islanders in 1983, but a year later the script was flipped, and Edmonton ended the Islanders' run of four straight championships. With the Islanders blanketing Gretzky in the 1984 final, Messier took control of the series — and the Conn

Smythe trophy — as playoff MVP. It was the first of four Cups in five years for the Oilers.

In 1989–90, as captain and undisputed leader after his running mate Gretzky had decamped for the Los Angeles Kings, Messier had his highest regular-season point total (129) and won his first Hart Trophy as league MVP. He also led the Oilers past Gretzky and the Kings in the second round of the playoffs and to the franchise's fifth Stanley Cup.

"I don't think I've ever seen any of the leaders that I've ever had do it as well as Mark did that particular year," said Oilers coach John Muckler.

But just as Gretzky ended up in a major American market, Messier was traded to New York in 1991.

According to Doug Weight, who broke into the NHL with the Messier-led Rangers in 1991 and later captained the Oilers and Islanders, "He was fierce, he led by example [and] things weren't going to be accepted. As a team, whether you were 18 or 19 like me or you were a veteran, he was going to let you know what he expected.

"It's a tactful thing, treating people with respect, but also being able to make people accountable when you need to. It's uncomfortable at times. It's something I forced myself to do. A lot of it was him; he had an aura about him. Even when you were pissed at him, you wanted to play for him. That's a real talent, and you knew he was genuine because

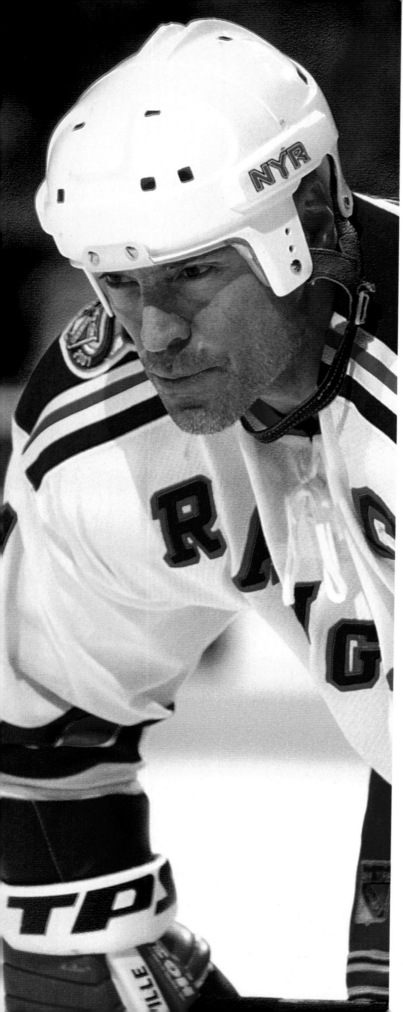

you had a relationship with him. I took a lot of that with me."

Messier won his second Hart Trophy in his first year in New York, and after missing the playoffs in 1992–93, the Rangers earned the Presidents' Trophy in 1993–94. But fans of the Blueshirts were keenly aware that finishing first in the regular season guaranteed nothing, and the curse of 1940 — the last year the Rangers won the Stanley Cup — was alive and well.

The Rangers lost just one game in the first two rounds of the 1994 playoffs, but in the Eastern Conference final, the New Jersey Devils won Games 4 and 5 convincingly to take a 3-2 series lead and push the Rangers to the brink.

Unprompted, Messier guaranteed to the media the day before Game 6 that the Rangers would beat their rivals across the Hudson River and bring the series back to Manhattan.

"The questions that elicited Messier's response had little to do with a prediction. But Messier's replies were pointed and direct," said John Giannone, who was a Rangers beat writer at the time. "And they carried a distinct message from the weary leader to the embattled troops: I've put my five Stanley Cup rings, my reputation and my neck on the chopping block, boys. Now save me."

Messier recalled 20 years later: "I didn't realize, or forgot, that 14 million other New Yorkers and people around the country — and, more importantly, the New Jersey Devils — would be reading the same article. But at that point, we were so far down the tracks, it didn't really matter."

Down 2–0 late in the second period of Game 6 and facing goalie Martin Brodeur — who would set career records for wins, shutouts and playoff shutouts — it looked dire for the Rangers' title hopes and for Messier as prophet.

In an effort to spark the offense, Rangers coach "Iron" Mike Keenan decided to put slick center Alexei Kovalev on Messier's wing midway through the second period. It paid off when Messier set up Kovalev for the Rangers' first goal late in the frame, making it 2–1 at the second intermission.

At 2:48 of the third period, Kovalev returned the favor with a pass to Messier, who scored on a backhander to tie the game. Ten minutes later, with the teams playing 4-on-4, a Kovalev slap shot bounced

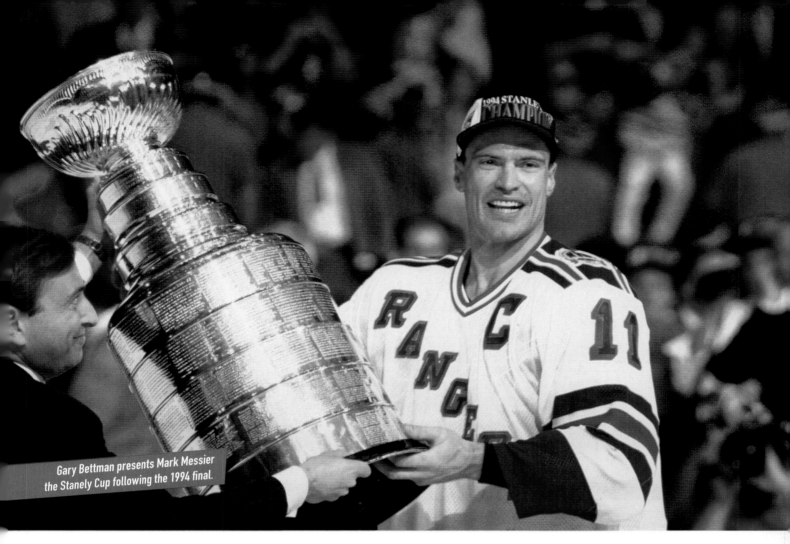

Gary Bettman presents Mark Messier the Stanely Cup following the 1994 final.

off Brodeur's chest and fell kindly for Messier, who bowled over a defender and slammed it into the net to give the Rangers the lead.

With Brodeur on the bench for the extra attacker and the Rangers killing a penalty, Messier intercepted a pass and sealed the win with an empty-netter from his own end.

"The stuff of legend. The called shot. The hat trick," said broadcaster Mike Emrick.

Keenan called it "one of the single most impressive performances by any hockey player in the history of this league."

But curses aren't easily broken. It took a double-overtime winner in Game 7 for the Rangers to reach the Stanley Cup Final, where they faced the Vancouver Canucks in another thriller that went to the limit. The Canucks rallied from a 3-1 series deficit, but Messier scored the winning goal in Game 7 to clinch the Rangers' first Stanley Cup in 54 years and become the only player in NHL history to captain two different teams to the title.

Not only had he brought the Cup back to

Manhattan, he mesmerized a city of endless distractions, where hockey was a niche sport. New York City Mayor Rudy Giuliani called Messier "Mr. June," and Rangers fans dubbed him "the Messiah."

Messier spent three more years in New York, including one with Gretzky, before joining the Canucks as a free agent in 1997. He returned to the Rangers in 2000 at the age of 39, and in 2004 in his 1,756th and final NHL game, he scored his 694th goal.

Messier retired with 1,887 points — the second-highest total in NHL history behind Gretzky — and only Gordie Howe played more games. He also created a legend that grows each passing year.

"So you make the guarantee, it makes headlines, and you score three goals in the third period? Seriously?" said Glenn Healy, the Rangers backup goalie on the Cup-winning team, in 2014. "How many of us have had these great plans, and they never come to fruition? Then the greatest leader in sports makes them and seals the deal with a hat trick, on his own, in the third. Never discount what Mess says. That's one thing I've learned."

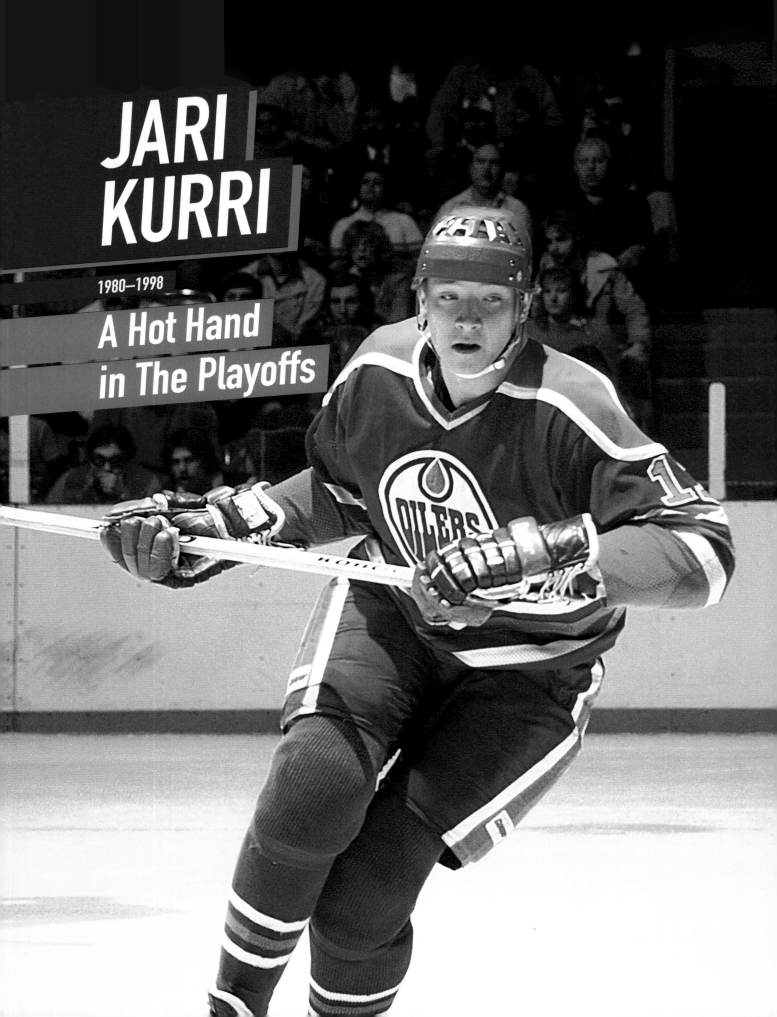

JARI KURRI

1980–1998

A Hot Hand in The Playoffs

IT TAKES A SPECIAL PLAYER TO STAND OUT IN HIS OWN RIGHT WHEN PLAYING ALONGSIDE PERHAPS THE GREATEST TALENT the game has ever seen.

The fate of Jari Kurri, the godfather of Finnish hockey excellence, could have been very different if not for the insistence of two of his countrymen, and a move by a coach looking for the right fit.

Kurri was born in Helsinki and rose through the ranks of the legendary Jokerit system as a budding professional. He was drafted 69th overall by Edmonton in 1980, but a reticent Kurri had to be convinced by Oilers Matti Hagman and Risto Siltanen — fellow Finns — to move to North America.

His plan was to stay two years, and when things started slowly in the 1980–81 season, he may have been considering cutting that short. But around Christmas, Oilers coach Glen Sather decided to put Kurri on Wayne Gretzky's wing. Together, they were magic.

Kurri had over 100 points in 1982–83, and the season after, he broke the 50-goal mark — the first of four consecutive seasons of 50 or more. He was the first Finnish player to reach both milestones.

It would be doing Kurri a disservice to suggest his 601 NHL goals were a result of being on a line with the best playmaker in NHL history. To be Gretzky's wingman, to keep up with the skill and mind of the player who was rewriting the way the game was played, Kurri needed to share Gretzky's head-space and see the game the same way as the Great One. The synergy of the duo — and Kurri's scoring exploits — allowed him to stand on his own as a premier threat. Kurri's strong defense also afforded Gretzky the offensive freedom he needed to be great.

The Oilers won the team's first Stanley Cup in 1984, and in 1984–85, Kurri had career highs of 71 goals — a single-season record by a right-winger — and 135 points, finishing second to Gretzky in the scoring race and winning the Lady Byng Trophy.

The Oilers beat the Philadelphia Flyers for their second-straight Stanley Cup that year, and Kurri had four hat tricks in the playoffs, including one four-goal game. He scored 19 goals, which tied the playoff record set by the Flyers' Reggie Leach in 1976.

The Oilers appeared to be an unstoppable dynasty in the making, but they lost in seven games in the 1986 Smythe Division final to the Calgary Flames when defensemen Steve Smith accidentally — and infamously — shot the puck into his own goal when a breakout pass hit goalie Grant Fuhr and caromed into the Oilers' net.

In 1987 the Oilers were back in the Stanley Cup, seeking redemption and their third championship in four years. It was a rematch with the Flyers, who now had Vezina Trophy winner Ron Hextall in net.

Edmonton won the first two games at home, with Kurri scoring the overtime winner in Game 2. The Oilers took a 3–0 lead in Game 3 in Philadelphia before the Flyers stormed back with five unanswered goals to win. They were the first team to come back from a 3–0 deficit to win a game in Stanley Cup Final history.

The Oilers won Game 4 to go up 3-1 in the series and had a 2-goal lead in Game 5 at home, but the Flyers rallied again to win 4–3.

The Flyers weren't daunted by another 2-goal deficit in Game 6, winning 3–2 to send the series back to Edmonton for Game 7. Hextall made 40 saves in the deciding game and won the Conn Smythe as playoff MVP, but the Oilers won the game 3–1 — and the series — thanks to Kurri's 15th goal of the playoffs, a wrist shot off a Gretzky pass with five minutes left in the second period, which held up as the Cup winner.

On a team with six future Hall of Famers, Kurri led the playoffs in goals each of the four years the Oilers won the Cup, from 1984 to 1988.

Kurri finished his career as the highest-scoring European-born player in NHL history, and his 106 goals and 233 points in 200 career playoff games both remain third in history, behind fellow Oilers and Hall of Famers Gretzky and Mark Messier.

As Oilers personnel director Barry Fraser said in the midst of their glory days, "We've got some outstanding people, eh? All-Stars, right? But Kurri is by far our most complete player."

DINO CICCARELLI

1981–1999

From Undrafted to Rookie Record Setter

DINO CICCARELLI HAD ALWAYS BEEN PRECOCIOUS, SO IT SHOULDN'T HAVE COME AS A SURPRISE WHEN HE BECAME an NHL playoff prodigy at the tender age of 21.

When Ciccarelli was 15, he played for his hometown Sarnia Legionnaires with 20-year-olds, after the coach convinced his father he wouldn't get killed. Vic Ciccarelli, who immigrated to Canada from Italy in the 1950s, may not have played hockey, but he was his son's inspiration on the ice.

"I think it's why I was never satisfied as a hockey player and always pushed for more," says Dino. "I didn't care how big opponents were or how much it hurt; I wanted to stick my nose in there. Dad did anything to make money, to support his family. He's been my biggest fan ... He drove me pretty hard. He's meant everything."

Ciccarelli joined the major junior London Knights at 16, and in his first season he had 82 points in 66 games and 24 points in 20 postseason matches. The following year he led the league in goals, with 72, but because of his relatively small stature (5-foot-10), he went undrafted. After another year of being passed over in the draft, the Minnesota North Stars wisely signed him as a free agent in 1979.

Called up from the North Stars minor-league affiliate in Oklahoma for the final 32 games of the 1980–81 regular season, Ciccarelli made a splash when he averaged almost a point per game leading up to the 1981 playoffs. But the unheralded right-winger was just warming up.

In the first round — a sweep of the Boston Bruins — Ciccarelli had 6 points, including a goal and 3 assists in a 9–6 Game 2 victory. Facing the Buffalo Sabres in round two, he had another 6 points, four of them goals. And in the Stanley Cup semifinal against the Calgary Flames, he had a hat trick in Game 4 and added a fourth goal in the series in the Game 6 clincher.

Awaiting the Cinderella North Stars in the Stanley Cup Final were the defending-champion New York Islanders. Ciccarelli posted 3 goals and 2 assists in the series, but the clock struck midnight on Minnesota's fairytale run, and the North Stars fell in five games.

Ciccarelli's consolation was a permanent spot in the NHL and rookie playoff records, with 14 goals and 21 points. The points record has since been equaled by Ville Leino of the Philadelphia Flyers in 2010, but still no rookie has scored more than 11 goals in the playoffs.

Ciccarelli's first full NHL season ended up being the best of his career. He set career highs in goals (55) and points (106) in 1981–82, marking his first of seven seasons of 30 or more goals — including two over 50 — in Minnesota. In nine seasons with the North Stars, he scored 332 goals and 651 points in 602 games.

After stints with Washington, Detroit, Tampa Bay and Florida, the player no one chose to draft had played 1,232 regular-season games, scored 608 goals and added 592 assists for an even 1,200 points. In 141 playoff games, he added 73 goals and 118 points.

The majority of those goals were scored within a stick's length of the net, and he absorbed a lot of opponents' lumber to earn them. He was also known to use his own, amassing 1,425 minutes in penalties, including a 10-game suspension and a day in jail for clubbing the Toronto Maple Leafs' Luke Richardson over the head with his stick in 1988.

The incident may have delayed induction, but Ciccarelli was welcomed to the Hall of Fame in 2010 in his eighth year of eligibility.

His dad died before he could see his son in the Hall of Fame, but Ciccarelli says that two of his favorite moments in hockey were having him there when he scored his 500th and 600th career goals.

As for the magical playoff run and record, Ciccarelli describes the alchemy of it as the "right time, right place, right team.

"Lou Nanne gave me an opportunity, put me with Tom McCarthy and Neal Broten. We gelled ... It was a great experience.

"It's nice [the rookie record is] still there."

RON FRANCIS

1982–2004

The Quiet Difference Maker

RON FRANCIS MIGHT BE THE MOST UNDERAPPRECIATED AND UNSUNG SUPERSTAR IN NHL HISTORY.

"I heard it put once that it is probably the quietest 1,500-plus points that anybody has ever scored," said Francis after he passed boyhood hero Phil Esposito in 2001 for fifth on the all-time scoring list, 20 years after he was drafted fourth overall by the Hartford Whalers.

"That's probably true. But it doesn't really matter to me what people say about me. As individuals you try to go out there and work as hard as you possibly can, and at the end of the day, you can look in the mirror and know that you've tried your best and given everything you have. That's when you have to be satisfied. That's all I've ever been concerned with."

Francis certainly gave his all to the Whalers. Called up partway through the 1981–82 season, he had 68 points in 59 games. It was the team's third season in the NHL, and over the next nine years, Francis became the face of the franchise as he dragged them to respectability. He led the team in scoring and to the playoffs five times before he was traded to the Pittsburgh Penguins in 1991.

In Pittsburgh, on a team with Mario Lemieux and Jaromir Jagr — not to mention legends and multiple-Cup winners like Bryan Trottier and Paul Coffey — Francis didn't have to bear the burden

of carrying the offense. But he quietly and naturally became a respected leader.

"He was a true professional, on and off the ice," says Mark Recchi. "He's a better person than he was a player — and he was a great player."

The Penguins won their first Stanley Cup later that year. "Coffey knew all about winning Cups, and he told me to enjoy the moment, but that it would get better every day the rest of my life," Francis said of the immediate aftermath of the title. "He was right."

The 1991–92 season started with a Stanley Cup hangover and the loss of beloved head coach "Badger" Bob Johnson to a brain tumor. The Penguins finished third in their division, and when the 1992 playoffs started, Francis was playing on a badly injured knee he suffered late in the season. "I didn't think [my knee] was going to make it through the Washington series," he says. "But when you're winning hockey games, you don't feel it as much. And when you see the finish line ahead of you, it gives you the incentive to just play through."

In Game 4 of the Patrick Division final against the New York Rangers, the Penguins were trailing two games to one in the series and 3–1 in the game when a Francis shot from his own blue line beat Rangers goalie Mike Richter at 19:54 of the second period.

Francis scored another in the third period and got his sixth of the series at 2:47 into overtime to

complete the hat trick and tie the series.

"I've never heard the arena that loud," recalled teammate Phil Bourque. "Ronnie Francis — that's what I remember from the series. That overtime goal for the hat trick was the stuff of legend."

That was the start of seven straight Pittsburgh wins, including a sweep of the Boston Bruins in the conference final to set up a Stanley Cup matchup against the Chicago Blackhawks.

The Penguins' winning streak reached 11 as they swept Chicago for their second consecutive Cup, and it was Francis's 8th goal of the playoffs that held up as the Cup winner in a wild 6–5 final in Game 4. The goal was Francis's 27th point in 19 playoff games.

Francis racked up 723 points in 533 games for Pittsburgh and 100 points in 97 playoff games. In 1994–95 he became the first player in history to win the Selke Trophy as the NHL's best defensive forward and the Lady Byng as the league's most gentlemanly player. He had a career-high 119 points in 1995–96, including a league-leading 92 assists.

Francis returned to the Whalers as a free agent in 1998. In his absence the team had relocated to Carolina and become the Hurricanes, and 10 years after clinching the Cup for the Penguins, Francis, at the age of 39, led the Hurricanes in scoring and a surprise run to the Stanley Cup Final. Carolina lost the championship, but Francis did win his third Lady Byng that year and added the King Clancy Memorial Trophy as the player who best exemplifies leadership qualities on and off the ice.

When he retired after 23 NHL seasons, Francis had played the third-most games in NHL history (1,731), scored the fourth-most points (1,798 on 549 goals and 1,249 assists), and was second in career assists to Wayne Gretzky's 1,963. Perhaps most impressive: he scored 20 or more goals in 20 seasons, a total surpassed only by Gordie Howe, with 22.

"Just a class guy," says former Pittsburgh teammate Kevin Stevens. "We would have never won the Stanley Cup without him."

DALE HAWERCHUK

1982–1997

Rookie Record Kick-Starts Jets Turnaround

LIKE MANY BOYS HIS AGE, DALE HAWERCHUK'S IDOL WAS BOBBY ORR, THE OFFENSIVELY GIFTED BOSTON BRUINS All-Star defenseman who first turned heads as an underage player in the Ontario Hockey League with the Oshawa Generals.

Hawerchuk too was turning heads at a young age, scoring all 8 goals in the final of a prestigious Montreal peewee tournament, breaking a record for goals in a game, first set by Guy Lafleur.

When Hawerchuk was 15, the Oshawa Generals — Orr's former club — offered him a try-out. He didn't make the team, and the Generals assigned him to their Junior B affiliate, coached by the legendary future NHL and Team Canada coach Mike Keenan. He did well enough there that the Quebec Major Junior Hockey League's (QMJHL) Cornwall Royals (who, despite being in the Quebec league, were able to select players in Ontario) drafted him sixth overall in 1979. "I wondered if they were a new team in the OHL," says Hawerchuk. "I knew nothing about them."

And like his idol before him, Hawerchuk's major junior debut was stellar, scoring 103 points and winning the QMJHL Rookie of the Year. He added a whopping 45 points in 18 games in the playoffs as the team captured the Memorial Cup.

At the time, the Memorial Cup winner represented Canada at the World Junior Championship,

and Hawerchuk tied for the tournament lead with 9 points.

In his second season in Cornwall, "all the pressure was on [Hawerchuk]" according to fellow Royal and future Hall of Famer Doug Gilmour. "It would be like [Connor] McDavid now or [Sidney] Crosby in his junior years. Dale came through with flying colors."

Hawerchuk had 81 goals and 183 points, won Canadian Major Junior Player of the Year and was named Memorial Cup MVP as the Royals repeated.

The NHL draft in 1981 was a no-brainer: the Winnipeg Jets picked Hawerchuk first overall and introduced him with great fanfare on August 13.

Hawerchuk was driven to the Jets' 10th anniversary party on the corner of Portage and Main in downtown Winnipeg in a Brinks truck. When he arrived he signed his first pro contract and was handed the No. 10 jersey while the mayor and members of the provincial legislature looked on.

It was a lot of hype for a shy teen to live up to, but fans and dignitaries would not be disappointed. In 1981–82, 18-year-old Hawerchuk led the Jets to the single biggest turnaround by any team in NHL history. After just nine wins the season prior, the Jets won 33 games and had 80 points — a 48-point improvement.

Hawerchuk played every game that season, scoring 45 goals and 103 points. He broke 17 franchise

records, including points in a season, and was the youngest player to ever be named the NHL's top rookie.

Hawerchuk was also the youngest player in history to have more than 100 points and the first rookie to have 40 goals and 100 points in the same season — the second-highest point total ever recorded by an NHL freshman.

That record was owned by Wayne Gretzky, who was two years older and two provinces over, in the city of Edmonton. The two shared a work ethic and a certain style of play; neither appeared to be the smoothest or quickest skater, but they just kept scoring.

Goal magazine called Hawerchuk "Mini-Gretzky," and Mike Doran, the Winnipeg Jets' director of player personnel when Hawerchuk was drafted, said, "He has the same instincts — that puck sense — of Gretzky."

In 1984–85, Hawerchuk had 53 goals and 130 points — both career highs — and he finished second in Hart Trophy voting. No prizes for guessing the winner.

Playing alongside Gretzky in the historic 1987 Canada Cup, Hawerchuk scored the fifth goal in the deciding game of the final against the Soviet Union and won the faceoff that led to the Gretzky-to-Lemieux, tournament-winning sixth goal.

In 1990, Hawerchuk was traded to the Buffalo Sabres. He had scored 379 goals in 713 games with the Jets. It took 1,422 games over 20 seasons for Shane Doan to break Hawerchuk's Jets/Phoenix Coyotes franchise record (which Doan did, fittingly, against the new incarnation of the Winnipeg Jets).

Hawerchuk spent five years with the Sabres before closing out his career in St. Louis and Philadelphia, becoming the first NHLer to play 1,000 games before his 31st birthday.

Hawerchuk retired in 1997 after losing in the Stanley Cup Final with the Flyers, the first final of his career. He left the game with 518 goals and 1,409 points in 1,188 career games, and was inducted into the Hall of Fame in 2001.

"People think because you are in the Hall of Fame it must have been easy for you, but that was not the case with me," said Hawerchuk in 2015. "I could get results, but I wasn't the greatest skater. I had to find a way to score."

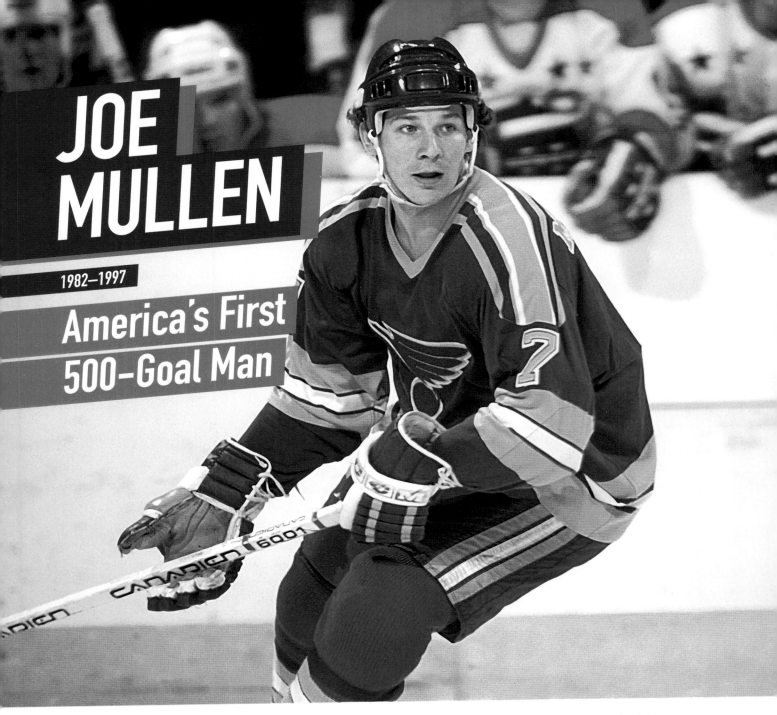

JOE MULLEN

America's First 500-Goal Man

GROWING UP IN HELL'S KITCHEN, ON MANHATTAN'S MEAN STREETS — WHEN SUCH A THING EXISTED —JOE MULLEN could see Madison Square Garden from his window. His dad worked at the iconic arena and brought home sticks for him and younger brother Brian to use on the asphalt of the schoolyard across the street.

The brothers learned on roller skates, using a wad of electrical tape as their puck. The cracked and craggy pavement that taught them to puckhandle was also a long way from the leafy campus of Boston College, where Mullen was offered a partial scholarship. He paid out of his own pocket as a freshman

before his play convinced the school to give him a full ride the rest of the way.

At 5-foot-9, Mullen was considered undersized by NHL scouts, and he went undrafted. But after averaging a point per game at the 1979 World Hockey Championship, the St. Louis Blues signed him as a free agent. It was Blues GM Emile Francis who, during his time with the New York Rangers, had started the New York Metropolitan Junior Hockey League, which Mullen had dominated in his youth.

The Blues' offer pushed Mullen to decide between keeping his amateur status — which would allow him

included Mario Lemieux, Jaromir Jagr and several other future Hall of Famers, he found a way to stand out, because he just kept scoring. In the 1991 postseason he contributed 17 points — including 8 points in the final — as the Penguins won their first Stanley Cup. The following season he had back-to-back games with 4 goals, part of a five-game, 11-goal streak. He finished the 1991–92 season with 42 goals, and Pittsburgh repeated as champions.

Already the all-time leading American scorer, on February 7, 1995, at Pittsburgh's Civic Arena, Mullen had 4 points, including an assist on a John Cullen goal 28 seconds into the second period, to become the first American-born player to register 1,000 NHL points.

After a year with the Boston Bruins, Mullen returned to Pittsburgh for the 1996–97 season, his last in the NHL. On March 14, 1997, with only 10 games left in his career and two weeks after his 40th birthday, Mullen went to the dirty area in front of the net and deflected a point shot past Colorado Avalanche goalie Patrick Roy at 16:01 of the second period.

With that marker, Mullen was the first American with 500 goals, and it was the first of a record three 500th career goals that Roy surrendered. He later allowed those of the Detroit Red Wings' Steve Yzerman and Brendan Shanahan.

Mullen was inducted into the Hall of Fame in 2000 with 502 goals and 1,063 points in 1,062 games, three Stanley Cups, two Lady Byng awards and one Lester Patrick Trophy for outstanding service to hockey in the United States.

As one of just seven players in NHL history who were 5-foot-9 or under to have 1,000 points, and as the first U.S.-born player to score 500 goals and 1,000 points, Mullen was an inspiration.

"The way people talk about Joe is pretty special. He was one of those guys who didn't have the flash, the tape on his stick was always screwed up, he kind of looked like he was fumbling the puck, but he was probably one of the smartest hockey players," says Michigan-born Doug Weight, who played with Joe's brother Brian.

"That almost sounds like a backwards compliment, but it's not. He just played the game the right way, and every year he scored goals. He just scored goals. He was a machine."

to play in the 1980 Olympics in Lake Placid (that team famously became the American "Miracle on Ice" squad) — or turning pro and playing in the NHL. Mullen chose pro and a paycheck to help take care of the family, because his father was ill. He made his Blues debut in the 1980 playoffs and joined the team permanently during the 1981–82 season, notching 59 points in 45 games. In 1983–84 he scored 41 goals, the first of six times he posted 40 or more.

Traded to the Calgary Flames midway through the 1985–86 season, Mullen helped the Flames reach the Stanley Cup Final that year, which they lost to the Montreal Canadiens.

Three years later he had a career-high 51 goals and 110 points, and added 16 more goals in the playoffs — the most in the NHL that year — to help the Flames avenge their loss to the Canadiens and win the 1989 Stanley Cup. Mullen capped the banner year with his second Lady Byng.

In 1990, Mullen was traded to the Pittsburgh Penguins, where, among an already potent lineup that

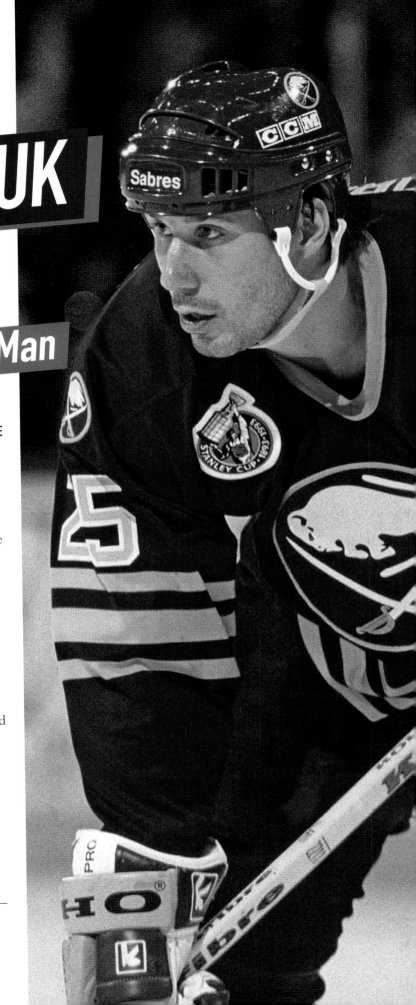

DAVE ANDREYCHUK

1983–2006

Portrait of the Artist as a Garbage Man

MOST HOCKEY PEOPLE WILL AGREE THAT SCORING GARBAGE GOALS IS A DIRTY JOB: IT TAKES A LOT OF GUTS TO STAND in front of the net and absorb the punishment necessary to tip in a shot or whack in a rebound. They're the goals scored by grinders who may not have the offensive skills to race end to end, outmaneuver an opponent, or fire in a one-timer. Yet some players have the talent to lift garbage goals to high art. Dave Andreychuk was one of those players.

"It started in junior," Andreychuk once said, "16, 17 years old. You realize [that the front of the net is] where my bread and butter was going to be. Not a lot of pretty goals, to be honest. Not sure if there's a highlight-reel goal." Yet over the course of a 23-season career between 1982 and 2006, Andreychuk managed to score 640 regular-season goals, ranking him 15th all-time in NHL history. And while Alex Ovechkin is likely to surpass him early in the 2020–21 season, as of 2019–20, no one has scored more career power-play goals than Andreychuk's total of 274.

At 6-foot-4 and 220 pounds, Andreychuk was a big man with soft hands. The Buffalo Sabres picked him 16th overall in the 1982 Draft after he had 57 goals and 100 points with the Oshawa Generals of the OHL. He scored 38 goals in his first full NHL season in 1983–84 and had a career-high 54 in 1992–93 in a season split between Buffalo and Toronto.

He had 53 with the Maple Leafs the following year. Andreychuk led the NHL with 28 power-play goals in 1991–92 and with 32 power-play goals in 1992–93, which is the second-highest single season total in NHL history behind Tim Kerr's 34 in 1985–86.

In 2002–03, a year before he captained the Tampa Bay Lightning to the Stanley Cup, Dave Andreychuk surpassed Phil Esposito as the NHL's all-time power-play leader. At the time, Espo was credited with 249 power-play goals. (A revision of NHL statistics in recent years knocked him down to 246.) Andreychuk scored #250 on November 15, 2002. He was camped out in front of San Jose netminder Evegny Nabokov with defenseman Scott Hannan trying to knock him out of the way.

"It was a good play by Richie [Brad Richards]," said Andreychuk afterwards. "All I had to do was get my stick on it. It was another one of those goals where I didn't have to do much."

Phil Esposito (now a Lightning radio analyst) was gracious when his record fell, just as he had been when Wayne Gretzky broke his single-season scoring record. "What can, I say?" said Espo of Andreychuk. "Terrific…. A power-play guy has to pay the price. He has to be there and stand in front of the net and take a beating. Dave takes a beating. That's why he has 250. He's the man."

STEVE YZERMAN

1984—2006

Fan-Favorite OT Winner Ushers in New Era for Detroit

Steve Yzerman hoists the Stanley Cup
following the 1998 final.

STEVE YZERMAN NOT ONLY CAPPED ONE OF THE GREATEST PLAYOFF GAMES IN NHL HISTORY BUT ALSO HELPED USHER in the nickname that has become as synonymous with Detroit as is the Motor City: Hockeytown, U.S.A.

His goal in the second overtime period of Game 7 of the Western Conference semifinal in 1996 gave his Detroit Red Wings a 1–0 victory — and the series — over the St. Louis Blues, who had finished 51 points behind Detroit in the regular season. Had the Wings lost, their reputation as postseason underachievers would have grown exponentially. The franchise hadn't won a Stanley Cup championship since 1955 and had been swept by the New Jersey Devils in the previous spring's final.

Although the Red Wings reignited their fans' passion by winning back-to-back elimination games after dropping three consecutive one-goal decisions to the underdog Blues, they would not win the Cup in 1996 either. They went on to lose the Western Conference final to Patrick Roy — against whom Yzerman had

scored his 500th goal in January — and the eventual Cup champions, the Colorado Avalanche.

The following year the Hockeytown logo made its debut in the faceoff circle at Joe Louis Arena's center ice, and the Detroit Red Wings won three of the next six Cups, in 1997, 1998 and 2002.

By the time he scored the goal that broke a scoreless tie in the second minute of the second overtime of Game 7, Yzerman had evolved from the 50-plus goal-scorer of the late 1980s into a complete two-way player and a team captain. And in Game 6 of the series, à la Mark Messier, he had predicted his team would force a seventh match. They won, 4–2.

"We never sat back and said, 'My God, what if?'" Yzerman said. "It really was a different atmosphere. There was a lot of excitement, a lot of energy. People were really positive. We proved to ourselves how to approach tough games and tough situations. If anything, our attitude got better, our will got stronger and our confidence grew."

The Blues were loaded with talented veteran

players, many of whom had made their reputations elsewhere. Throughout most of Game 7, Yzerman was matched against Wayne Gretzky's line.

St. Louis dominated the first overtime period, but 14 seconds into the second extra frame, Jon Casey, replacing the injured Grant Fuhr, had to make a brilliant save against Sergei Fedorov. A minute later Slava Fetisov coolly retrieved the puck in his own zone and got it to defenseman Vladimir Konstantinov, who wobbled a poor pass over the blue line that Gretzky nearly intercepted on the left side of the ice.

But the puck bounced off Gretzky's stick and then his skate and caromed to Yzerman, who angled to the right and unleashed a slap shot from just inside the blue line that caught Casey by surprise and turned the relatively quiet Joe into a screaming madhouse. Many Wings fans still call it their favorite goal of all time.

"I remember thinking in the first overtime, 'I'm just going to start shooting the puck from wherever. I'm tired and they're not calling penalties,'" Yzerman would later explain of his eighth shot of the game, 8th goal of the playoffs and 11th point of the series.

"The defensemen were just wrapping us up. I wasn't getting a whole lot done. So I picked the puck up in the neutral zone — I think Murray Baron was the defenseman — and I thought, 'Just shoot it and try to get it past his feet and not hit him.' Sure enough, I found a clear path and it found the top corner. It was kind of a lucky shot because I was just trying not to get it blocked. That was my only playoff overtime goal."

In more than one fan poll, Yzerman's series winner has ranked among the top-10 moments in Stanley Cup history. It broke more than 81 minutes of scoreless hockey in which both Casey and Detroit goalie Chris Osgood had been flawless. It was the second 1–0 game in the series: Gretzky had scored the only goal of Game 4 to tie the semifinal at two games apiece.

"I couldn't believe it went in," Yzerman said amid the Detroit delirium. "I don't score a whole lot of goals from out there. To score a goal in overtime, particularly in Game 7, is a tremendous thrill. Every player dreams of that."

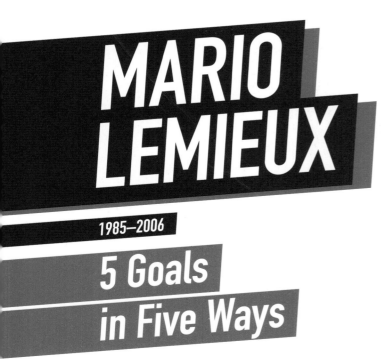

MARIO LEMIEUX

1985–2006

5 Goals in Five Ways

UNLIKE MOST OF MARIO LEMIEUX'S OUTRAGEOUSLY BRILLIANT ACCOMPLISHMENTS — SO IMMEDIATE AND SO GASP inducing — this one took a little while to sink in.

And it will take a lot longer to match, although most hockey observers believe it never will be. It would take a perfect storm, including a score close enough to produce an empty-net situation, and it would take somebody as skilled at marquee production as the Magnificent One.

On December 31, 1988, playing in front of a hometown crowd of 16,025 revelers taking in a Pens game against the New Jersey Devils before ringing in the New Year, Lemieux scored 5 goals. That's a rare enough occurrence in itself, although a little more frequent for the likes of him and fellow outlier Wayne Gretzky, but Lemieux went one mammoth step further on this celebratory night.

Each goal was scored in a different manpower situation: at even strength, on a power play, short-handed, on a penalty shot and into an empty net. No player had ever scored in five different ways before the Cinco de Mario, and no player has ever done it since.

"Quite frankly, nobody was aware until the score sheet came down and you looked at it," longtime Penguins broadcaster Mike Lange recalled later.

"The first thing you think is, 'Has anybody ever done this before?' The actual truth was that nobody

Mario Lemieux hoists the Stanley Cup following the 1991 final.

said, 'Look, if he scores an empty-netter …' No, it wasn't that way at all."

Lemieux scored his final goal of the record-setting game at 19:59, with goalie Chris Terreri, who had replaced starter Robert Sauvé, sitting on the New Jersey bench as the Devils tried to even the score at 7–7. There was some talk that time should already have expired, but the fifth goal counted.

By then, he had scored an even-strength goal at 4:17 of the first period followed by a short-handed goal at 7:50, and he then completed his opening-frame natural hat trick with a power-play goal off a slap shot at 10:59. That gave him his fourth hat trick of a season that was not yet half over. All were scored against Sauvé, who allowed five goals on 10 shots. He was starting in place of regular goalie Sean Burke, who was injured.

In the middle of the second period, Terreri, replacing the struggling Sauvé, found himself caught out of his own net with Lemieux bearing in on the only Devil in the defensive zone. In desperation,

the goalie threw his stick, resulting in the penalty shot call. Of course Lemieux scored, leaving only an empty-net goal remaining in the *Mission Impossible* he didn't really know he was on. Some karma had to be involved as the Devils kept it a one-goal game, enabling them to pull their goalie late, but that's the kind of year it was for Lemieux.

The Mario Cycle, as it became known, is considered by many to be the greatest individual scoring performance ever, especially when you consider he also assisted on each of the other three Penguins goals, giving him 100 points for the season — less than a week after Christmas.

"That was Mario's Christmas gift, a little late, to me and the fans," Penguins coach Gene Ubriaco said after the game. "I'm not going to say it was awesome — I've said that too many times before. What can I say? Someone once said we are a one-man team and certainly tonight … when he makes up his mind, no one can stop him."

Many of the game's leading players of the era

acknowledge that the already-ascendant Lemieux had taken a massive step forward 16 months earlier, when he stood out among more seasoned players on Team Canada in the 1987 Canada Cup. His tournament was capped by scoring the winning goal on a drop pass from Gretzky in the championship game at Copps Coliseum in Hamilton, Ontario. And that perception of greatness arrived was borne out over the next couple of seasons. He went directly from Team Canada to a 168-point regular season, up 61 points from the previous year, then had the best statistical year of his career in 1988–89, with 85 goals and 199 points.

What is stunning is that in NHL history a player has scored 8 or more points in a single game only 16 times. Lemieux accounts for three of them, all in that 1988–89 season, including one in the playoffs against cross-state rival Philadelphia. In that rampage against the Flyers, he tied the NHL records for most goals and points in a playoff game, most goals in a playoff period (4), and most assists (3) in a single postseason period. Of the nine other players who have recorded 8 or more points in a game, only Wayne Gretzky had done it more than once.

"It was a good game," he grossly understated after the historic performance. "It seems everything I did went the right way. I had the day off yesterday and that helps me, particularly at this time of the year."

According to Joe Starkey's *Tales from the Pittsburgh Penguins Locker Room*, Lemieux asked locker-room attendant Tracey Luppe, who'd been with the club for a few years but had never taped the star's sticks, if he wanted to do so that night.

"Well, he goes out and scores 5 goals in five different ways," Luppe recalled in 2004. "Needless to say, I'm still doing them today."

Lemieux lost the Hart Trophy to Gretzky that year, sparking an industry-wide debate. He had not only led the league in most scoring categories — goals, assists, points, power-play goals, shorthanded goals and hat tricks — but he was also a plus-41 for the Penguins, a team that scored two fewer goals than it allowed. Lemieux's two linemates (Bob Errey and Rob Brown) were the only other players on the team with a plus rating.

Powered by Lemieux's 8-point nights and his

199-point regular season, the Penguins made the playoffs for the first time in seven years. They were eliminated in the second round, but Lemieux had 17 points in 11 games, establishing himself as the same undeniable force in the playoffs that he had become in the regular season.

"He did things on the ice that 95 percent of us in this league only dream of doing," said Hall of Famer Ron Francis, who joined Lemieux in Pittsburgh for his two Stanley Cups.

Seventeen years after his 5-in-five New Year's Eve, Lemieux played his last game, and, befitting of a man who had always attracted the spotlight (he scored on the first shift — and first shot — of his NHL career), he had a goal and an assist against the Flyers in a losing playoff effort. He was asked on the eve of his retirement how he would like to be remembered.

"As a winner," he said. "As someone who started with the worst team in the NHL back in 1984 and was able to win a Stanley Cup seven years later. This was a big challenge for me. To be able to do that is something I am very proud of and something I can take with me and cherish for a long, long time."

BRETT HULL

1987—2006

Controversy in Buffalo

I T WAS THE SECOND-LONGEST GAME EVER PLAYED IN A STANLEY CUP FINAL, AND AS FAR AS HARDCORE BUFFALO SABRES FANS are concerned, it should still be going on.

In the early hours of June 20, 1999, Brett Hull's shot past a sprawling Dominik Hasek was reviewed and ruled a legal goal. It stands as the 1999 Cup winner even though Hull's skate appeared to be illegally in the goal crease.

During that 1998–99 season, a number of similar goals had been called back: a new rule stated that an attacking player couldn't stand in the goal crease unless the puck was already there. The rule was intended primarily to protect goalies from the increasing traffic in and around the blue paint.

But other than goalies, few embraced the regulation because it resulted in a number of good goals being canceled for nothing more than having a skate in the blue paint. In addition, reviewing goals delayed and defused post-goal celebrations and adversely affected the flow of the game.

Hasek's Sabres and Hull's Dallas Stars entered Game 6 at Buffalo's HSBC Arena on the evening of June 19 with the visitors holding a 3-2 lead in the series and hoping to capture the franchise's first Stanley Cup. As the Minnesota North Stars, the organization had lost in the 1981 and 1991 finals.

As the seventh seed in the Eastern Conference, the upstart Sabres were clear underdogs to the Stars, who had won the Presidents' Trophy and finished with 23 more points. Coached by Ken Hitchcock, the Stars were in win-now mode. When Hull signed a three-year contract in July 1998 after 11 seasons in St. Louis, he was regarded — correctly, as it turned out — as the final component in a Stanley Cup contender.

"It ranks number one to me," Hull recalled of the goal a few years later. "There was a boatload of people saying when I was leaving St. Louis, 'You're never going to win with Brett Hull on your team.' To go to Dallas and be the missing piece of the puzzle that's going to help them win their Cup, and then to go out and score the goal in overtime — who hasn't sat as a kid on the ice with his buddies and dreamt or pretended that's the goal they've scored?

"To do it in real life was something special."

It wasn't so special to hockey fanatics in Western New York, who argue to this day that the ruling on Hull's goal was inconsistent with what had been called during the regular season.

In the 55th minute of overtime, the puck came to Hull (Jere Lehtinen and Mike Modano are credited with assists) in front of Hasek, who used his stick to stop Hull's initial backhand. Hasek couldn't smother on the rebound, but he did outbattle Hull to push the puck out of the crease. The puck deflected off Hull's left skate towards his right — his stick side — as Hull's skate left the crease. As the puck landed on Hull's stick blade in front of the crease, his left skate re-entered the painted area before he swept the puck — in unerring Hull style — through the only space Hasek had left him and into the net.

The Stars stormed onto the ice in celebration, but Buffalo coach Lindy Ruff and an arena full of his supporters were yelling, "No goal!" Meanwhile, the on-ice officials waited by the penalty box until they received the signal from the NHL's war room that the goal was legit.

"We saw that red light, and we just jumped on the ice. It was a big celebration," recalls Guy Carbonneau, who was the Stars' checking center at the time. "Once you get it to a second or third overtime, you're just happy to get that goal. There was an issue about the goal an hour later, but I don't think anyone thought about it at the time. It never came up in my mind. And then, I would say maybe an hour later, once we were in the room and drinking champagne, that's the first time we ever heard about it. But it was too late.

"It was a bad rule," Carbonneau continued. "That's why they changed it the next year. I understand the rule, but they should have written it differently. I think they realized after that that the rule didn't make sense."

The NHL's ruling was that the sequence of shot, rebound, kicked puck off the skate and second shot constituted continuous possession by Hull, which made his skate in the crease — and the Cup-clinching goal — permissible.

"Hull had possession and control of the puck," Bryan Lewis, then the NHL's director of officiating, explained to a media horde hours after the game.

"The rebound off the goalie does not change anything. It is his puck then to shoot and score, albeit a foot may or may not be in the crease prior to."

A memorandum clarifying the continuous possession concept had been circulated to NHL teams prior to the playoffs, although the media and therefore the public had not been alerted to the clarification.

"We all knew they had changed the rule," Hull recalled on a conference call just before his 2009 induction into the Hockey Hall of Fame. "But obviously, the NHL decided they weren't going to tell anybody but the teams. They changed the rule to say if you have control in the crease, you can score the goal, and that's exactly what it was.

"But nobody knows that. You can tell people that a million times, and they just will not listen."

More might have listened had the NHL thought to inform the public about the rule clarification at the same time they informed the teams.

Hull has constantly had to defend that goal, and the always-playful wisecracker has had some fun on Twitter at the expense of Buffalo fans, who are still waiting for their first Stanley Cup championship. Ironically, Hull was a teammate when Hasek won his first Stanley Cup title, with the 2002 Detroit Red Wings.

The goal that clinched Hull's first championship was his second major moment of the 1998–99 season. On New Year's Eve he had scored his 600th goal, which made him and Bobby Hull the first father-and-son duo to achieve that significant milestone.

But Brett's Cup winner almost wasn't. As Carbonneau remembers, Hull was sitting most of the

overtime: "Brett got hurt earlier in the game — his knee, I think. And in the third overtime, Benoit Hogue broke a stick blade, or something happened to his equipment. I remember Ken Hitchcock asked Brett if he could give him just one shift, because the period was almost ending. So he jumped on the ice and …

"We still talk about it all the time. He happened to be in the right place at the right time. It's one of those stories you like to hear because Brett had an unbelievable career and had this chance to win the Cup."

It's only in Buffalo that they don't like to hear it.

JOE NIEUWENDYK

1987–2007

A Steady Hand in Turbulent Times

THE DAY AFTER THE CALGARY FLAMES CHOSE JOE NIEUWENDYK IN THE 1985 ENTRY DRAFT — WITH a second-round pick received in a trade for local favorite Kent Nilsson — a local newspaper headline screamed, "Joe who?"

Nieuwendyk would spend his entire career giving positive answer after positive answer to that question — a career that lasted through 20 seasons, led to a place in the Hall of Fame and included three Stanley Cups with three different teams in three different decades.

A prolific scorer from the outset, he helped the Flames to the 1989 Stanley Cup, then led the Dallas Stars to the title in 1999 and got a third ring with the 2003 New Jersey Devils.

It was the middle one, with Brett Hull missing time because of an injury and Mike Modano hampered by a wrist injury, that solidified Nieuwendyk as a quietly efficient money player. A year after he tore an ACL being checked by Bryan Marchment in Game 1 of the first round of the playoffs, Nieuwendyk won the Conn Smythe Trophy as the most valuable player of the postseason. His nomination came on the strength of his playoff-leading 11 goals, along with 10 assists, and his tying of Joe Sakic's record for most game-winning goals in the playoffs, with 6.

Some goals are potted early in a game and declared the game-winner only after the final margin of

victory has been determined. Few of Nieuwendyk's goals in 1999 matched that description.

When the veteran Stars swept Edmonton in the first round, giving themselves a much-needed rest, it was Nieuwendyk who scored in the 58th minute of extra play in Game 4 to eliminate the Oilers, several hours of real time after he'd opened the game's scoring.

In the next round, Nieuwendyk scored at 8:22 of overtime to give Dallas a 5–4 victory over St. Louis and a 2-0 lead in a series the Stars would eventually win in six games. In Game 2 of the Western Conference final, Nieuwendyk scored against Colorado's Patrick Roy just after the halfway point of the third period to break a 2–2 tie. The Stars went on to win in seven games and advance to the Cup Final against the younger Buffalo Sabres.

The Stars won their only Stanley Cup to date when Brett Hull scored a still-debated goal in the third overtime of Game 6, but Nieuwendyk helped Dallas get there by scoring both goals — one of them the winner, of course — in a 2–1 victory in Game 3. He also continued to display the supremacy in the faceoff circle that had made him the NHL's leader in draws won during the regular season.

It was a remarkable spring for Nieuwendyk — and not just because of the plethora of game-winners. He had spent a grueling summer in the Dallas heat rehabbing from his ACL injury, and he had to take

periodic rests during the regular season. With Hull's and Modano's nagging injuries, much of the onus of scoring fell on him.

Many Dallas fans still remember where they were when Nieuwendyk — wearing the captain's C for a week because Derian Hatcher was suspended — had Sergei Zubov's point shot bounce off him into the Edmonton net to end what was then the 12th-longest game in playoff history and launch the Stars on their Cup crusade.

"We had nothing left. They had nothing left," the soft-spoken Nieuwendyk said after the game. "Thank God it's over."

As you'd expect of a career 564-goal, 1,126-point player who honed his already-strong hand-eye coordination with years of top-level box lacrosse, Nieuwendyk had a touch around the net. He scored 51 goals in each of his rookie and sophomore seasons and 45 or more in each of his first four seasons. He capped his second year with 10 postseason goals as the Flames won their only Cup.

But it is the Dallas championship that seems to resonate most with him.

"You hate to say one is better than the other," he said. "But there was something special about that team that you could feel in the locker room. You never think about it at the time, but that was a talented team. We were very fortunate to all be together at one time.

"I was lucky that I had a Cup in 1989, but I went 10 years without getting close again, so when I went through it in '99, I savored every moment," Nieuwendyk said. "I remember so much of that run in '99. That's when you realize how hard it is to get there. I cherished every moment of it."

So much so that he got the Cup for two days that summer, taking it to Ithaca, New York, where he had attended Cornell University, and to his hometown of Whitby, Ontario, where he and some friends put a bowl of gravy in it at a local hamburger joint and dipped their french fries.

"To me, it's the people's Cup," he said. "I just get pleasure out of watching everyone's reactions to seeing the Cup."

It was a pleasure he got to experience three times for three different teams.

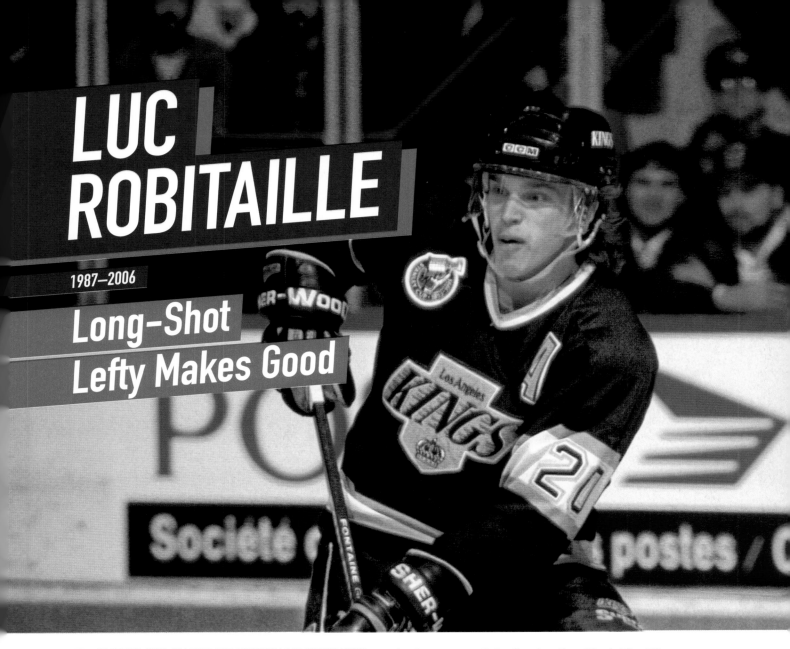

LUC ROBITAILLE

1987–2006

Long-Shot Lefty Makes Good

PAT BURNS, WHO COACHED LUC ROBITAILLE IN JUNIOR HOCK-EY AND COACHED AGAINST HIM IN THE NHL, HAD THIS TO say about the sniper that scouts had decided was too slow to play in the big leagues: "Coaching against him in the NHL, I would always tell my teams to pay close attention to him. But while he isn't always the first to the puck, he will eventually hurt you."

The Montreal native really hurt Burns and his Toronto Maple Leafs in the spring of 1993, when he scored the tying goal to send Game 6 of the Campbell Conference final into overtime. His Los Angeles Kings won the game on Wayne Gretzky's famous (in Toronto, infamous) goal, keeping the Los Angeles Kings alive for Game 7, which they also won.

Robitaille continued scoring, adding two goals in

the first game of the Stanley Cup Final. The Kings eventually lost in five games to the Montreal Canadiens, but the franchise's very first trip to the biggest series in hockey helped cement the NHL's broadening foundation on the U.S. West Coast and in the Sunbelt. Robitaille registered 9 goals and 22 points in 24 games in the Kings' run. His playoff success was an extension of the most prolific season ever enjoyed by an NHL left-winger. In 1992–93 with Wayne Gretzky sidelined by injury for about half the season, Robitaille assumed the captaincy and scored 63 goals, the most ever by a portside player until Alexander Ovechkin's 65 in 2007–08. He also had 125 points to slip by Kevin Stevens's single-season points record for left-wingers, established only the year before.

Despite battling flu on the final day of the season,

Robitaille surpassed Stevens's mark of 123 in striking style, with a goal and 3 assists in the Kings' 8–6 loss to Vancouver, their second defeat in three nights at the hands of the Canucks.

The losses to the division-winning Canucks, who finished 13 points ahead of the third-place Kings, was a brief glitch in their otherwise stellar closing weeks.

"We had a great start to the season, then we seemed to get tired and got a couple of injuries," Robitaille recalled. "But I know that in the last three weeks or four weeks of the season, we were as good as anybody in the NHL.

"Certainly, it was a lot of fun for me [to score 63], but I think it was more the success of the team that was so much fun, because we played every game like a playoff game that whole year because we knew we were always the underdog. Until Wayne came back, we were constantly the underdog. We had a team that was really together, and we were accomplishing things that no one ever expected us to accomplish."

That could also describe Robitaille, who had only one NHL scout, the Kings' Alex Smart, take any interest in him. And even with that, Los Angeles didn't select him until the 171st spot in the 1984 draft. Three years later he was the NHL's rookie of the year with 45 goals and 84 points.

Robitaille had a very quick release. His game was about finding scoring chances, and he worked to get himself into open areas where it was easy for

his centers to locate him. According to teammates, Robitaille would do anything to put the puck in the net.

"I have never been around a player who liked to score goals more than Luc," his former Kings teammate Rob Blake told the Frozen Royalty website. "He loved to score goals whether it was a game or practice. Not only did he love to score, he also knew how to score. That is what made him one of the best."

With Gretzky out of the lineup until January 1993, Robitaille was moved up to the first line for essentially the first time in his NHL career. And it was a converted winger and future Hall of Famer in Jari Kurri who became Lucky Luc's pivot and helped him to his record-breaking goal and point totals.

"I had a new center almost every few months. Funny enough in 1992–93, they put Jari Kurri as my center, and that's the best year I ever had statistics-wise." The fact that Kurri first shot to fame as the right-winger for Wayne Gretzky was not lost on Robitaille. "It's the irony of how things go sometimes," he said.

In March 2015 the Kings commemorated Robitaille's 14 seasons in Los Angeles (over three separate terms) with a bronze statue outside the Staples Center.

"I was 13 years old in 1979, and I had a picture of Wayne Gretzky in my room," he said appreciatively at the time of the unveiling. "And I watched him on TV every time I could. Now there are statues of both of us here."

BRENDAN SHANAHAN

1988–2009

Meaningful Goal Caps Unforgettable Season

BRENDAN SHANAHAN NEVER FORGETS THE MOST IMPORTANT GOALS SCORED BY OTHER PLAYERS.

As he puts it, "I remember goals, and not just mine ... I have a photographic memory of a lot of people's goals — the meaningful ones at least."

Shanahan scored a pair of meaningful goals, including the Cup winner, in the fifth game of the 2002 Stanley Cup Final, which was also his last appearance in the championship series. His Detroit Red Wings defeated the Carolina Hurricanes, the direct descendants of the Hartford Whalers, the team that traded him to the Motor City just two games into the 1996–97 season.

The 2013 Hockey Hall of Fame inductee, who is now president of his hometown Toronto Maple Leafs, has no problem summoning an instant mental replay of his Stanley Cup–winning goal.

The prototypical power forward — the first NHL player to score 600 goals and incur 2,000 penalty minutes — scored the deciding goal on a power play with just under six minutes left in the second period.

"When I scored against [Arturs] Irbe, it was important, but I didn't know it was going to end up being a Stanley Cup–winning goal," Shanahan recalls. "My goal ended up being the game-winning goal, but I think the special ones are the Jason Arnott ones, the [Bob] Nystrom ones, the [Patrick] Kane ones — breaking a tie late in the game. And

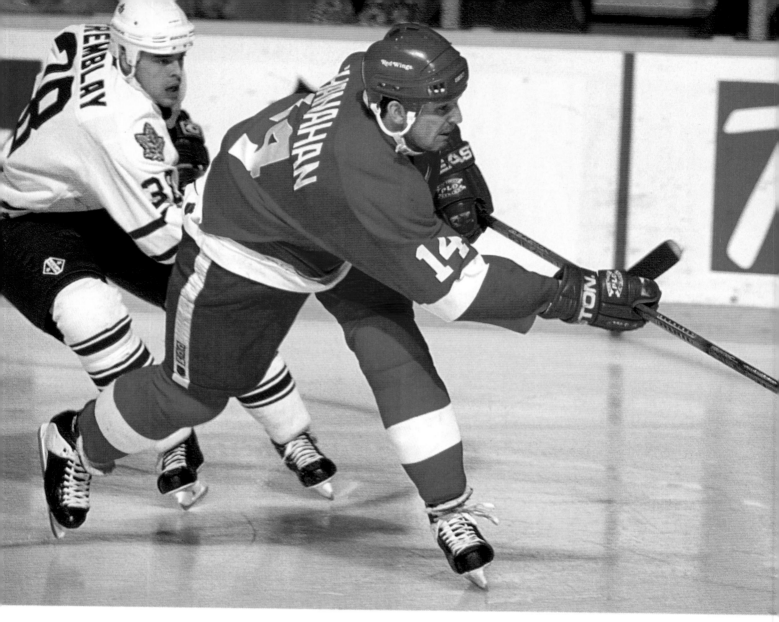

Darren McCarty's Stanley Cup–winning goal in '97 — my first year in Detroit — when it had been so long. I'd put all those ahead of mine."

Shanahan had been a big part of that 1997 Cup win — Detroit's first since 1955 — scoring 9 goals in the playoffs. Just the year before, he had been appointed captain of the Whalers after coming over from St. Louis in a trade for Chris Pronger. But after scoring a team-high 44 goals and 78 points in his one full season in Hartford, he asked for a trade.

It was no secret the Whalers were destined to leave Hartford, but where or when they would move remained uncertain. Shanahan says that as he entered his 10th year in the NHL, he wanted to "know where I was going to be and to have a chance to win." Whalers GM Jim Rutherford honored his request in early October 1996, sending him to Detroit for

fellow power forward Keith Primeau, defenseman Paul Coffey and a first-round draft choice. Defenseman Brian Glynn also went to the Wings.

Six seasons later, by which time the Whalers had moved to North Carolina, Shanahan was facing his old club with the Cup on the line.

"Sergei [Fedorov] was down low in the right corner," Shanahan recalls of Game 5, played on June 13, 2002, "and I was on the right side farther up. Stevie [Yzerman] was down low on the other side. The puck got over to Sergei's corner, and I held up defenseman Glen Wesley to give Sergei a bit of time to get it.

"It looked like Glen Wesley and I were tied up, but when I let him go, I was open. Sergei was able to pull it from his backhand to his forehand and saucer a little pass that I was able to shoot with a short

Brendan Shanahan hoists the Stanley Cup following the 1998 final.

backswing — I always had a very short backswing. I one-timed it from a bad angle, but I think it caught Irbe off guard, and it didn't go in clean. I went in through what we sometimes call the eight-hole. There was actually a split second where I was taking a step in to see if I could bang in a rebound.

"It was quick. When I shot it, it looked like it was going at him, but it went through him. It went in out of my sight. The people behind the net reacted to it … so I had a bit of a half-delayed reaction, then realized it went in and threw my arms up."

The goal made the score 2–0 with nearly half a game to play, but two things — both of which involved Shanahan — ensured his goal would stand as the winner. Late in the second period, he took a penalty, and while he was in the box, Jeff O'Neill scored for the 'Canes to halve the deficit and make

the Wings' second goal the potential winner. Then Shanahan insured the win with an empty-netter from the blue line with 45 seconds left, just as he was slammed into the boards.

"I always kid around with Jeff O'Neill: 'You and I conspired to give me the Cup-winning goal,'" Shanahan laughs.

That made Shanahan and Yzerman just the second and third players (Ken Morrow was the first, in 1980) to win an Olympic gold medal and the Stanley Cup in the same year. The win also capped a season in which the Red Wings became the first team to lose its first two playoff games and go on to hoist the Cup, and in which Shanahan scored his 500th goal (March 23, versus Colorado) and 1,000th point (January 12, against Dallas).

MARK RECCHI

1989–2011

A Man of Any Era

THROUGH THE 2019–20 SEASON, ONLY FIVE MEN IN NHL HISTORY HAVE PLAYED MORE GAMES THAN MARK RECCHI, WHO took part in 1,652 regular-season contests over 22 seasons from 1998 through 2011.

And all that playing resulted in a lot of scoring. Recchi ranks 12th all-time in points with 1,533, including 577 goals and 956 assists. He topped 100 points for the first of three times with 113 for Pittsburgh (including a career-high 70 assists) in 1990–91 and established personal bests with 53 goals and 123 points for Philadelphia in 1992–93. He was a top-10 scorer four times.

Recchi won numerous titles throughout his career, including a World Junior Championship in 1988 and a World Championship in 1997. He won the Turner Cup (International Hockey League) with the Muskegon Lumberjacks in 1989 in his first years as a pro and then won his first Stanley Cup championship in 1990 as an NHL rookie with the Penguins. Recchi won the Stanley Cup again with Carolina in 2006 and with Boston in 2011, making him one of only 10 NHL players to win the Stanley Cup with three different teams and one of only eight to win it in three different decades.

Despite his stellar stats, multiple championships and Hall of Fame career, Recchi was never really ever considered the "big" star on any team he played for. In fact, with the exception of, perhaps, the

dismal Montreal squad he joined partway through the 1994–95 lockout-shortened season, Recchi was almost always considered a secondary or tertiary draw. His early years were spent in Pittsburgh behind Mario Lemieux and Jaromir Jagr. His middle years were largely spent behind Eric Lindros — even though for the first two years of the big stud's career, Recchi outpaced him in points twice and goals once. In his later years, Recchi was brought in as a veteran presence and secondary scoring punch for players like Ilya Kovalchuk, Sidney Crosby and Evgeni Malkin. As Pittsburgh's general manager Ray Shero said of bringing Mark Recchi back to Pittsburgh (for his third time with the franchise) for the 2006–07 season, "I've seen Mark Recchi play for 15 years … I know the sort of leadership he brings on and off the ice."

Shero knew Recchi was no longer the 40 and 50-goal scorer of his youth. He'd turned into a consistent 20-goal scorer and an all-around player who could give a team 15 to 20 quality minutes and notch timely goals.

With the Bruins in 2011, the 43-year-old veteran became the oldest player ever to score in the Stanley Cup Final. He scored once in a 3–2 overtime loss to Vancouver on June 4, 2011, and then twice in an 8–1 win in Game 3 two nights later to kick-start Boston's comeback from a 2-0 deficit to a seven-game victory. Recchi announced his retirement immediately after

the series, and many of his teammates credited him as a key part of their championship.

"I wouldn't be here right now if it wasn't for him," said Boston rookie Brad Marchand. "Everything I learned from him on and off the ice is unbelievable. It's such an honor to be part of this with him."

"Recchi is amazing — he's such a tremendous leader," added Bruins forward Daniel Paille.

"Everyone loves him," said Shawn Thornton, "and appreciates everything he's done for us."

Summarizing his own career a few years later,

"pretty relentless," were the words Mark Recchi chose to describe himself. "I had a work ethic that I didn't want to be stopped and I would do whatever it took," he said. "I felt I could have played in any era because of that."

In a career that lasted from the glory years of Gretzky and Lemieux to the early days of Crosby and Ovechkin, it could be said that Recchi had already played in several eras.

He played, and he won.

JOE SAKIC

Dueling Hat-Tricks and Game-Winning Goals

PAT QUINN WAS TALKING ABOUT THE OPENING SERIES OF THE 1996 STANLEY CUP PLAYOFFS, BUT HE COULD JUST AS easily have been referring to that whole spring — or, for that matter, the entirety of Joe Sakic's career.

"Joe is a talented player and, over the years, has become a complete player," the consummate coach said of Burnaby Joe, who had just scored 3 goals against his Vancouver Canucks in Game 5 of the 1996 Western Conference semifinal, turning the tide towards a six-game Colorado Avalanche victory.

"I'm not too sure how we deal with him. What he does is capitalize on mistakes we've made."

In a 21-year Hall of Fame career that included a 16-season run as captain of the Avalanche and their original incarnation, the Quebec Nordiques, Sakic was always a quiet assassin, leading by example and letting his exploits speak for themselves with their loud impact.

"I'm quiet," Sakic told *Hockey Player* magazine. "I don't say too much in the dressing room. We have a lot of guys — or a few guys — that speak up in the dressing room. I'm not one of the talkers. I just try to do it by working right and working hard in practice."

And by translating that hard work in practice into mind-numbing exploits in big games.

There were many astounding moments yet to come: unselfishly handing the Stanley Cup to Raymond Bourque so he could hoist it first after the Avs'

second championship, scoring the winning goal in the 2002 Olympics to break Canada's 50-year gold-medal drought, becoming the second-oldest player ever to surpass 1,000 points. But none of those exploits speak louder than Sakic's 1996 Stanley Cup campaign.

Despite the presence of franchise-changing Patrick Roy in his team's net, Sakic won the Conn Smythe Trophy after leading the Avalanche to the first championship in a major professional team sport in Denver history, putting a cherry on top of the team's debut season after it moved from Quebec City.

Sakic led the playoffs with 18 goals, just one shy of the record set by the Flyers' Reggie Leach 20 years earlier and later matched by Jari Kurri. He also added 16 assists for 34 points in just 22 games.

Sakic had 51 goals and 120 points in 1995–96, the best regular-season production of his career, and none of those 51 goals came as part of a hat trick. But on the evening of April 25 in Denver, he scored three times, including the tying goal in the third period and the winner in overtime to match Trevor Linden's hat trick, as two quiet, let-their-game-do-the-bragging captains carried their teams

in Game 5. It was the last time two men scored hat tricks in the same playoff game until Sidney Crosby and Alexander Ovechkin went equally toe to toe in 2009.

"Joe's a great player, and this doesn't surprise me," Linden said the day after the game. "We're giving him a little too much space."

With his thunderous and quick wrist shot, it could usually be said that any space was too much to give Sakic. There was no time in his career — even in minor and junior hockey — when he wasn't a star

and when he wasn't working to get better. Cut from Canada's World Cup team in 1991, he worked incessantly on his skating until it was no longer an issue but a strength, and on the advice of his father, he worked on his wrists and his wrist shot from the time he took up the game.

"I would shoot pucks for hours, from all kinds of different positions," Sakic recalled to the *Denver Post*. "It became something that I had to do every day, right to the end of my career. If I ever missed a day of that, I would stress out."

Joe Sakic (top row, fifth from left) celebrates winning the Stanley Cup with his team following the 1996 final.

Instead, he stressed out goalies. Game after game.

"Joey is very hard-nosed and quick," goalie Corey Hirsch said when they were facing each other regularly in the Western Conference.

"He's got a quick release. If the puck's in the corner, he's hard after it. He doesn't let you beat him to it. When he's got the puck, it's off his stick — boom! Smart."

Hirsch was in goal for the Canucks when Sakic and Linden traded hat tricks in Game 5.

Sakic's 1st goal was the result of a great defensive play in the offensive zone when he, seemingly innocuously, corralled with one hand a puck that was rolling out of the Vancouver zone, wheeled to the right side where he scored so many of his 51 goals that year, and let go an unexpected wrister off the wrong foot, off the post and past Hirsch.

The game-tying goal came partway through the third period from between the circles, dead in front of the net, where he had all five holes to pick from.

Then, in overtime, Sakic demonstrated just how tiny a space was, in Linden's estimation, too much to give

him. Taking a nifty back pass from Sandis Ozolinsh while stationed almost against the boards at the right hash mark, he let another wrist shot go, again off the wrong foot. Goal, Avalanche win, series momentum.

Two nights later, Sakic gave the Avalanche their first playoff series win when his snapshot off another pass from Ozolinsh with less than three minutes to go broke a 2–2 tie for his 7th goal of the series. It was his second game-winner in a row — of six he would score in the playoffs — breaking the record held by Mike Bossy, Jari Kurri, Mario Lemieux and Bobby Smith.

Sakic had 8 points in a six-game series against Chicago, then added 10 points, including two goals and an assist, in the series clincher against Detroit in a Western Conference final that set the stage for a bitter, angry rivalry that persisted for the next decade and a half.

His sixth and final game-winner of that remarkable spring came in Game 3 of a four-game sweep of the upstart Florida Panthers, who were in just their third season in the league. He scored early in the second

period to break a 2–2 tie. The Avalanche then won their first Cup in Game 4, on Uwe Krupp's famous triple-overtime goal.

Colorado became the third team to win the Stanley Cup after relocating (behind the 1989 Calgary Flames, formerly of Atlanta, and the 1995 New Jersey Devils, who had once played in Denver), but the true significance of the 1996 playoffs lay in the way they established Colorado as a solid NHL team in a viable market and heralded Sakic as one of the great playoff performers of all time.

Inside the game, Joe had always been recognized as a star, but prior to the Cup run, he had been playing in the league's smallest market, and his Nordiques had appeared in only 12 playoff games in his seven years there.

"The spotlight is on the playoffs, and if you haven't been there, you're not going to get noticed," Sakic said during the 1996 postseason. "This is definitely the biggest chance I'll ever get."

And he made the most of it, rising with a young team from a 12-win rookie season through a difficult move from Quebec to Denver and finally hoisting the Stanley Cup as captain, with a Conn Smythe Trophy as a bonus.

"Early on," Sakic added, "it didn't look like we were ever going to get there. Now, just to get my name on the Cup is something special. A lot of great players in this league have never won it. To be one who has, that is so special. It's something you never forget."

MIKE MODANO

1990–2011
American Success Story

I T WAS A ST. PATRICK'S DAY TO REMEMBER FOR MIKE MODANO. On March 17, 2007, four days after scoring his 500th goal, Modano took a pass from defenseman Darryl Sydor at the blue line, pulled up at the left faceoff dot and fired a wrister through the legs of Nashville Predators goalie Tomas Vokoun at 10:54 of the second period. The power-play goal was the 502nd of his career, and it tied the record for U.S.-born players, previously held by Joe Mullen.

At 17:08 of the third, he slapped a one-timer from Jere Lehtinen for his second power-play goal of the game and the 503rd goal of his career. The record was his and still is.

Eight months later, on November 7, 2007, Modano scored 2 goals in the first 4:24 of a game against the San Jose Sharks to earn career points 1,232 and 1,233. He beat Sharks goalie Evgeni Nabokov on a short-handed breakaway to break Phil Housley's record for points by an American-born player, and he did it in 1,253 regular-season games — 242 games less than Housley.

A native of Livonia, Michigan, Modano grew up a Red Wings fan, wearing the iconic No. 9 of Gordie Howe. After graduating from the Detroit Little Caesars select program, he went west to the Prince Albert (Saskatchewan) Raiders of the Western Hockey League.

While Modano was scoring 47 goals and 127 points in 65 games with the 1987–88 Raiders, the Minnesota North Stars were winning all of 12 games, earning them the right to pick Modano first overall in 1988. He was just the second American to be the top draft choice.

Known for his silky smooth skating and shot — slap, wrist or backhand — Modano became the face of the franchise as its fortunes turned around. Minnesota reached the Stanley Cup Final in 1991 but lost to Mario Lemieux and the Pittsburgh Penguins. Two years later the team moved as part of the NHL's southern expansion and became the Dallas Stars.

"The way he played the game, the way he carried himself, made him a natural role model for a number of kids," says friend and former Dallas Stars teammate Brett Hull. "I think it went from two arenas [in Dallas] when Mike came [to town] to more than 35 — and from a handful of kids playing hockey to well over 5,000. That's strictly because of Mike."

The Stars' Stanley Cup win in 1999 with an American superstar leading the way helped capture the imagination of young athletes raised on Texas football. Modano led the Stars in scoring that post-season with 23 points in 23 games, despite breaking his wrist in the second game of the final against the Buffalo Sabres.

Modano played 21 of his 22 seasons with the Minnesota/Dallas franchise and always had a flair for the dramatic — right to the end. In his final game

with Dallas, he tied it up with 1:47 left in regulation and scored the deciding goal in the shootout, as the Stars beat the Anaheim Ducks 3–2 at the American Airlines Center.

His lone season away from the Stars was his last, which he spent in Detroit, hoping for one more shot at a Cup. But a wrist injury cut his homecoming short, and on September 23, 2011, he signed a one-day contract with the Stars and retired. He remains the career leader in both goals (561) and points (1,374) among American players, and his 146 post-season points (58 goals and 88 assists) are also an American record.

"He probably would have had three or four hundred more points had he played in a different system, but I think Mike is going to go down as maybe the best two-way player to ever play the game," says former Dallas general manager Doug Armstrong. "He had to play [defensively] against the other teams' top players, but it was still a necessity for him to produce offense for us. Mike was a great player."

Former Stars netminder Marty Turco, who was on the ice when Modano became the top American scorer, agrees. "Mike's pure hockey … He's about as elegant a hockey player as you'll ever see. To be on the ice when he became the all-time leading American goal-scorer, I know how special it was to him, so that was pretty cool to be part of that. But you never heard him talk about his individual stuff. Never. Maybe his long bombs on the green but never his hockey. He was too classy."

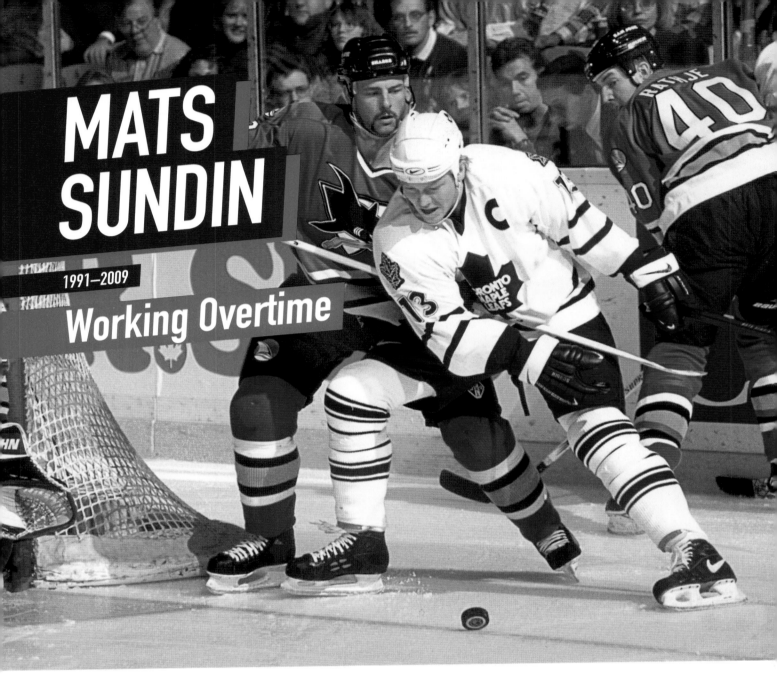

MATS SUNDIN

1991–2009
Working Overtime

IT WAS ONLY FITTING THAT AN OVERTIME VIRTUOSO WOULD HIT ONE OF HIS HIGHEST NOTES IN AN EXTRA PERIOD.

Mats Sundin, showing a flair for the dramatic possessed by only the game's most elite players, scored 15 regular-season overtime goals in his 18 NHL seasons. When he retired in 2009, he was tied with Patrik Elias, Jaromir Jagr and Sergei Fedorov for the all-time lead. (As of 2015–16 he remained tied with Fedorov for fourth.)

But no one else — not even the ageless wonder who is Jagr — has ever hit the 500-goal plateau after regulation time has expired.

Sundin entered the Toronto Maple Leafs' sixth game of the 2006–07 season with 497 goals and exited it with an even 500, scoring the landmark goal 50 seconds into overtime with a screaming, slightly screened slap shot from just inside the blue line that evaded Miikka Kiprusoff of the Calgary Flames.

Sundin's marker not only gave the Maple Leafs a 5–4 victory over the Flames but also completed an impressive hat trick for the Toronto captain, who was accorded a lengthy standing ovation and was named as the first, second and third stars of the game. Sundin's 1st goal of the night came on a Leafs power play, goal number 499 was at even strength and the overtime winner came with Darcy Tucker in the penalty box. The 1st and 3rd goals were from the left side of the ice; the 2nd, from the right. But

all 3 were delivered with prototypical Sundin laser-beam accuracy.

Only one other player, Gordie Howe, had ever hit the 500 mark with a shorthanded goal, and Sundin is one of just seven players — all of them Hockey Hall of Fame inductees — who registered 3 goals in a game to reach 500. The other six are Jean Béliveau, Wayne Gretzky, Mario Lemieux, Mark Messier, Brett Hull and Jagr.

With his younger brother, Per, among the fans roaring their unfettered appreciation, Sundin became the first Swedish-born-and-trained player to score his 500th goal. After he scored he was mobbed by his teammates, who tapped their sticks on the ice in his honor as they left the ice.

"It was a very special moment for a lot of guys on the team," said Tucker, who had scored earlier in the game (on a Sundin assist). "It's only fitting that he scored that huge, big goal in overtime because he's done it so many times before for us. It was nice to see the ovation from the crowd and all the guys sitting around waiting at the end of the ice.

"Even when he came in after doing his interviews, the guys gave him a good cheer in the dressing room. It was great, great to see."

Sundin, like many Hockey Hall of Famers as they approach a major signpost in their careers, was glad he could erase the distraction of number 500 early in the season.

"Certainly, I'm proud of the accomplishment, and it makes it special the way it happened — to get the win in overtime too," he said right after the game. "I'll remember it all my life.

"More than anything, it's nice to get it over with.

"I didn't want to go 15 or 20 games into the season and still be looking for it."

The goal came in Sundin's 10th year as captain and his second-last as a Maple Leaf — the last leg of his time in Toronto unfortunately coinciding with a franchise downturn and a fan base that had become bitter and disillusioned. Sundin, however, with his determined and often-dominant game presence, as well as his poise and class both on and off the ice, usually gave fans hope. Though the Toronto faithful were slow to warm to the talented Swede after his arrival via a trade that sent fan favorite Wendel Clark the other way, by the time of his 500th goal, they had long since realized they were watching one of the greatest Maple Leafs of all time.

"We have the best fans. The team hasn't won a championship since 1967. They don't want anything else than for us to do well," Sundin said after the game. "I realized the applause and the people standing and staying in the rink for me — it was appreciation of that on my part. That just doesn't happen very often. I've been here for many years, and it was a special moment for me.

"It was very emotional. I'm obviously very proud, and I'm very humbled by the reception that I got. It was awesome."

TEEMU SELANNE

1993–2014

Rookie Goal Record Kicks Off Storied Career

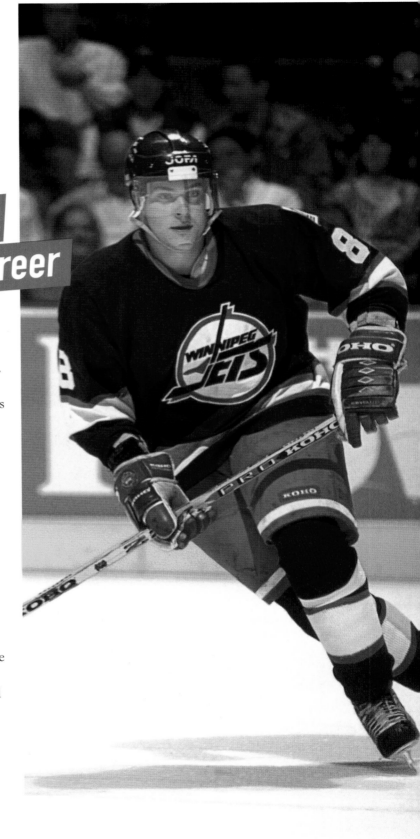

TEEMU SELANNE WASN'T EXACTLY WET BEHIND THE EARS WHEN HE ARRIVED IN WINNIPEG FOR HIS FIRST NHL SEASON. The Jets had drafted him 10th overall in 1988 but chose to let him develop his game against players in Finland's top professional league, with Helsinki's Jokerit. Finally, after winning a Finnish title and the Aarne Honkavaara Trophy as league's top goal-scorer in 1991–92, Selanne was ready to make the move to North America.

The 22-year-old scored 3 goals in his fifth NHL game and 11 goals in his first 12 outings of the 1992–93 season. The Jets, however, went just 5-12-1 in the first month. The team was laden with rookies, and losing got to Selanne. He was thrown out of a game against the Montreal Canadiens after swinging a high stick, but the season turned for him on December 28 when Eddie Olczyk was traded to the New York Rangers for Tie Domi and Kris King. The two tough guys opened up space and looked after Selanne, and it would be nine years before he earned his next game misconduct.

After the trade, the Jets went 11-1-2, with an eight-game goal streak by Selanne spurring an eight-game winning streak. At the end of January 1993, the Jets were above .500, and Selanne — the "Finnish Flash" — had 40 goals. The eyes of the hockey world were now on Winnipeg and the league's new superstar.

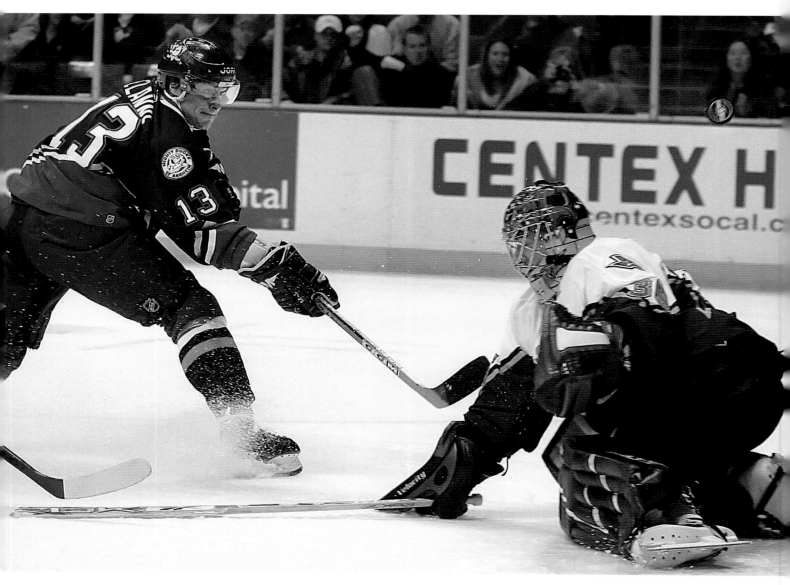

Mike Bossy of the New York Islanders had set the rookie record of 53 goals back in 1977–78. By February 28, 1993, Selanne had 47 goals but had gone three straight games without scoring, his longest drought since the opening month of the season. There were concerns that the long NHL season had worn him down, but playing at home that night against the Minnesota North Stars, Selanne exploded for 4 goals, breaking the magical 50-goal barrier and making the record inevitable. Only two nights later, on March 2, he scored 3 goals against the Quebec Nordiques, and the record was his. He punctuated number 54 — a one-handed goal on a partial breakaway — by throwing his glove in the air and shooting it down with his stick.

The old record was dead; long live King Teemu.

By the end of the 1992–93 season, Selanne had 76 goals, 56 assists and 132 points. Selanne was the unanimous choice for the Calder Trophy as rookie of the year, and he was sixth in Hart Trophy voting for league MVP. "It was unbelievable," Selanne has said of his debut season. "Something that you couldn't even realize what I did until next year or the year after…. The whole year was like a dream."

Although scoring has been on the rise in recent seasons, hockey may never see another 76-goal scorer, let alone one in his first year in the NHL. The most goals any rookie has scored since Selanne broke the record was 52, by Alexander Ovechkin in 2005–06, and only Ovechkin (65 in 2007–08) and

Steven Stamkos (60 in 2011–12) have even scored 60 goals since 1995–96.

In February 1996, the Jets traded Selanne to the Anaheim Ducks. He played three years with the San Jose Sharks and one with the Colorado Avalanche between two stints with the Ducks, with whom he won the Stanley Cup in 2007. When he retired in 2014 at the age of 43, Selanne had 684 goals, 773 assists and 1,457 points in 1,451 career games.

Teemu Selanne never matched the huge numbers of his rookie season but he was always a dangerous scorer. He topped 50 goals two more times, including the 1997–98 season when he tied Peter Bondra for the NHL lead with 52 goals, and led the league again with 47 goals the following season. When he scored 48 goals for Anaheim in 2006–07, it was the seventh time in his career that he'd scored 40 or more. At the age of 36, he just missed topping John Bucyk as the NHL's oldest 50-goal scorer, but did become the oldest player in NHL history to score more than 45 in a single season.

Over all those years, speed remained a key part of Selanne's game, but so was his good nature. "Every day, Teemu finds something to be happy about," longtime teammate Paul Kariya once said. "[He] gets as mad as anyone else when we lose, but I think he forgets it quickly."

"You keep shooting," Selanne reasoned. "You hope it goes in, and you smile."

JAROME IGINLA

Setting the Standard

I T'S NEVER EASY BEING THE CHOSEN ONE. BUT DON'T TELL THAT TO JAROME IGINLA, THE SOFT-SPOKEN, TOUGH-AS-NAILS Albertan who became the first black player to be named an NHL captain.

Heading into his first Flames' training camp in 1996, after being the centerpiece of a trade that saw the Flames part with captain and franchise star (and future Hall of Famer) Joe Nieuwendyk, Iginla had only one thing on his mind. "I'd really like to make the team," he told the *Calgary Herald*. "Then, if I make the team, I will set some goals."

Coming off his final junior season in which he was named MVP of the Western Hockey League, won a gold medal at the World Junior Championships and had already skated in two NHL playoff games as a call-up with the Flames (earning a goal and an assist), Iginla making the team should have been a given. But for the modest junior star, there was no skipping a step. Step one: make the team. Step two? Rewrite the franchise record books.

Always quick to highlight the efforts of others, Iginla was a natural leader and became a club spokesperson right out of the gate. Sure, he didn't post the 51 goals Nieuwendyk did in his rookie year. Nor did he snag the Calder Trophy like Nieuwendyk had. But his 21 goals and 29 assists had him second in Calder voting. A sophomore slump had some worried, but the Flames were already in disarray. In fact, since his

pre-rookie playoff call-up, Iginla didn't taste postseason action again until 2003–04.

By then, Iginla was a household name. His breakout season of 2001–02 is the stuff of childhood dreams. He won gold with Canada at the Olympics in February and in the NHL posted league highs in points (96) and goals (52) on his way to winning the Rocket Richard Trophy and the Art Ross Trophy and also being voted the league's most valuable player by his peers.

Iginla's Art Ross win was the first by someone other than Wayne Gretzky, Mario Lemieux or Jaromir Jagr since Marcel Dionne captured the hardware in 1980. And Iginla's style earned him comparisons to another legend known for his easy demeanor off the ice but sharp elbows on it — Gordie Howe.

Early in his first Rocket-winning season when, with Mr. Hockey in attendance at the Red Wings home opener, Iginla stood up to tough guy Darren McCarty. The Detroit enforcer had taken a cheap shot on one of Iginla's linemates, and no sooner had it happened

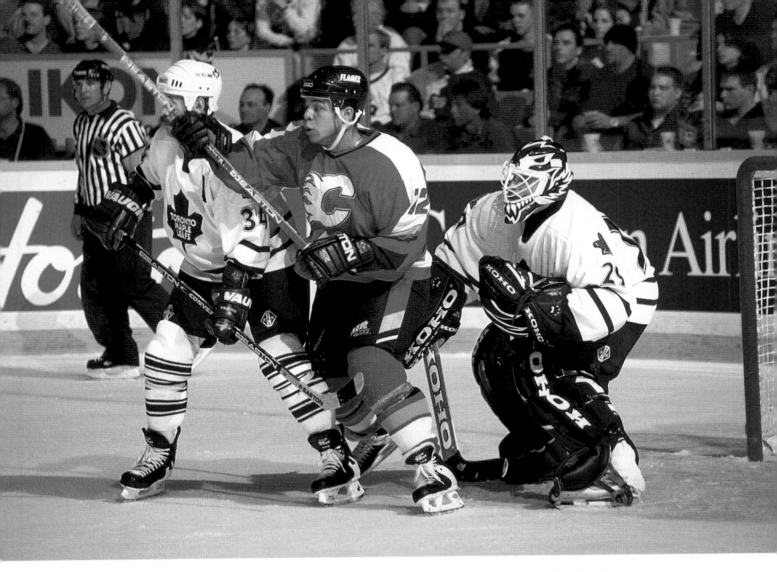

did the sturdy right winger jump in for retribution. Iginla was given 17 minutes in penalties. He later added a goal and two assists to notch a Gordie Howe hat trick as the Flames spoiled Detroit's night.

There would be more fireworks to come for the affable Flame. Iginla won his second Rocket trophy in 2003–04, the same season the Flames' seven-year playoff drought ended. The run had all the makings of a fairy tale, but the Flames narrowly missed out on raising the Stanley Cup. A contentious no-goal call in Game 6 of the Cup Final, which would have handed them a championship on home ice, paved the way for a tight-checked Game 7 in which the Tampa Bay Lightning emerged victorious. Iginla led all playoff performers in goals, short-handed goals, even-strength goals and shots on net. And when an extra spark was needed, he memorably dropped the gloves with Tampa star Vincent Lecavalier in the first period of Game 3.

But that magical run would be the closest Iginla

came to the NHL's top prize. He played seven more seasons in Calgary before a deadline deal sent him to Pittsburgh in 2013. In his 16 years with the Flames, Iginla had 11 seasons with 30 or more goals, including four with 40 or more and two 50-goal seasons. He is the Flames career leader in games played (1,219), goals (525) and points (1,095). He's second all-time in assists behind former Flames defenseman Al MacInnis. He's currently tied at 16th with Joe Sakic on the NHL's all-time goals list with 625.

As for being a trailblazer for black hockey players, Iginla has always been deferential. He'd rather cite those who he idolized — Grant Fuhr, Tony McKegney and Claude Vilgrain — and aspire to be as meaningful to others as they were to him. As he told the *Los Angeles Times* during his breakout year, "If young kids of color want to play the game, I'd love it if I could be a role model for them and if they would look up to me."

Mission accomplished.

MARIAN HOSSA

1997–2017

Third Time's the Charm

LOSING A STANLEY CUP FINAL IS AN AGONIZING EXPERIENCE. PARTLY IT IS THE EFFORT AND SACRIFICE IT TAKES TO GET there: an 82-game season followed by four rounds of grueling playoff hockey. Also, though — and likely the greater source of anguish — is the fear a player may never get there again.

Given all of that, the 2008 and 2009 postseasons were gut wrenching for Marian Hossa.

The silky-smooth winger had just completed a pair of career-best seasons in Atlanta, which saw him elevate his offensive game to superstar level (92 points in 2005–06 and 100 points in 2006–07) while leading the Thrashers to their first ever postseason. He'd been scoring 29-or-more goals since his second full season in the league (1999–2000), and the feeling was Hossa and Atlanta, with fellow superstar Ilya Kovalchuk, were on the rise. However, the 2007–08 campaign started poorly, and before it ended, Hossa was dealt to Pittsburgh at the deadline.

It was, as it turned out, a life-changing moment for Hossa. Pittsburgh, loaded with young talent, made a big playoff push, and Hossa was at the heart of it. He finished third in playoff scoring and led Pittsburgh in goals, including an OT-winner in Game 5 to ice the New York Rangers in Round 2. Even with all the good vibes, the Penguins fell short, losing to the Detroit Red Wings in six games in the Cup Final.

Hossa watched Detroit celebrate, with his summer of free agency on the horizon. And on July 2, 2008, Hossa signed a one-year deal with the Red Wings. As he told the *Detroit Free Press*: "I know I could get more money somewhere else, but I was looking for the best chance to win the Stanley Cup. I think Detroit is that destination."

The Red Wings looked the part, cruising to first in the central division with a 112-point season, led by their new right winger who netted 40 goals. But as the hockey gods would have it, Detroit's march to a second straight Cup would have to go through the Penguins, and after seven bitter Cup Final games, Hossa was on the outside looking in, again. Struggling to find words to describe his luck, Hossa merely said, "That's life."

It was a bitter pill, no doubt. But the 31-year-old winger, known as much for scoring goals as for his solid two-way game, had his pick of suitors. This time it was the Chicago Blackhawks who landed him. He'd spend the rest of his career with the storied franchise.

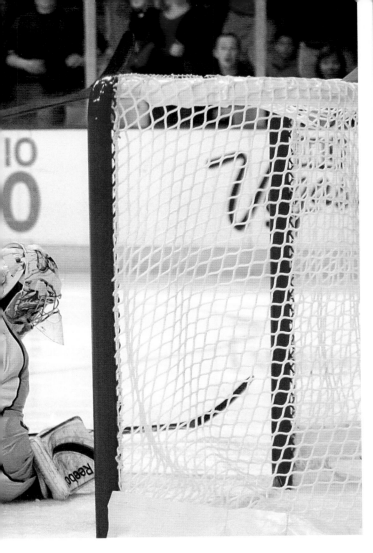

The 2009–10 season was an offensive down year for Hossa, as he scored the fewest goals of his career since his rookie season. But on a Blackhawks squad loaded with talent, his defense was as critical as his scoring touch. Driven by young superstars Patrick Kane and Jonathan Toews and a deep roster of skilled players, Chicago plowed their way to the Cup Final in Hossa's first year on the team. In Game 6, with the Stanley Cup in the building, the Blackhawks were up 1 and less than four minutes away from their first Cup win since 1961.

That's when Philadelphia's Scott Hartnell banked a puck off Hossa's skate for the goal that knotted the contest at 3 apiece. It seemed the Hossa-hex would live another day.

"I was happy we were in the Finals," Hossa said after the series. "But at the same time a little scared, you know?"

In the end, there was no reason to be afraid. Patrick Kane scored a seeing-eye shot in overtime before the ice had barely dried, and Hossa was,

finally, a Stanley Cup champion. Captain Jonathan Toews then made the best pass of the playoffs when he handed the Cup to Hossa after receiving it from NHL commissioner Gary Bettman. "The right guy got it first," Chicago coach Joel Quenneville said to the agreement of almost every hockey fan.

Hossa, the first player to play in three-consecutive Cup Finals for three different teams, went on to win two more Cups with Chicago, playing an important two-way role and chipping in offensively by netting two-game winners en route to each championship. Clearly the curse had been broken.

As Hossa told reporters after the Blackhawks 2010 win, "Third time's the lucky charm."

PART 2

THE GOALIES

Early-Era Goalies 128

134 TURK **BRODA**	**137** FRANK **BRIMSEK**	**140** CHUCK **RAYNER**
143 BILL **DURNAN**	**146** HARRY **LUMLEY**	**150** TERRY **SAWCHUK**
154 GLENN **HALL**	**158** JACQUES **PLANTE**	**162** GUMP **WORSLEY**

166 JOHNNY **BOWER**

170 GERRY **CHEEVERS**

174 EDDIE **GIACOMIN**

178 BERNIE **PARENT**

182 ROGIE **VACHON**

186 TONY **ESPOSITO**

190 KEN **DRYDEN**

194 BILLY **SMITH**

198 GRANT **FUHR**

202 PATRICK **ROY**

206 ED **BELFOUR**

210 DOMINIK **HASEK**

213 MARTIN **BRODEUR**

EARLY-ERA GOALIES

by Eric Zweig

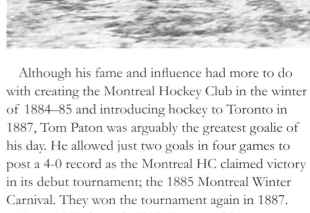

I N THE EARLIEST IMAGES OF HOCKEY, IT'S DIFFICULT TO TELL WHO'S THE GOALIE. NO MASKS, CERTAINLY, BUT NO SPECIAL gloves, pads or sticks either. Well into the 1890s, the official photographs of Stanley Cup champions show players in uniform with no noticeable difference between them.

Early hockey pictures were sometimes taken at a rink, but they were most often taken in photographers' studios. While it's possible the goalies of the day chose not to wear any extra padding under hot lights, consider what is perhaps the best-known image of hockey players in action from the 1890s. It's not a photograph, but a painting showing the hockey team from the Montreal Amateur Athletic Association (they preferred to call themselves the Montreal Hockey Club, or just the Montreals) taking on the Montreal Victorias in the city's famous Victoria Skating Rink circa 1893.

In this often-reproduced painting, all 14 players — seven on each team, including a rover — are visible. The largest player seen, in the lower lefthand corner of the image, is the goalie for the Montreal Hockey Club. He is guarding a post with no netting and looks identical to all the other players on both teams, even hunched over his stick with the same two-handed grip. This goalie is likely the most famous and influential netminder of his era, Thomas Laird Paton.

Although his fame and influence had more to do with creating the Montreal Hockey Club in the winter of 1884–85 and introducing hockey to Toronto in 1887, Tom Paton was arguably the greatest goalie of his day. He allowed just two goals in four games to post a 4-0 record as the Montreal HC claimed victory in its debut tournament; the 1885 Montreal Winter Carnival. They won the tournament again in 1887.

From 1888 through 1893, Paton and his Montreal teammates were rarely defeated in winning

Roy Worters displays goaltending of the 1930s. He is the beneficiary of those who first introduced pads and wide sticks to the game, as well as the ability for a goaltender to go down to the ice to stop a puck.

six straight championships in the Amateur Hockey Association of Canada (AHAC). The 1893 victory brought with it the Stanley Cup, which was presented that year for the very first time. The team would win the Cup again as AHAC champions in 1894, although Paton was no longer playing.

The two-handed grip that early goalies used to hold their sticks remained in vogue until the 1920s, but changes in goalie equipment were already under way in Paton's day. One of the earliest stories of a goalie wearing special padding on his legs comes from Dartmouth, Nova Scotia, in 1889. There are

Whitey Merritt

Hugh Lehman

also reports of goalies in Winnipeg wearing leg guards as early as 1891, and it was quite common for goalies in the Manitoba capital to be wearing cricket pads by 1892.

When an all-star team from Winnipeg toured Ontario and Quebec in 1893, the Montreal Gazette reported on February 16, that the equipment worn by the Winnipeggers, "was somewhat of a revelation to Montrealers. The goalkeeper wore a pair of cricket greaves and every man on the team wore shin pads." Some goalies in Ontario were also wearing cricket pads by that time, but they had obviously not been seen yet in the hockey hotbed of Montreal.

Three years later, almost to the day, goalie George "Whitey" Merritt wore cricket pads in Montreal when his Winnipeg Victorias played the Montreal Victorias for the Stanley Cup. The Montreal team protested, but Merritt was allowed to wear his pads and he posted a 2–0 shutout that gave Winnipeg a victory in the one-game championship challenge. Over the years, many hockey writers have claimed that Merritt (who may have been the first to use a wider goalie stick) was the first goalie ever to wear pads. He wasn't, but he was the first to wear them in a Stanley Cup game and his success that night was a probably a big reason why more goalies started wearing pads, too.

Even so, when writing about goaltending in Art Farrell's 1899 book *Hockey: Canada's Royal Winter Game*, Frank Stocking of the Quebec Bulldogs — "generally recognized throughout Canada as the peer of his position," according to Farrell himself — makes no mention of any specialized equipment.

Stocking, who was already at work on bringing a more modern style of goalie net to the top league in hockey (which was now the Canadian Amateur Hockey League), didn't say much at all about equipment. "Goalers should use a good broad bladed skate," he writes, "not too sharp so as to allow easy change of position from one side to the other of the goal. He should dress warmly and protect his body and limbs with the usual pads which at the same time help to fill up the goal."

More than 120 years later, it's impossible to know if Stocking meant that cricket pads had already become "usual" or if he was referring to the standard type of padding every player wore. Stocking is much clearer when he discusses a goalie's mental make up.

"He must not get 'rattled' by the spectators," says Stocking, "and never lose confidence in himself…. Nothing should fluster a goalkeeper, nothing discourage him."

And as for playing:

Goalkeeping is one of the easiest and at the same time one of the most difficult positions to fill successfully on the team. It is simple because it is not altogether essential to be an expert skater or stick handler. It is difficult because it requires a quick and true eye together with agility of motion and good judgment.

Aside from their sparse equipment, the biggest difficulty early-era goaltenders faced was the rule stating that they must not lie, kneel or sit upon the ice during play but must maintain a standing position. Hockey innovators Frank and Lester Patrick were the first to change this rule prior to the 1916–17 season of the Pacific Coast Hockey Association, a league whose champions played for the Stanley Cup from 1914 until 1924.

Future Hall of Fame goalies Hugh Lehman and Hap Holmes, playing with the Vancouver Millionaires and Seattle Metropolitans in 1916–17, were among the goalies able to put the new rule into effect immediately, but anyone playing in the NHL when the league began on December 19, 1917, still had to remain standing. However, just three weeks later, on January 9, 1918, NHL president Frank Calder sent the following message to team managers and referees:

> Section 13 of the rules, and that portion of Section 9 dealing with the goalkeeper, are hereby deleted, thus permitting the goalkeeper to adopt any attitude he pleases in stopping a shot. Please be governed accordingly.

Art Ross, a lifelong friend of the Patrick brothers and a great hockey innovator himself, was pushing for the move behind the scenes, but the NHL's decision to change its goalie rule is often credited to another future Hall of Famer, Clint Benedict of the original Ottawa Senators.

Benedict's habit of dropping to his knees to stop the puck had led Toronto fans to mockingly call him Praying Benny. "It was against the rules then," Benedict told the *Ottawa Journal* for a feature about

Notable Early-Era Goalies

EDDIE GIROUX
Although he's not in the Hockey Hall of Fame, he played for the Stanley Cup in 1904, 1905 and twice in 1907 — winning with the Kenora Thistles in January of 1907 — and was among the earliest goalies to wear a mask, which he did in preseason practice with the Toronto Marlboros of the Ontario Hockey Association in 1903 to protect a cut on his face.

RILEY HERN
Playing pro from 1901 to 1911, he was a championship goalie wherever he went. He won U.S. titles with the Pittsburgh Keystones in 1902, and the Portage Lake team (Houghton, Michigan) in 1904 and 1906 before winning the Stanley Cup with the Montreal Wanderers in 1907, 1908 and 1910. He also earned All-Star honors in four different leagues in two different countries.

BOUSE HUTTON
An all-around athlete, he played hockey at the highest level for his hometown Ottawa team from 1899 to 1904, winning the Stanley Cup with the "Silver Seven" in 1903 and 1904. He also won national championships with Ottawa teams in lacrosse and football and had to give up playing hockey (an amateur sport at the time) after accepting money to play lacrosse professionally.

PADDY MORAN
Playing at hockey's highest level from 1901 to 1917, he spent all but one of those years with the Quebec Bulldogs. Though the team was usually a weak one, he was always considered a star and helped the Bulldogs win the Stanley Cup in 1912 and 1913. He was known for having a temper and would sometimes slash skaters who got too close to him.

PERCY LESUEUR
Though he joined Ottawa too late to salvage a 1906 Stanley Cup defense, he later won the Cup with the Senators in 1909 and 1911. He wrote the book *How to Play Hockey* in 1909, developed specialized gloves for goalies with longer cuffs for better protection, and designed a better style of goalie net that was used by the NHA and the NHL from 1912 until 1925.

HUGH LEHMAN
In a pro career that began in 1906–07 and ended with the Chicago Black Hawks in 1927–28, he spent most of his playing days in leagues that either predated or rivalled the NHL. Best known for his years in the PCHA with the Vancouver Millionaires, he was a 10-time All-Star who played for the Stanley Cup eight times but won it only in 1915.

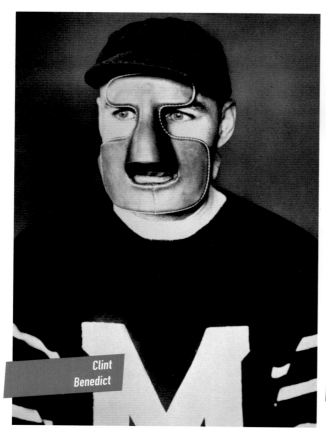

Clint Benedict

Georges Vezina

him in 1962, "but if you made it look like an accident you could get away without a penalty. I got pretty good at it."

Starting in 1918, Benedict no longer had to pretend, and a goalie who was already great became even better. Benedict led the NHL in wins in six of the league's first seven seasons. He led or shared the lead in shutouts (not that there were many in his day) in each of the first seven seasons. He led in average six times between 1918–19 and 1926–27. There was plenty of team success too. Benedict won the Stanley Cup with Ottawa in 1920, 1921 and 1923 and added another with the Montreal Maroons in 1926.

Benedict may be best known today for being the first goalie in NHL history to wear a mask, which he did late in the 1929–30 season after missing several weeks due to two facial injuries. It would be almost 30 years before Jacques Plante made the mask a standard piece of goalie equipment, but once the PCHA and the NHL allowed goalies to fall to the ice, it became obvious that these goalies needed better protection.

The first advancement came with chest protectors — or belly pads, as most goalies called them — that

were very similar to what baseball catchers used. These were made of leather, canvas and felt. Soon, goalies also added arm pads that they wore like thick felt sleeves beneath their hockey sweaters. Frank Brimsek, a future Hall of Famer with the Boston Bruins in the 1930s and '40s, created the first blocker glove. Emile Francis (later a Hall of Fame builder) created the prototype of the modern catching glove when he had a first baseman's mitt attached to the cuff of a standard hockey glove while playing with the Chicago Black Hawks in 1947–48.

But even among all these pioneers and innovators, the name of one early-era goalie stands above them all: Georges Vezina.

By all accounts, Vezina was stoic and silent. He was known as the Chicoutimi Cucumber for his hometown and his ability to remain calm ("cool as a cucumber") under pressure. Vezina played a standup style and preferred the two-handed grip even after the rule about falling to the ice was changed.

The Montreal Canadiens of the National Hockey Association discovered Vezina when they played an exhibition game against his Chicoutimi hockey club during the winter of 1909–10. He joined them in 1910–11 and never missed a game (regular season or playoffs) over the next 15 years.

Vezina recorded the first shutout in NHL history on February 18, 1918, and led the league in goals-against average that season. Previously, he'd helped the Canadiens win the first Stanley Cup in team history in 1916, and he'd win it again in 1924. His 1.97 goals-against average at age 37 set a new NHL record in 1923–24, which he broke with a 1.81 mark in 1924–25.

Tragically, Georges Vezina took ill before the 1925–26 season. He collapsed during the first period of the Canadiens first game on November 28, 1925, and never played again. He died of tuberculosis on March 27, 1926, and in 1927, ownership of the Montreal Canadiens donated the Vezina Trophy. Ever since, it has been awarded to the best goalie in the NHL — first as determined by goals-against average, later as voted by club general managers — and has assured Vezina's lasting legacy above all other early-era goalies.

Hap Holmes

HAP HOLMES

Playing in all the top professional leagues of his era in a career that stretched from 1912 to 1928, he won his first Stanley Cup with the Toronto Blue Shirts of the NHA in 1912, won again with Seattle of the PCHA in 1917, the Toronto Arenas of the NHL in 1918, and the Victoria Cougars of the Western Canada Hockey League in 1925.

GEORGE HAINSWORTH

Replacing Georges Vezina in Montreal, he gave the Canadiens everything they could have hoped for and more. The Vezina Trophy winner the first three years it was presented, he set all-time records with 22 shutouts and a 0.92 goals-against average in 1928–29 and won the Stanley Cup in 1930 and 1931. Retiring in 1937 with 94 shutouts, he still ranks third in NHL history.

ALEX CONNELL

Often overlooked in discussions of the greatest goalies of all time, he holds the NHL career record for lowest goals-against average at 1.92. He led the NHL in shutouts five times, including a career-high 15 in 1927–28 when he set a record with a streak of six consecutive shutout games, and was a Stanley Cup champion in 1927 and 1935.

CHUCK GARDINER

If not for a career cut short by tragedy, he might have become the greatest goalie in NHL history. Starring mostly for terrible Chicago teams, he won the Vezina Trophy in 1932 and 1934 and led the Black Hawks to a Stanley Cup victory in 1934, making him the only goalie ever to captain his team to the title. He died of a brain hemorrhage a few weeks later.

TINY THOMPSON

The first goalie in history to win the Vezina Trophy four times, he began his NHL career with a shutout in his first game, leading the Boston Bruins to a 1–0 win over the Pittsburgh Pirates on November 15, 1928. He is the only goalie in the Hall of Fame to begin his career with a shutout, and he also led Boston to its first Stanley Cup championship that season.

ROY WORTERS

At 5-foot-3 and only 135 pounds, he is the smallest player in NHL history and was known as "Shrimp." Playing mostly on terrible Pittsburgh Pirates and New York Americans teams, he never won the Vezina Trophy or the Stanley Cup but became the first goalie ever to win the Hart Trophy as NHL MVP for the 1928–29 season.

TURK BRODA

1937–1952

The Brilliant Bulging Battler

THERE ARE A FEW TALES AS TO HOW WALTER BRODA EARNED HIS NICKNAME, "TURK," AND ONE OF THE MORE POPULAR IS that he got it for his freckles, which resembled the spots on a turkey egg. Turk was small as a child (he only grew to be 5-foot-9), and the other origin story for the famous moniker came from his school days in Brandon, Manitoba. There, Broda was a skinny, short-legged boy with a large upper body, which prompted his friends to dub him "Turkey Legs," and then, of course, "Turk."

The stout Broda was deemed too short to play any position other than goal, and he ended up playing his junior and minor league hockey with the Detroit Red Wings organization before Toronto Maple Leafs' owner Conn Smythe bought him for $7,500 to replace George Hainsworth for the 1936–37 season. Broda was a mainstay for the Leafs for the next 15 years, interrupted only by two years of military service.

Broda's outgoing style made him hugely popular with Leafs fans. They tossed cigars onto the ice in appreciation after a game, and Broda was quick to scurry around and gather them up. He was equally loved by his teammates, who knew firsthand his dedication to the team. Despite his chubby appearance, Broda worked harder than most in practice. "The Leafs pay me for my work in practices," he joked, "and I throw in the games for free." In truth, Broda established himself as a "money" goaltender, as his

best games came when it mattered most. Although he backstopped the Leafs to the Stanley Cup Final three times in his first four seasons, to his coach's dismay, Broda was notorious for getting distracted and letting in some long shots when the game wasn't on the line.

"Turk has been known to boot the odd soft one, miss a two-foot putt and trump a partner's ace," teased his coach Hap Day, who took over the Leafs' bench duties in the fall of 1940 and worked on Broda's reflexes and awareness by having him play without a stick while teammates fired shots from 20 and 30 feet out.

In 1940–41, Broda won his first of two Vezina Trophies, but the Leafs were eliminated in the first round of the playoffs. The team seemed destined, again, to also-ran status the following year, falling behind 3-0 against Detroit in the 1942 Cup Final. Broda, however, allowed only seven goals in the next four games, as Toronto executed an unprecedented comeback. Broda notched a shutout in the sixth game and let in only a single goal in the deciding seventh match, and Toronto had its first Stanley Cup victory in 10 years.

In 1943, Broda joined the army, as did many of his contemporaries. A public controversy erupted when the Royal Canadian Mounted Police stopped his train en route to Montreal and arrested Broda, who had been offered a $2,400 bonus to enlist in Montreal and tend net for a Quebec military team. Returned to Toronto so that he would join the Toronto Army Daggers, Broda was sent off to England for two years, primarily to play hockey.

When Broda was discharged in 1945, he went straight to Maple Leaf Gardens and resumed practicing with the team. He was back in the nets, and there he stayed for four more Stanley Cup finals, winning three in a row from 1947 to 1949. Broda played the entire season in goal in 8 of his 11 seasons, and part

Broda seen in net enjoying a large stack of pancakes.
Broda's weight was the subject of much ridicule.

of two others, leading the league in shutouts twice. But for all his fame and glory, he's also remembered for his weight problems, which Conn Smythe used as a publicity stunt.

When the Leafs stumbled early in the 1949–50 season, Smythe ended Broda's run of more than 200 starts in a row by ordering five of his players onto diets, including his star netminder, who was reported to weigh 197 pounds. "The honeymoon is over," blustered Smythe. "I'm taking Broda out of the nets and he's not coming back until he shows some common sense. Two seasons ago, Broda weighed 185 pounds. Last season he went up to 190 — and now this. A goalie has to have fast reflexes and you can't move fast when you're overweight." Smythe added some gravitas to his decision by calling up the slim Gil Mayer, goaltender for the farm club team in Pittsburgh, and then sending four players and cash to the AHL's Cleveland Barons for up-and-coming lanky netminder Al Rollins.

For days afterward, however, newspaper articles showed Broda smiling, sometimes sitting on a scale. His wife, Betty, became famous for being the one person who could help him win "The Battle of the Bulge" and save the city's team. "I don't know what I

can cut off Turk," lamented Mrs. Broda. "He hardly eats a darn thing now and has the smallest appetite in the house. Why, the girls and I eat more than he does." After getting down to the prescribed weight of 190 pounds in a well-publicized weigh-in, Broda started his first game in a week.

"There may be better goalies around somewhere," laughed Smythe, "but there's no greater sportsman than the Turkey. If the Rangers score on him tonight, I should go out and buy him a malted milk just to show I'm not trying to starve him to death." Broda posted a shutout that night, and with the permission of his boss, announced he'd be enjoying a small steak that evening. He went on to notch a career-best nine shutouts that season.

Although reduced to backup status in the following campaign, Broda sparkled in the 1951 playoffs, playing 8 of the 11 games it took the Leafs to win the Stanley Cup. All five games of the final against Montreal went into overtime. "I couldn't beat him. Toe Blake couldn't. None of the Canadiens could," Maurice Richard said after that series. It was Broda's swan song, however, and he retired after playing only half a game the next season.

FRANK BRIMSEK

Mr. Zero Made His Mark

FRANK BRIMSEK MADE AN AUSPICIOUS NHL DEBUT IN THE FALL OF 1938. ALTHOUGH INITIALLY UNHERALDED AS A replacement for the legendary Tiny Thompson, he made such a strong impression in two games as a substitute that the Boston Bruins traded the veteran Thompson to Detroit.

"The kid had the fastest hands I ever saw," said Boston coach and general manager (and former NHL star) Art Ross. "Like lightning." The Beantown fans were irate at the trade, however, and so were many of the Boston players, some of whom even threatened to quit in frustration.

"When I hit the ice, things were so quiet that I could hear the people breathing," recalled Brimsek, looking back at a game against the Montreal Canadiens on December 1, 1938. "They were just waiting for me to blow one." Under incredible pressure from both his uncertain teammates and the usually raucous fans, Brimsek and the Bruins lost the game 2–0, and the crowd was on Brimsek's back throughout.

But Brimsek shut out his opponents in each of the next three games. When he finally surrendered a goal, after 231 minutes and 54 seconds of shut-out hockey (breaking Thompson's team record), the Boston fans paused only a moment before breaking out into a prolonged ovation. Brimsek had won his doubters over. He posted a victory

that game, too. In his first eight NHL games the rookie posted six shutouts.

Henceforth tagged with the moniker "Mr. Zero," Brimsek finished the 1938–39 season with a league-leading 10 shutouts. He was awarded the Calder Trophy as Rookie of the Year, the Vezina Trophy for the best goals-against average (1.56) and a First All-Star Team berth. More important, he took the Bruins to Stanley Cup victory, which they won four games to one over Toronto in the league's first best-of-seven final series. Boston's biggest challenge that year came in the semifinal, when it took three overtime wins to vanquish the New York Rangers. Tiny Thompson was not forgotten, but Frank Brimsek had passed every test with flying colors.

One of the first NHL stars ever to hail from the United States, Brimsek was born in Eveleth,

Minnesota, the home of the U.S. Hockey Hall of Fame (where he was enshrined as a charter member in 1973). A classic stand-up goalie, he showed great confidence, often leaning back calmly against his net when an opponent started in on a breakaway or a penalty shot. There was nothing passive about Brimsek's play, however. His glove hand, often described as "Brimmy's lightning," was a potent weapon, and his heavy custom-made stick was used to sweep away pucks — or the skates of a foe taking liberties near his net. He played a smart mental game, too, always looking for an edge. "I tried to make the opposition player do what I wanted him to," he once explained. "I always felt that the glove side was the strongest side for a goaltender. And I would make the shooter believe this, too. In that way, I would make most shooters fire the puck to my stick side, which is what I wanted them to do in the first place."

Brimsek earned All-Star status in each of his first eight seasons, an unprecedented streak, winning a second Stanley Cup ring in 1941 and another Vezina Trophy in 1941–42. The latter season may have been his most spectacular, as the Boston lineup had lost the famed Kraut Line of Milt Schmidt, Bobby Bauer and Woody Dumart to the Canadian Armed Forces. Brimsek enlisted the following season. "You just get established in a business like hockey, and you have to give it all up," complained Brimsek. "A damned war comes along." World War II interrupted Brimsek's NHL hockey career for two seasons. He played for the U.S. Coast Guard Cutters for the 1943–44 season, on a team that was intended to bolster morale, but when American participation in the war intensified and casualties were increasing, Brimsek found himself on active duty in the South Pacific in 1944–45.

A year on a patrol boat left Brimsek "jumpy" when he returned to the NHL early in 1946. "I was a little shaky when I got back," he said later. "My legs and my nerves were shot." Although he later confessed that he came back too soon, primarily because he needed the money, Brimsek picked up much where he had left off. The Bruins made it to the 1946 Stanley Cup Final but were vanquished by the Montreal Canadiens, who were led by a star

who had emerged during Brimsek's military years: Maurice "Rocket" Richard.

Brimsek felt his skills were diminishing, and the Bruins overall were a shadow of their pre-war squad. Nevertheless, "Mr. Zero" continued to keep his team in many games. He finished second to the New York Rangers' Buddy O'Connor in the 1947–48 Hart Trophy voting for the NHL's Most Valuable Player, and made the NHL's Second All-Star Team in three consecutive seasons. Brimsek saw the end in sight, though. "When I got out of the war, I knew I

wasn't going to play long. I didn't have that same feeling for the game," he said. "I had a hard time even going back to training camp."

Thinking of future career opportunities, Brimsek had the first of his conversations with Art Ross about his post-Boston career in 1947, but he more or less demanded a trade to Chicago in 1949. "My brother was starting a business there," he explained, "and I thought I might help him open a few doors." Soon sold to the Black Hawks, reportedly for the largest cash outlay since Toronto's

$35,000 purchase of King Clancy from Ottawa in 1930, Brimsek played every game of the 1949–50 season, adding five shutouts to his career record despite Chicago's last-place standing. Brimsek then retired but left an indelible mark on the game. In 1966, his decade of NHL service was recognized when he became only the third American elected to the Hockey Hall of Fame. In Minnesota, the Frank Brimsek Award is presented annually to the state's top high-school goalie.

CHUCK RAYNER

1941–1953

Bonnie Prince Charlie

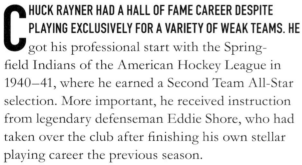

CHUCK RAYNER HAD A HALL OF FAME CAREER DESPITE PLAYING EXCLUSIVELY FOR A VARIETY OF WEAK TEAMS. HE got his professional start with the Springfield Indians of the American Hockey League in 1940–41, where he earned a Second Team All-Star selection. More important, he received instruction from legendary defenseman Eddie Shore, who had taken over the club after finishing his own stellar playing career the previous season.

Shore's "creative" but notorious coaching methods and parsimonious ways generally made enemies of his students, but Rayner acknowledged him as "the greatest goaltending coach I ever had. Before that, there wasn't such a thing as a goaltending coach. Nobody told you anything. You went out and did your best, got hell for the goals you didn't stop, and no praise for the ones you did."

"Tap-dancing improves balance and balance is the foundation of an athlete's ability," said Shore, explaining one of his more unorthodox coaching methods. "From balance you get power and maneuverability. I want a player who can move forward, backward, one side or the other without actually taking a step; just shifting his balance." Shore once tethered a goalie to the crossbar with a rope around his neck to train him not to fall to the ice, but as a four-time NHL MVP, Shore also had genuine skills, insights and a fierce work ethic.

Through Shore's insistence, Rayner participated in every skating drill with his teammates and fired pucks until he couldn't move from fatigue. This training helped Rayner develop outstanding skating and shooting abilities, which became hallmarks of his own innovative style. In turn, fellow Hall of Famers Gump Worsley and Johnny Bower both credit Rayner with teaching them invaluable lessons in what we now know are essential NHL goaltending skills, like the poke check.

Rayner was called up from Springfield to the New York Americans for a 12-game tryout in 1940–41, and became a full-time NHLer in 1941–42. That season Rayner appeared in 36 games and posted a 3.47 goals-against average for the newly christened Brooklyn Americans, who didn't enjoy any more success financially or on the ice with the franchise name change. Rayner notched one shutout for the lackluster squad, but the team remained in the league basement with a 16-29-3 record over the 48-game season.

The Americans folded after that 1941–42 campaign, marking the actual beginning of the "Original Six" era, but Rayner was changing his address regardless. He enlisted in the Canadian Navy and missed three NHL seasons. He played some hockey for Navy teams in Halifax and Victoria, but eventually shipped out on a frigate that

traversed the North Atlantic. When the war ended, he signed with the New York Rangers, where he split goaltending duties with "Sugar" Jim Henry for three seasons. The pioneering move toward the "two-goalie" system was instituted by Ranger coach Frank Boucher, who, like Eddie Shore, was a former star player and creative thinker. The system worked well as the two goalies became close friends, but the Rangers eventually decided they couldn't afford the luxury of two NHL netminders on the payroll and traded Henry.

Although the Rangers had fallen into the league cellar during the war years, Rayner often brought the crowd to its feet with his unprecedented roaming from the crease. Boucher called him "brilliantly aggressive," and Rayner's poke check became a signature move. He surprised many attacking forwards when he dove headfirst, his goal stick outstretched in front of him, to knock the puck away.

"Bonnie Prince Charlie" led the league with five shutouts in 1946–47, although he also had an offensive flair. He went behind his net for pucks, fielded

them in the corner, and fired passes to his team-mates, and he even made rink-long rushes, attempting to become the first NHL netminder to score a goal. Boucher didn't need to pull his goalie when there was a delayed-penalty call, as Rayner functioned effectively as a sixth attacker.

Rayner lost much of the 1947–48 season recovering from a broken cheekbone, and he was one of the first goaltenders to use a face mask, although he wore it only in practice. He made the NHL's Second All-Star Team in 1949, 1950 and 1951, playing almost every single game for the Rangers. He guided New York to a surprisingly successful trip to the 1950 playoffs, helping to vanquish the Montreal Canadiens in surprisingly short order (leading to the resignation of his friend Bill Durnan in the Canadiens' net). After falling behind two games to Detroit in the Stanley Cup Final, a team that had finished 21 points ahead of them in the 70-game regular season, Rayner backstopped the Rangers to three straight wins, including two overtime victories. Sadly, New York lost the Cup to the Red Wings in the second

overtime period of the seventh game. Their near win was all the more remarkable when one realizes the Rangers had to play all the games of the final on the road because the circus had taken over Madison Square Garden. Rayner received the 1950 Hart Trophy as the league's Most Valuable Player, the second goalie after Roy "Shrimp" Worters to win the prestigious award, and one of only five to receive the trophy to date.

The Rangers didn't qualify for the playoffs again during Rayner's tenure, and in the 1952–53 season he played only 20 games, replaced by Gump Worsley, who won Rookie of the Year honors. Rayner went back to his home province of Saskatchewan the following season, signed as a free agent by the Saskatoon Quakers of the Western Hockey League. He played a handful of games spread over the following two campaigns with the WHL's Nelson Maple Leafs before hanging up his skates.

BILL DURNAN

1944–1950

The Quick Change Artist

Durnan strikes a pose. Notice his ambidextrous catching gloves.

WHEN THE MONTREAL CANADIENS CAME CALLING, BILL DURNAN WAS NOT EAGER TO ENTER PROFESSIONAL hockey, despite earning at most $15 per week between playing hockey, softball and doing a variety of odd jobs. Initially signed by the Toronto Maple Leafs, Durnan was invited to attend his first pro camp in 1936 at age 20. Just before camp, he injured his knee in a playful tussle on the beach with a friend.

When the Leafs heard he had torn all the ligaments in his knee and displaced some cartilage, they dropped Durnan like a hot potato. Durnan felt he'd been treated shabbily and lost his enthusiasm for the pro game, even drifting completely away from hockey for a spell. He then spent four seasons in the northern Ontario mining town of Kirkland Lake, where he helped the Blue Devils win the 1940 Allan Cup, senior hockey's top prize.

Friends in Montreal then convinced Durnan to take a job with the Royals in their city, and after three years in the Quebec senior league, he had the full attention of the Montreal Canadiens' general manager Tommy Gorman. Durnan's play at the Habs' training camp in 1943 had Gorman convinced he had a new starting goalie, but Durnan drove a hard bargain. He was content to make less money as an amateur in return for less stress, but he did have his price. Gorman made a final counteroffer 10 minutes before the Canadiens' first game of the season. The ink on his $4,200 contract was barely dry when Durnan stepped between the pipes of the Montreal net for what would prove to be a brief but brilliant NHL career.

Durnan was skilled at cutting off angles and a superb athlete, but unusual ambidexterity was one of the keys to his goaltending mastery. Hockey hasn't seen this skill, before or since, but Durnan wore specially fingered trappers that allowed him to hold his stick or catch the puck with either hand, and he could make the switch with lightning speed. No matter which way a shooter came in at him, Durnan would ensure he had his catching hand at the optimum side. He credited Steve Faulkner, his boyhood coach in a Toronto church league, for the development of his unique skill. "He worked me by the hour," recalled Durnan, "until I had the technique down pat, and we won five city championships in six years. At first, it felt as though I was transferring a telephone pole from one hand to the other, but after a while, I'd hardly realize I was doing it."

Over seven seasons at the NHL level, from 1943–44 to 1949–50, Durnan confounded shooters enough to win the Vezina Trophy six times, including his first year when he finished runner-up as Rookie of the Year and earned his first of six First All-Star Team berths. In the playoffs that year, he posted a 1.53 goals-against average and won his first Stanley Cup ring.

"Durnan was toughest for me," recalled Boston's Milt Schmidt, when asked about goaltenders during his lengthy playing career. "I could never do much with the guy. At the outset, he troubled me, and it got to be a complex, I guess. It got to the point where I'd break through on him and have the feeling he had me beaten anyway. Durnan had an uncanny way of cutting off all the angles, and waiting patiently for you to commit yourself."

Durnan backstopped the Habs to Stanley Cup victory again in 1945–46, and to the final the following season. Although genial in temperament off the ice, Durnan was serious during games and constantly vocal in directing his teammates on the ice. His leadership was acknowledged when Toe Blake suffered a broken leg in January 1948 and

Durnan shares a laugh in the dressing room with Coach Dick Irvin (top). Maurice Richard (left) and Butch Bouchard (right).

Durnan was handed the captain's "C." Durnan's frequent forays to discuss game matters with the referee had the opposition fuming and arguing he was just seeking an opportunity to catch his breath. The league instituted a new rule for the following season, disallowing a goaltender from executing the captain's duties on the ice.

Montreal failed to make the playoffs in 1947–48 and Durnan received sustained booing for the first time. "I don't know whether you've ever heard 13,000 people all calling you the same bad name at the same time," he later recalled, "but it sure makes a loud noise." He was an easygoing man by nature, but with his heavy workload and extra responsibilities as captain, compounded with the team faltering, Durnan felt the pressure starting to get to him. "It got so bad," he said, "that I couldn't sleep the night before a game or the night afterwards, either. Nothing is worth that kind of agony." He contemplated quitting but the Canadiens talked him out of it — temporarily.

"I'll admit, if they were paying the kind of money goaltenders get today, they'd have to shoot me to get me out of the game," conceded Durnan in 1972. "But at the end of any given season, I never had more than $2,000 in the bank, I wasn't educated and had two little girls to raise. All this worried me a great deal, and I was also hurting."

Durnan posted career highs in 1948–49, with 10 shutouts and a 2.10 goals-against average, but he looked back at the 1949–50 season as "the beginning of the end." Although he tallied eight shutouts and led the league with a 2.20 goals-against average, most of the fun of the game had gone for him. A bad gash in his head from an errant skate, late in the season, had him pondering retirement, but more significant, he felt his play was faltering and he was letting down his teammates.

When Montreal fell behind three games to none in the playoff semifinal in 1950, Durnan abruptly quit. Montreal had signed a promising young goalie named Gerry McNeil, and Durnan felt McNeil might as well get started. This time, despite McNeil's and his coach and teammates' protestations, there was no convincing Durnan to change his mind again. McNeil won one match before the Canadiens were eliminated that season, and Durnan never played another game.

HARRY LUMLEY

The Nomadic Netminder

HARRY LUMLEY DIDN'T LOOK AS THOUGH HE WAS NHL MATERIAL AT FIRST, BUT HE FASHIONED A HALL OF FAME CAREER for himself before he was done. Known as "Apple Cheeks" for his ruddy complexion when he blushed, Lumley holds the record as the youngest goalie to play an NHL game. He signed his first professional contract at age 16 and was a 17-year-old rookie when he was called up for two games in 1943–44 with the Detroit Red Wings.

After giving up 13 goals and losing both games, Lumley had been officially sent back to the minors but was still in town when Detroit hosted the New York Rangers. Watching from the stands, he saw Detroit take the lead before the Rangers' goalie went down with an injury near the end of the second period. As teams only carried one goalie in those days, it was expected that the home team would provide a substitute, should one be necessary. Detroit called upon Lumley, who donned a Ranger sweater for the third period as a "loaner." He blanked the Wings, causing coach Jack Adams to rage to his team that, "the best Red Wing player tonight wasn't even wearing a Red Wings uniform!"

Lumley was sent back to the Indianapolis Capitols of the AHL for half of the next season before earning a starting job with the Wings. He was especially effective in the playoffs, backstopping Detroit to within a game of the 1945 Stanley Cup. The Toronto

Maple Leafs rookie goalie, Frank McCool, won the first three games of the series by shutouts to set an NHL record. Lumley, the first teenager to ever play goal in the Stanley Cup Final, rebounded and posted a shutout of his own in Game 5. Toronto's owner and manager Conn Smythe thought he could rattle the young netminder in the following game and seal the Leafs win.

"Smythe lurked behind Lumley's net in the late stages of the game and gave Harry the full benefit of his inimitable verbal blasts," wrote Jim Coleman of the *Globe and Mail*. "Every time Lumley turned aside another Maple Leaf thrust, he would turn and smile

sweetly upon Smythe." Lumley posted his second consecutive shutout, making a lasting impression upon Smythe, and forcing a seventh and deciding game, a 2–1 thriller won by Toronto.

Over the next five years, Lumley and the Red Wings established themselves among the league's best in a very competitive era. Considered large in his day, at 6 feet tall and 200 pounds, Lumley was not noted for quickness or a flashy style, but he was consistently effective. Twice with Detroit he led the league in wins and games played, and he had the most shutouts (seven) in 1947–48. Near the end of the 1949–50 regular season, Lumley was injured

and young Terry Sawchuk was called up to guard the Detroit net for seven games. He showed great promise, but it was Lumley back in net for the 1950 Stanley Cup playoffs, as Detroit overcame the loss of Gordie Howe to a serious injury in the semifinal series against Toronto, and then beat New York in the final. Lumley won his first and only Stanley Cup ring, with three playoff shutouts and a minuscule 1.85 goals-against average.

Only a week after hoisting the Cup, Lumley was traded to the lowly Chicago Black Hawks in a nine-player deal. He spent two seasons in the league basement, facing a nightly barrage of rubber behind

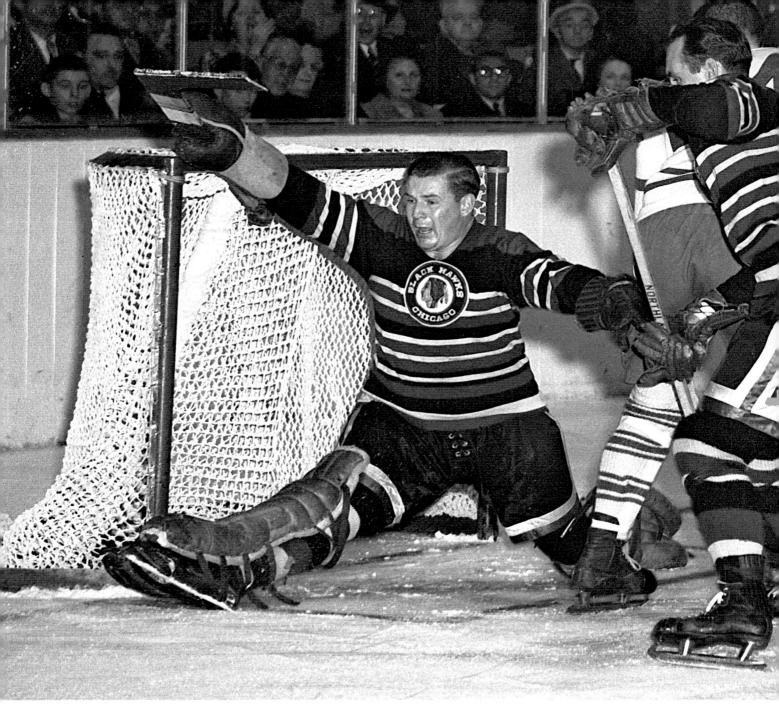

the NHL's weakest offense and defense. Lumley fashioned only 29 victories over 134 games with the Hawks before being traded to another struggling franchise in 1952. Conn Smythe sent four players — Al Rollins, Gus Mortson, Cal Gardner and Ray Hannigan — in return for Lumley, who had foiled Toronto so many times while with Detroit. Lumley rewarded Smythe's judgment by posting his best individual seasons with the Maple Leafs.

In 1953–54, Lumley won his only Vezina with a 1.86 average and led the league while posting a modern-day record of 13 shutouts, a feat not

bettered until Tony Esposito notched 15 in 1969–70. Lumley also was selected to the league's First All-Star Team, a distinction he'd earn again the following season. Unfortunately, he lost the 1954–55 Vezina to Detroit's Sawchuk by a single goal (unlike today where the NHL GMs vote for the best goalie, the trophy then went to the netminder that allowed the fewest goals), despite the fact that he led the league with a 1.94 goals-against average over 69 games versus Sawchuk's 1.96 average over 67 games and one period. To further illustrate Lumley's dominance in 1954–55, the rouge-cheeked netminder

Lumley suits up at 17 years old.

posted his league-low goals-against while backstopping the weakest offense in the NHL, as Toronto only scored 147 times compared to Detroit's 204 goals (Montreal notched 228). Lumley kept his team in every game, posting 23 wins, 24 losses, and a still-standing record of 22 ties.

As perhaps the most underrated goalie of his era, Lumley found himself cast off once again in the summer of 1956. He was sold (along with Eric Nesterenko) back to Chicago. Lumley wanted no part of the struggling Black Hawks again, however, and refused to report. He played instead with the

AHL's Buffalo Bisons for most of the next two seasons. Lumley returned to the NHL in 1957 when Boston needed help, his fifth club of the Original Six, and he split duties with Don Simmons for the Bruins until he retired in 1960. Lumley's 71 career shutouts leave him currently in the number 12 spot in NHL history.

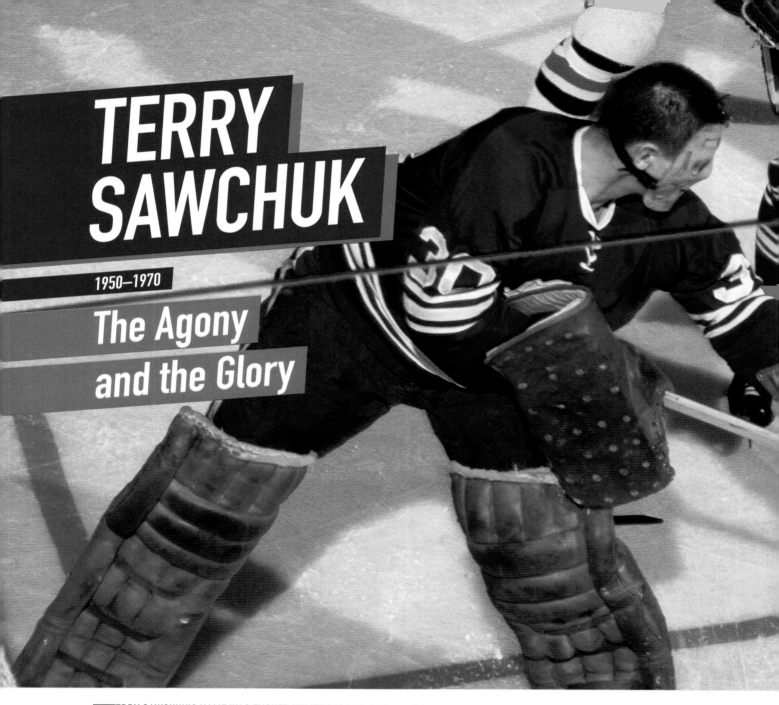

TERRY SAWCHUK

1950–1970

The Agony and the Glory

TERRY SAWCHUK'S NAME WAS EVOKED NUMEROUS TIMES IN 2009, AS MARTIN BRODEUR ENCROACHED UPON, AND THEN surpassed, Sawchuk's almost 40-year-old career record of 103 regular-season shutouts. The mark, long considered unassailable, was the last of the major goaltending records Sawchuk had established as, arguably, the greatest goalie of the Original Six era, and perhaps the best ever. Sadly, however, Sawchuk's career was as noteworthy for tragedy as glory.

Terry Sawchuk's brother died of a heart attack at age 17, and 10-year-old Terry inherited his goalie equipment. Within five years, the superbly talented athlete was playing junior hockey, and he signed

his first pro contract with a Detroit Red Wings farm club while still a teenager. Sawchuk got his first NHL action when Detroit's Harry Lumley sprained an ankle near the end of the 1949–50 season. Sawchuk sparkled in seven games, notching his first shutout, and despite the fact that Detroit was an NHL powerhouse, winning the Stanley Cup that season with Lumley back between the pipes, Sawchuk was handed the full-time job for 1950–51.

The pressure of joining the defending Cup champs and replacing a future Hall of Famer didn't faze the 20-year-old Sawchuk an iota. He not only won the

Calder Trophy as top rookie, he led the league with 44 wins and 11 shutouts and made the First All-Star Team. Over the next four seasons, Sawchuk won the Vezina Trophy three times while backstopping the Red Wings to three Stanley Cup victories. He had brilliant reflexes, but he also pioneered a new goal-tending stance.

"I found that I could move more quickly from the crouch position," explained Sawchuk. "It gave me better balance to go both ways, especially with my legs. Scrambles and shots from the point were becoming the style in hockey when I broke into the NHL. From the crouch, I could keep the puck in my

vision much better when it was coming through a maze of players."

Of course, this new stance put Sawchuk's unmasked face in danger, and he bore the scars to prove it. In truth, none of his successes came easily. Battling through a long list of physical injuries, his life was fraught with pain. Additionally, although generally weighing about 195 pounds, he had to work hard to maintain that weight, ballooning to 230 in the fall of 1951 before dropping to a gaunt 175 pounds. But his internal demons were also a constant pressure.

"The first time I met Terry Sawchuk," recalled Joe Falls of the *Detroit Free Press*, "he was raging with

anger and shouting obscenities and throwing his skates at a reporter. This was in 1953. In all the years to follow, he never really changed."

Despite his tremendous success with Detroit, Adams tried to maximize his assets and sent Sawchuk to Boston, as part of a then-record, nine-player trade, two months after his star netminder helped hoist the 1955 Stanley Cup. Sawchuk, as usual, had played hurt many nights for Detroit, but, partly because of frayed nerves, there were occasions when he just couldn't play. Glenn Hall filled in for him twice in his last season in Detroit, and Adams liked what he saw in the younger netminder.

Sawchuk's confidence was severely shaken when he joined the Bruins, a far weaker team than Detroit. Although he still tallied nine shutouts in his first season in Boston (1955–56), he suffered a nervous breakdown and then temporarily quit

midway through the 1956–57 campaign. Sawchuk's wife and children had remained in Detroit after the trade, and he felt that their support would help him cope better. At Sawchuk's request, Boston traded him back to Detroit for John Bucyk the following summer. The Red Wings sent Hall to Chicago, where he became a star, and Sawchuk spent seven more seasons as a Red Wing. While his skills were still remarkably sharp, the team was heading into some lean years, and Sawchuk was plagued with injuries. "When it came time to waken him," his wife later recalled, "I often had to help him out of bed and, later, into the car for the trip to the rink. Then he'd take a painkiller pill, timing it so he would unstiffen by the time the buzzer sounded to skate out onto the ice." Needless to say, with such a regimen, Sawchuk earned no accolades as a practice goalie, but he made the Second All-Star Team in

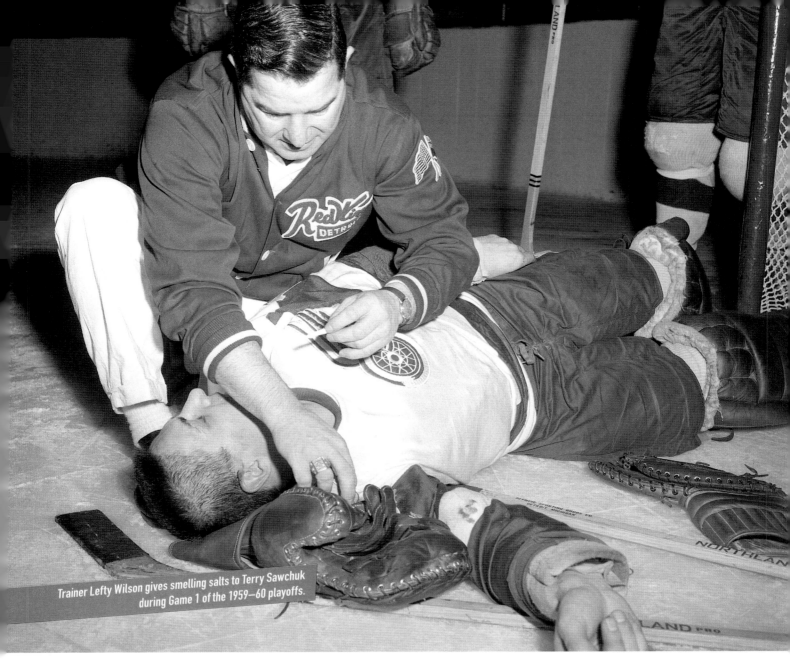

Trainer Lefty Wilson gives smelling salts to Terry Sawchuk during Game 1 of the 1959–60 playoffs.

1959 and 1963, as he established the career records for wins and shutouts.

With the emergence of the two-goalie system, Toronto claimed Sawchuk in the 1964 intra-league draft, and he shared the net with Johnny Bower for three seasons. "Terry was a real loner," recalled Bower, who is quick to acknowledge he learned much just from watching his teammate. "He was certainly a great competitor whose record speaks for itself, but I just couldn't talk to him. I asked him for help a couple of times, but he only reassured me without really offering any insight or assistance." The two shared the 1965 Vezina Trophy, and Sawchuk relieved Bower in the 1967 playoffs to help the underdog Leafs unexpectedly defeat the Montreal Canadiens for the Stanley Cup. That victory would prove to be the last highlight of his career.

Sawchuk was picked in the NHL's expansion draft by Los Angeles, where he played the 1967–68 campaign, but at 38, his age was beginning to show. He bounced back to Detroit for 13 games the following season and concluded his career with the New York Rangers in 1969–70, appearing in only eight games. Sadly, shortly after the end of the season, he died of heart failure following two operations that were the result of a wrestling match with teammate Ron Stewart. The usual waiting period was waived and Sawchuk entered the Hall of Fame, posthumously, in 1971.

GLENN HALL

1953–1971

Ironman and the Butterfly

GLENN "MR. GOALIE" HALL EARNED HIS NICKNAME FOR HIS CONSISTENTLY STERLING PLAY OVER MORE THAN 1,000 games, including an "iron-man" record that will likely stand the test of time. Beginning with the first game of 1955–56, through part of the 1962–63 season, Hall played every minute of every game before a back injury forced him out of action. His streak ended at 502 games (552 including playoffs) and what is even more significant is that Hall played those games without a mask. There was nothing cautious about his play, either.

Hall pioneered the "butterfly" style of goaltending when he discovered that crouching and keeping his legs spread below the knees allowed him to go down rapidly but keep his body erect to cover more of the net, and then spring back up again quickly. Hall's innovative method was ridiculed by many, who saw it as "flopping" and contrary to the accepted stand-up style. "I didn't realize at the time how much criticism was being directed at me through the media, because I didn't read the hockey section of the newspaper until I retired," he recalled. "I'm thankful for that. I knew the style was good for me. The critics didn't understand what I was doing. The butterfly keeps the body erect. When the body is erect, you can recover easily. It's actually the opposite of flopping."

Of course, Hall's butterfly method also put his unprotected face directly into harm's way. "The styles have changed so much since the mask came in," Hall said. "We tried to get our feet over in front of the puck and the head out of the way. Making the save was thought number two; it was survival, number one. Sometimes you sacrificed that to stop the puck, but survival was always on our mind."

Hall grew up in Saskatchewan, but played his junior hockey with the Windsor Spitfires in the Ontario Hockey Association and was signed by the Detroit Red Wings in 1951. He entered Detroit's farm system, where he continued to perfect his style. "I liked the deep crouch that I saw Terry Sawchuk use," recalled Hall. "Most goalies would try to look over the players screening them, but Terry would often look underneath the screen. That worked well for me too, but in those days, goalies never talked about goaltending. I was called up a few times to fill in for Terry when he was injured, but he never told me a thing. No goalie ever did."

Hall was called up for six games with the Wings in 1952–53, and just two more in 1954–55, posting a 6-1-1 record over those eight games. And even with the small sample size, Detroit thought highly enough of his potential that the great Sawchuk was deemed

expendable. Hall began his ironman streak in the Detroit net in 1955 and won the Calder Trophy as Rookie of the Year with a league-leading 12 shut-outs. He made the First All-Star Team the following season, yet it was his last in Detroit.

Annoyed at Hall's outspokenness when his team-mate Ted Lindsay was forging the first NHL Play-ers' Association, Red Wings' general manager Jack Adams traded both players to the lowly Chicago Black Hawks, a move at the time comparable in NHL terms to exile in Siberia.

"Being around Ted Lindsay did a lot for my approach to the game," recalled Hall. "I think I was reasonably talented, but he taught me that if you forced yourself to play harder, you'd get better results." Hall's mental preparation before a game involved getting so keyed up that he would be sick to his stomach, but it wasn't nervousness. For him, this was a sign that he was ready to compete to the best of his ability. "I always felt I played better if I was physically sick before the game," he said, and Hall's vomit bucket became part of goaltending lore. "I had

no trouble getting 'up' for a game," he added. "I was always completely ready. Five minutes before a game or between periods, I didn't hear what a coach was saying because I was in total preparation. All I would be thinking about was what I had to do. During a game, when someone got ready to shoot, I'd already looked at the shot in my mind. I tried to prepare myself for every option."

Hall didn't miss a beat — or a game — with the move to the Windy City and the Hawks were immeasurably improved by the addition of other "rebels" from various teams and the arrival of junior sensations such as Bobby Hull and Stan Mikita. Hall made the First All-Star Team in 1958 and 1960, and the Second Team in 1961, when he also backstopped the Hawks to the team's first Stanley Cup victory since 1938. Before the decade was out, Hall made both the First and Second All-Star Teams three more times, and thrice got his name on the Vezina Trophy.

The St. Louis Blues wisely chose Hall as their first pick in the expansion draft of 1967. At age 36,

"Mr. Goalie" showed he still had plenty of game left. He backstopped the Blues to the Stanley Cup Final three seasons in a row, earning the 1968 Conn Smythe Trophy as the playoffs' Most Valuable Player even though his heroics couldn't prevent his club being swept 4-0 in the best-of-seven series. "The Original Six teams gave nothing to the expansion clubs but old guys they thought couldn't play anymore or young kids they didn't think would ever amount to much," recalled Hall. "We had a team of 20- and 40-year-olds, but I feel good about how well the Blues represented the expansion teams. I don't think the NHL would be enjoying the success it is today if we hadn't done so well."

Fellow veteran Jacques Plante came out of retirement and joined the Blues for the 1968–69 season, and the veteran tandem shared the Vezina with Hall snagging a First All-Star selection. Perhaps it was Plante's influence, but Hall finally donned a face mask that season and continued to wear it until his retirement in 1971. "I had no confidence in the masks we wore," he said, "but the game was changing. Instead of beating the defenseman wide, the forwards often put the puck back to the point and went for the screen and the deflection. As a result, there were more injuries to the goalies." At the time of Hall's retirement, his 84 career shutouts was second best in NHL history, behind only Terry Sawchuk's remarkable 103; he is currently fourth on the all-time list.

JACQUES PLANTE

1953–1975

Jake the Snake

JACQUES PLANTE MARCHED TO THE BEAT OF HIS OWN DRUM, ALL THE WAY TO THE HOCKEY HALL OF FAME. AS WELL AS being one of the best goalies of all time, Plante was among the most innovative. He is best known today as the first NHL goalie to regularly wear a mask.

His approach to the mask was that it could prevent injury, not just protect an injury, which had previously been its use when Clint Benedict debuted his leather contraption in 1930. "They figured a goalie had to be scared to play well," Plante later recalled. "When shots are coming at you at 100 miles per hour, you're scared whether you have a mask or not." But it took an ultimatum to overcome the notion that a mask was a sign of cowardice.

On November 1, 1959, New York Rangers' sniper Andy Bathgate ripped open Plante's nose with a backhand shot. Plante had worn a mask in practice since 1956, never in a game, but, while getting stitched up in the dressing room, he told his Montreal Canadiens coach Toe Blake that he wouldn't go back into the net without his mask on. In the single-goalie era, Blake had little choice but to capitulate, with the stipulation that the mask came off when Plante's nose was healed. The Habs then went on an 11-game win streak, yet Blake held Plante to their deal, and the mask came off. When Montreal lost the following game, Blake allowed Plante to decide whether the mask was a help or a hindrance.

The mask soon became standard equipment, not just for Plante, but for goalies everywhere.

Of course, it took a premier netminder to change the face of the game. Plante, known as "Jake the Snake" for his quick reflexes, made his first appearances with the Canadiens in November 1952, playing three games and going undefeated. He spotted starter Gerry McNeil for four games in the 1953 playoffs, notching a shutout against the Chicago Black Hawks in his postseason debut, and earned his first of six Stanley Cup rings. Plante started the 1953–54 campaign with the AHL's Buffalo Bisons, but before season's end, he was with the Habs to stay. He backstopped his team to within one win of the Stanley Cup that spring — falling to Detroit in seven games — and then an unequalled string of five consecutive Stanley Cup victories (1954–55 to 1958–59). "For five years, he was the greatest goalie the league has ever seen," observed Blake.

Plante also changed the game with the way he interacted with the puck and opposing shooters. While other goalies before him periodically came out of their crease to play the puck, Plante made it a regular practice. He was the first to skate in behind the net to stop the puck from ringing the boards on a shoot-in, and was the first goalie to raise his arm to signal an icing call for his defensemen. Plante perfected a stand-up style of goaltending that

emphasized positional play, cutting down the angles and staying square to the shooter. "So often, your skilled players are not dedicated," noted fellow net-minder Glenn Hall. "But Plante was."

His eccentricities were legendary, some harmless, such as knitting his own hats and undershirts (although his first Canadiens coach, Dick Irvin, forbade him from wearing his tuque on the ice, as Plante desired). Some other "quirks" were deemed harmful to team camaraderie, such as staying in a different hotel than his teammates because he felt the air was better for his asthma (a questionable practice at the time). It was actually Plante's asthma that had led him to become a goaltender in the first place, as the ailment prevented him from skating for long

periods. He gravitated to the net, where he quickly found his niche.

Although he picked up his sixth Vezina Trophy and won the Hart Trophy as the league's MVP in 1961–62, Plante eventually wore out his welcome in Montreal. Traded to New York in June 1963, Plante bragged that he would win another Vezina Trophy in Manhattan. Instead, tired of losing with the sad-sack Rangers, he retired in 1965 and took care of his ailing wife.

Three years later, Plante was lured out of retirement by the St. Louis Blues to share goaltending duties with the great Glenn Hall. Plante shared the 1968–69 Vezina Trophy with Hall at the age of 40, his seventh, and a new NHL record. "I don't think I

Plante's time with the Rangers was plagued with losing.

ever played better than I did with St. Louis," claimed Plante, "even in my best years with the Canadiens." The veteran tandem took the Blues to the 1969 and 1970 Stanley Cup Final. In the latter series, against the Boston Bruins, Phil Esposito tipped a blazing Fred Stanfield slap shot, splitting Plante's mask in two. When he regained consciousness in hospital, the doctors and Plante concurred that the mask had saved his life. That proved to be Plante's final game in a St. Louis uniform.

Sold to Toronto in May 1970, Plante made the NHL's Second All-Star Team the following season. At the age of 42, he led the league with a 1.88 goals-against average. He also tutored fellow Maple Leaf up-and-coming goaltender Bernie Parent,

who soon afterward emerged as the NHL's premier netminder. Plante finished his NHL career with the Boston Bruins at the tail end of the 1972–73 campaign, then came out of retirement one last time to play a season for the Edmonton Oilers in the World Hockey Association in 1974–75. Plante was inducted into the Hockey Hall of Fame in 1978. He died of stomach cancer in 1986, and the Montreal Canadiens recognized his outstanding contribution by officially retiring his No. 1 in 1995.

GUMP WORSLEY

1953–1974
Goaltending Gump-tion

LORNE "GUMP" WORSLEY MAY HAVE BEEN THE FUNNIEST MAN TO PLAY IN THE NHL. HE PICKED UP HIS NICKNAME AS A child for his resemblance to Andy Gump of the funny papers, and his round face, short stature and pudgy physique made him appear to be more of a wit than an athlete.

Yet his accomplishments were exemplary and his longevity was rare. Worsley played 21 years in the NHL, but his career didn't begin until he was 23 years old. Born in Montreal in 1929, Worsley played his first amateur hockey in Verdun (a borough of Montreal), but was signed into the New York Rangers' organization when he was 19 and played the rest of his amateur hockey with the New York Rovers. Prior to his 1952–53 NHL rookie season in the Big Apple, Worsley played in five different semi-pro leagues, winning honors and trophies at virtually every stop along the way.

Worsley attended the Rangers' training camp for three straight seasons before he was given a real crack at the NHL. The month-long camps gave the up-and-coming netminder some time to develop his game alongside pro players. "Charlie Rayner tutored me on how to play goal," said Worsley, recalling the Rangers' star netminder. "I had some of the basics, but he taught me most of what I know. Charlie was very good to me, staying after practice and getting a couple of guys to shoot on us. He showed me

how to cut the angles and play the position. He was coming to the end of his career, and I eventually took his spot on the Rangers when he retired." Although New York was mired deep in the league basement, Worsley won the Calder Trophy in 1953 as NHL Rookie of the Year. Thinking he'd earned a raise, Worsley asked for more money but was instead sent back to the minors (Vancouver Canucks of the WHL) for a season, where he led the Western Hockey League with 39 wins and a 2.40 goals-against average.

In 1954–55, he resumed his NHL career in the New York net and spent most of the next decade there. "Facing a lot of shots was an occupational hazard in New York," recalled Worsley, who often

saw the opposition put 50 to 60 shots on net, but his sense of humor remained intact. Asked by a reporter which team gave him the most trouble, Worsley quipped, "The Rangers."

At first it looked as if "The Gumper" had won the lottery when the stalwart Montreal Canadiens sent Jacques Plante to New York in 1963 in a multi-player swap that sent Worsley to the Habs. "I've yet to be informed by the Rangers," claimed Worsley in 1996, saying the Rangers never informed him and he only ever got the news from Montreal's Frank Selke Sr., who welcomed him to his new club. Worsley got off to a strong start as a Hab, but only eight games

into the 1963–64 season, he suffered a knee injury. Sent to the AHL's Quebec Aces to get into shape after his injury healed, Worsley had a difficult time breaking back into the Montreal lineup. "I was 34 years old and thought it was the end of my career," he said. "I didn't get the callback for a year." When he did, midway through the 1964–65 season, Worsley performed heroically, backstopping Montreal all the way to Stanley Cup victory. "The last five minutes of the seventh game seemed to last five years. I kept looking at the clock, and the hands never seemed to move. We were leading 4–0, and I was sure I'd never let five goals in, but I was incredibly nervous. I was

13 years in the league by then. I can't really put the feeling into words, but I could have walked home without my feet touching the ground. Every Cup win was the same."

In 1965–66, Worsley shared the Vezina Trophy with Charlie Hodge and made the Second All-Star Team, before playing every playoff game and again sipping from the Stanley Cup. "Worsley wasn't even tested," griped Detroit's great defenseman Bill Gadsby. "His underwear can't even be wet." Told of the comment, Worsley joked, "What most people don't know is that my underwear is wet even before the game begins."

Worsley shared the 1968 Vezina with the up-and-coming Rogie Vachon, and made the First All-Star Team with a league-best and career-low 1.98 goals-against average. He went on to win another Cup ring that season and the next. But

the pressure of playing for the Canadiens is often relentless. "Montreal can be a difficult place to be if you're not winning," said Worsley, whose wife at times would have strangers shouting at her in the grocery store. Even his son once faced pressure to get playoff tickets for his school teachers or see his marks suffer. "I had to go raise hell at the school," he said.

Worsley suffered an emotional collapse midway through the 1968–69 season but came back to contribute important playoff wins for the Canadiens. However, Vachon started getting most of the work. When Montreal attempted to send Worsley to the minors in November 1969, he retired instead.

The Minnesota North Stars convinced Worsley to join them late that season, and he went on to play four more seasons with them. "I loved it there," said Worsley. "Cesare Maniago and I became a 'Mutt

and Jeff' goaltending tandem." Maniago, a lanky 6-foot-3 veteran, but 10 years younger, was indeed a comical counterpart to 5-foot-7 Worsley — much like the famed comic-strip odd couple. "Cesare eventually convinced me to have a mask made, and I tried it in practice but couldn't get used to it," said Worsley. "I found it very warm and couldn't see the puck between my feet." But just before he hung up his pads for good, and almost 45 years old, Worsley donned a mask for the final six games of the 1973–74 season. "I knew I was retiring, and Minnesota was mathematically eliminated from the playoffs. [General manager] Wren Blair said, 'Save your eyes, Gump. Put it on.' But I didn't like it."

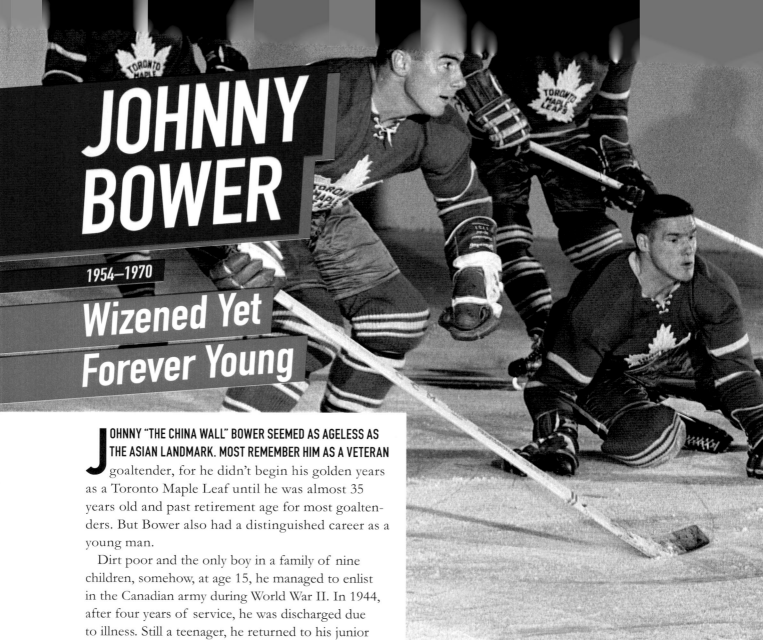

JOHNNY BOWER

1954–1970

Wizened Yet Forever Young

JOHNNY "THE CHINA WALL" BOWER SEEMED AS AGELESS AS THE ASIAN LANDMARK. MOST REMEMBER HIM AS A VETERAN goaltender, for he didn't begin his golden years as a Toronto Maple Leaf until he was almost 35 years old and past retirement age for most goaltenders. But Bower also had a distinguished career as a young man.

Dirt poor and the only boy in a family of nine children, somehow, at age 15, he managed to enlist in the Canadian army during World War II. In 1944, after four years of service, he was discharged due to illness. Still a teenager, he returned to his junior hockey team in Prince Albert, Saskatchewan, for the remainder of the 1944–45 campaign and made the jump to the American Hockey League (AHL) the following season.

"You had to bide your time," recalled Bower, who rode the buses with the Cleveland Barons for nine seasons before getting his first chance in the NHL. He made the 1951 AHL Second All-Star Team and joined the First Team in the following two seasons, at which point the New York Rangers swung a deal for his services. Bower posted a strong 1953–54 campaign for the Rangers, playing all 70 games even though goalie Gump Worsley had been the NHL's Rookie of the Year with the Rangers the previous season. Later on, Bower faced a similar disappointment to Gump's, when, to his surprise, he found

himself back in the minors the following season, and Worsley got his NHL job back. Although Bower won a multitude of AHL awards over the following four seasons, the perennial All-Star and three-time AHL MVP played only seven games as a call-up for the Rangers over that span.

Bower, like many professionals in the six-team era, was resigned to having a rewarding minor league career, but fate intervened in 1958. He had played a particularly strong playoff series that spring against the Springfield Indians. Punch Imlach, who ran the Indians, was hired as coach and general manager of the Toronto Maple Leafs that year, and he drafted Bower. Although initially

reluctant to join the Leafs, Bower was persuaded to report to training camp. "I was scared, literally shaking in my boots, for my first game in Maple Leaf Gardens," confessed Bower, but he quickly established himself as a No. 1 NHL goalie in the fall of 1958. Over the next 11 seasons, he won four Stanley Cup rings and two Vezina Trophies.

Bower was a standup goalie with surprisingly quick reflexes. He worked as hard in practice as he did in games, a habit that endeared him to Imlach, and although he was as affable a man as any who ever played in the NHL, he had an equally strong competitive streak. Bower is remembered for his famous poke check, a move he says he learned from his New York Ranger mentor Chuck Rayner at a training camp early in his career. But Bower certainly made the dangerous but effective technique his own. Diving headfirst — and maskless of course — he'd spear the puck off the stick of an attacking forward, and frequently take out the forward at the skates right after. Although facial injuries were common — from cuts and bruises to broken teeth — Bower never donned a mask until the very tail end of his career. His lined and scarred face led many to suspect he was even older than his reported age, and Bower was intentionally vague about dates, but his play was stellar, and Imlach never hesitated to use veteran players.

Johnny Bower during his time in the American Hockey League with the Cleveland Barons.

Bower helped the last-place Leafs into the playoffs his first season in Toronto, and then backstopped them to two consecutive Stanley Cup Finals, winning the 1960–61 Vezina Trophy along the way. Then, in 1962, he led the Leafs to the Promised Land. "It was such a thrill to win the Cup," said Bower. "I got so excited that at the end of the game, I threw my stick up in the air. I saw my teammates coming toward me to celebrate and realized I'd better get my stick. I looked up and — boom! — it came down on my forehead and cut me for seven stitches. I didn't feel a thing, bleeding all over the guys who were hugging me."

Toronto won the Cup in 1962, 1963 and 1964, with Bower averaging 2.01 goals-against in the

playoffs. "Anytime you win in the Stanley Cup, the goaltender is the big reason," said Imlach. "We've got a lot of good hockey players on our team, but they're not worth a darn unless the old guy is making the big saves."

"I wasn't all that glad to see the two-goalie system come in," maintained Bower. "I wanted to play in all the games I possibly could." But Imlach was always alert to squeezing the last juice possible from NHL veterans and Bower shared the Vezina with Terry Sawchuk in 1964–65. While Sawchuk was ever the loner and not really willing to offer tips to Bower, both benefited by watching the other, and resting while the other flashed a hot hand. In what would prove to be the last hurrah for both, the two

goalies combined efforts to help an underdog team of old-timers win the Cup again in 1966–67. That victory remains to date the last time the Stanley Cup belonged to the Toronto Maple Leafs.

Bower retired in 1970 as the oldest goalie ever to play in the NHL at the age of 45. He remained with the Leafs for many years as a scout and then goalie coach, putting the pads on and helping Leaf goalies in practice. He entered the Hockey Hall of Fame in 1976, but later, during the Maple Leafs' injury riddled 1979–80 season, the China Wall came within a whisker of dressing as Toronto's backup goalie — and had he been called to action, no one would have been surprised if the 56-year-old stoned the opposition.

GERRY CHEEVERS

1962–1980

A Stitch in Time

ALTHOUGH HIS CAREER RECORD SHOWS LITTLE IN THE WAY OF HONORS FOR PERSONAL ACCOMPLISHMENT, GERRY Cheevers made an indelible mark on the game. Team victories were what he valued most, and so long as his club scored more goals than he let in, he was satisfied. "Circumstances dictated what I did," explained Cheevers, who was well known for his sense of humor. "When a goal meant nothing to the outcome, I wouldn't always play the puck.

"My teammates laughed for a long time about one bouncing puck that I intentionally ignored. I heard it hit the post — closer to the net than I predicted — but I felt relieved that I had played it properly. Unfortunately, it was the middle post that it hit." But only a star can get away with playing the clown at times, and in truth, Cheevers was a clutch performer.

"I don't know how I got a reputation for being a 'money' goaltender, because I probably lost almost as many big games as I won," he maintained, humble enough to question his legacy. "Perhaps I'm remembered for playing well in some games that meant a lot to the team. If you aren't ready to perform well in a game that means elimination, then you shouldn't play professional hockey. I enjoyed those games, but you never win them all — no one does."

While his Boston teammates Bobby Orr and Phil Esposito got more of the limelight, Cheevers was a critical component of the club that won the Stanley Cup in 1970 and 1972. In the latter campaign, he notched a remarkable 33-game undefeated streak, a record that still stands. It was an improbable peak to a career that began inauspiciously during the Original Six years.

Born in 1940 in St. Catharines, Ontario, Cheevers was raised in Toronto and grew up in the Maple Leafs organization. The Leafs sent him to the St. Michael's Majors in the Ontario Hockey Association to develop. The Majors' coach, trying to cure Cheevers of roaming so far from his crease (a skill that became part of his professional repertoire), and for his disinterest in practice, made him, as punishment, play a dozen games at left wing. Nevertheless, Cheevers acquired strong goaltending skills over his five years at the famous hockey finishing school. But when he graduated in 1961, Johnny Bower was entrenched in the Toronto goal. Sent to the farm team in Pittsburgh, Cheevers played two games with Toronto in 1961–62, but without making much of an impression.

"I trusted that my day would come," recalled Cheevers, noting that with Bower, then Don Simmons and Terry Sawchuk, the Toronto goalies were getting old. But the Leafs left Cheevers exposed two years in a row in the intra-league draft (protecting Bower and Sawchuk), and he was claimed in 1965, much to his disappointment. "Not only would I not

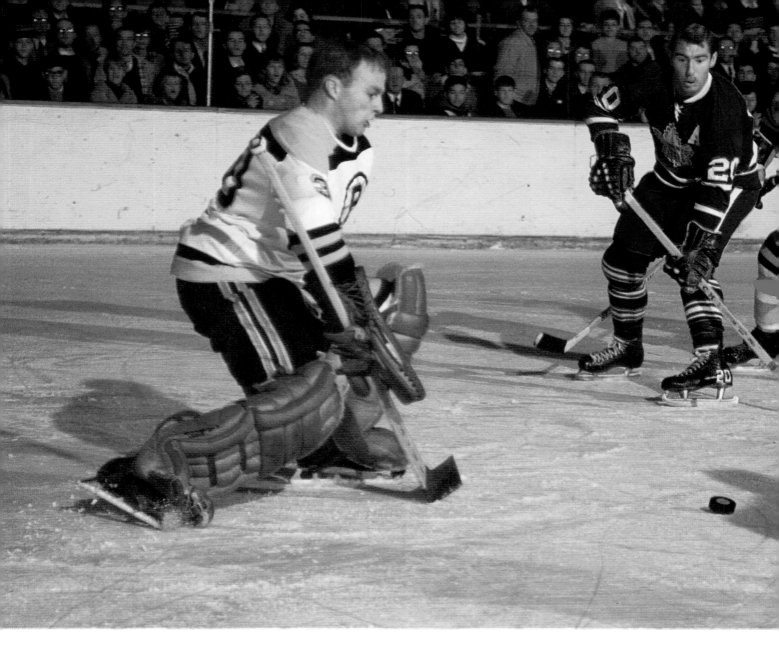

get my chance with the Leafs," he explained, "but the Bruins were a team going nowhere." Cheevers, however, found both a friend and a mentor in Boston teammate Eddie Johnston. "We competed in a friendly manner," said Cheevers, "but more than anyone, he helped me to become a big-league goaltender. He had an uncanny knowledge of the game that he was willing to share."

Cheevers played seven games for the Bruins in the 1965–66 season, and 22 the next before establishing himself as the No. 1 man in Boston. "It wasn't until 'No. 4' showed up that I started to enjoy myself," said Cheevers. "I knew immediately that we were going to win a championship." Boston got the incomparable Orr in 1966–67 and, soon afterward, Esposito and a plethora of other great scoring stars,

and while the team worked hard at putting the puck in the net, "Cheesy" was frequently left to his own devices to prevent goals. Acrobatic and aggressive, he swung his stick freely to clear his crease of opponents and accumulated a large number of penalties as one of the "Big Bad Bruins."

During practice in the 1968–69 season, Cheevers began creating his trademark mask. "I was trying to get out of practice one day," he explained, "when this shot that couldn't have broken an egg hit me in the mask. I faked a serious injury and went into the dressing room. I was sitting there having a Coke when [coach] Harry Sinden came in and told me to get back out onto the ice. All the guys were laughing, so I knew I had to do something. I told the trainer to paint a 30-stitch gash on the mask. Then I went out and told Harry, "See

Cheevers as a Cleveland Crusader. His jump to the WHA came on the heels of Boston's 1972 Stanley Cup.

how bad it is?" In ensuing years, Cheevers periodically added more stitch marks and his mask became less a joke and more an iconic symbol of the first generation of mask-wearing goalies.

In the summer of 1972, fresh from a Stanley Cup victory, Cheevers was one of a number of superstars to leave the NHL and join the upstart World Hockey Association (WHA). He signed a massive, seven-year, $1.4 million contract with the Cleveland Crusaders and earned his only professional hockey All-Star nominations: First Team in 1973, and Second Team in 1974 and 1975. But when the team's finances got rocky, Cheevers asked for a buyout. He returned to the Bruins and the NHL in January 1976.

Although he wasn't in game shape, Boston immediately dressed him as backup against Toronto. "I never

felt so badly for someone as I did for [Boston goalie] Dave Reese, but with every goal that went in, I went farther down the aisle," confessed Cheevers, recalling his first game back. Maple Leafs' captain Darryl Sittler had a game for the ages, tallying a record 10 points. "I didn't want our coach Don Cherry to see me. Don knew I wasn't ready, but if the Leafs had scored any more goals, I would have been hiding up in the stands with all my equipment on."

Cheevers helped the Bruins back to the Stanley Cup Final in the spring of 1977 and 1978, but they lost both times. He retired after the 1979–80 campaign, then immediately stepped behind the Boston bench as coach for an impressive four-and-a-half seasons.

EDDIE GIACOMIN

1966–1977

Ready, Steady, Eddie

H E HASN'T PLAYED NHL HOCKEY FOR OVER 30 YEARS, NEW YORK RANGER FANS CAN STILL BE HEARD CHANTING "EDDIE! Eddie! Eddie!" — a tradition in honor of Ed Giacomin. His success and the exciting manner in which he executed his game earned him everlasting affection, although that was never expressed in so heartfelt a way until he was with an opposing club.

Early in the 1975–76 season, Giacomin got off to a terrible start with New York, posting a 4.74 goals-against average, with three losses and a tie in his first four games. The Rangers had a new general manager in John Ferguson that season, and he decided that Giacomin's 10-year reign was over. The Rangers veteran was both saddened and embarrassed when he was claimed on waivers by Detroit. "I remember having such an empty feeling," he recalled. "I had given 10 years of my life to that team and the worst part about it was there was nobody around. My team-mates were on their way to Montreal. And here I am in this empty parking lot walking to my car. I had visions of walking straight into the bay."

On November 2, 1975, two days after becoming a Red Wing, he made a quick return to New York. Giacomin feared the reaction the fans might have upon seeing him in an opponent's uniform, and his family didn't dare attend the game. But the fans had been almost as upset as their star goaltender at the turn of events. The crowd's continual roar

of "Eddie!" began when they drowned out the national anthem, and he received numerous pro-longed standing ovations throughout the game. "I've never been an emotional man, but I couldn't hold back the tears tonight," said Giacomin in a post-game interview. "When the people started cheering me at the beginning, the tears came down my face. A couple of times, I thought I would collapse from the emotion." He sparkled, however, in facing 46 shots in a 6–4 victory. The fans booed the Rangers goals, and one former teammate apolo-gized for scoring.

Giacomin's career in New York did not begin with immediate success. He served a six-season minor-league apprenticeship before getting his first NHL shot. In 1958–59, the Washington Eagles of the Eastern Amateur Hockey League had called upon Sudbury Wolves' backup goalkeeper, Rollie Giacomin, to play the final four games of their season. Rollie didn't want to leave the Wolves of the Northern Ontario Hockey Association, so instead he sent his brother Eddie, five years his junior. Giacomin won all four games for the Eagles and earned a spot on the team for the next season. The Providence Reds of the American Hockey League purchased the rights to Giacomin in 1960, and once there, Giacomin caught the eye of a Rangers' scout from the area.

"The Reds were a last-place team most of the time I was with them," said Giacomin, recalling his five years on Rhode Island, "but this was a blessing in disguise. I saw a lot of rubber and learned how to play goal." In 1965–66, he began the season with the New York Rangers, but a rocky start led to another two-week stint in the AHL. When Giacomin returned, everything fell into place, and he was in the NHL for good.

Almost perennial also-rans in those days, the Rangers didn't fare well in Giacomin's rookie season. "I was so excited," he later recalled. "I was 26, and I didn't think I was ever going to make it to the NHL. I forgot that I was there to stop pucks." But in 1966–67, Giacomin led the league with 68 games played, nine shutouts and 30 wins, and he

was elected to the First All-Star Team. The Rangers made the playoffs for the first time in five years, and never missed the postseason again until they released Giacomin in 1975–76.

Unmasked until 1970 ("I do think you see the puck better without a mask," he stated that year. "I tried [Jacques] Plante's newfangled creation for a while, but I don't like it"), Giacomin played a fearless style, wandering far from his crease, sprawling acrobatically with great success and snapping crisp passes to teammates. "I hear Chuck Rayner of the old Rangers used to come right up and take part in the power play in the last minute of the game," he laughed in 1971, admitting he would love to score a goal. "Unfortunately, the rules no longer let goalies go past the center-ice line. Maybe I should have

been a forward!" He actually hit the opposition's goal post with one long shot, and he was the first NHL goalie to record two assists in one game.

He was the league's busiest netminder for several seasons while with the Rangers, leading the league in games played, and making the 1968, 1969 and 1970 Second All-Star Teams. When the game of No. 2 goaltender, Gilles Villemure, came into form, he proved the perfect goaltending partner. The two shared the 1970–71 Vezina Trophy, while Giacomin was named to the First All-Star Team with a league-leading eight shutouts in 45 games. He backstopped the Rangers to the 1972 Stanley Cup Final, pushing Bobby Orr and the Boston Bruins to six games. Giacomin helped vanquish Boston the

following season, but never got past the semifinal, and finished his career without a Cup ring.

The Wings failed to make the playoffs in 1975–76, and Giacomin played 29 games that season, relegated to a backup role for netminder Jim Rutherford. His average rose to 3.58 in 1976–77, the team missed the postseason again, and Giacomin quit after playing only nine games the following season. "My biggest thrill would have been winning the Stanley Cup," he said at his entry into the Hall of Fame in 1987, "but an individual can get no greater honor than this." A year and a half later, the Rangers bestowed further tribute, making Giacomin's No. 1 only the second sweater ever retired by the club.

BERNIE PARENT

1966–1979

Forever a Flyer

BERNIE PARENT BROKE INTO THE NHL STRAIGHT OUT OF JUNIOR HOCKEY, LANDING IN BOSTON FOR THE FINAL TWO years of the Original Six era. With only brief stints in the minors with the Oklahoma City Blazers, Parent had an unimpressive 15-32-5 combined win-loss-tie record as a Bruin. Boston management chose to leave Parent unprotected in the league's first expansion draft in June 1967, and the Philadelphia Flyers selected him to share goaltending duties with Doug Favell, another goaltender plucked from the Bruins.

Parent and Favell were partners for the better part of four seasons, and enjoyed a modicum of success. The Flyers won the 1967–68 divisional championship, and Parent established himself as a strong, but not dominant, goaltender, shouldering the majority of the work in the Philadelphia net. So he was genuinely shocked when he was traded in February 1971. "I heard the words and opened my mouth to say something but nothing came out," recalled Parent, who got the news from the Flyers' general manager Keith Allen. "I couldn't speak."

Before Parent learned to skate, he played a lot of goal in the street while growing up in Montreal in the 1950s. Naturally, he idolized the Canadiens' star netminder Jacques Plante. Therefore, there was a silver lining in the trade that sent Parent to the Toronto Maple Leafs. Plante, by then a 42-year-old veteran, had joined the Leafs earlier that season, and

he helped Parent take a more systematic approach to goaltending.

"There was no one in the world quite like Plante," noted Parent. "I learned more from him in two years with the Leafs than I did in all my other hockey days. He taught me a great deal about playing goal both on the ice and in my head off the ice. He taught me to be aggressive around the goal and take an active part in play instead of waiting for things to happen. He showed me how I kept putting myself off balance by placing my weight on my left leg instead of on my stick side. He taught me how to steer shots off into the corner instead of letting them rebound in front of me. That old guy made a good goalie out of me."

With Plante's tutelage, and more NHL experience under his belt, Parent was emerging as a top NHL talent when the World Hockey Association was birthed in 1972. He was drafted and signed by the Miami Screaming Eagles, who folded before even building an arena to play in. The WHA's Philadelphia Blazers quickly picked up Parent's rights, and he played the 1972–73 season back in his adopted hometown. Disenchanted by having to face an excessive barrage of pucks, and paychecks that sometimes bounced, Parent expressed a strong interest in returning to the NHL, but with the Flyers rather than Toronto, which held his rights.

Toronto management agreed, reluctantly, and traded Parent back to the Flyers in May 1973, and he immediately fashioned back-to-back Stanley Cup–winning seasons. "When Parent is out there," said Philadelphia coach Fred Shero, "we know we can win games that we have no business winning."

With 73 starts in a 78-game season in 1973–74, Parent tallied 47 wins — a record that stood until Marty Brodeur notched 48 in 2006–07. (Parent still retains the record for "most regulation time wins" as he posted a dozen ties that season, without the benefit of overtime or shootouts.) He also earned a league-best and career-high dozen shutouts, guiding Philadelphia to first place in the West Division while compiling a 1.89 goals-against average. Parent won the Vezina Trophy (in a tie with Chicago's Tony Esposito) and was selected to the First All-Star

Team. In the playoffs, he won the Conn Smythe Trophy as playoff MVP in leading the Flyers to victory over Bobby Orr and the Boston Bruins, winning the sixth and deciding game of the final with a 1–0 shutout.

"Only the Lord saves more than Bernie Parent" became a popular bumper sticker in Philadelphia, and Parent's 1974–75 campaign finished in almost identical fashion to the previous one. He posted 12 shutouts again (with four more in the playoffs), retained ownership of the Vezina with a league-best 2.03 goals-against average, and made the First All-Star Team. He then earned his second consecutive Conn Smythe Trophy while helping the Flyers successfully defend the Stanley Cup, punctuating another season for the ages with a 2–0 shutout against the Buffalo Sabres in the deciding sixth game of the final. After

the game, Parent was reluctant to pose with the Smythe, a personal rather than team award, a second time. "If you want to take a picture of me with a trophy," he said, "take me with the Stanley Cup. That's what this game is about."

Parent was absent from much of the following season due to a neck injury, and the Flyers were without him when the Montreal Canadiens and star goalie Ken Dryden swept them from the 1976 Cup Final. Parent played the majority of the Flyers' games over the next three seasons, and led the league with seven shutouts in 1977–78, before his career came to a sudden halt.

On February 17, 1979, during a goalmouth scramble, an errant stick hit Parent in his right eye. A sympathetic reaction in his other eye had him lying in a hospital bed for two weeks, completely blind.

"The doctors were honest with me and told me they could do very little to restore my sight," recalled Parent. "Ninety-five percent of the damage could be repaired only by my body's ability to heal itself. I was fearful, but I prayed and hoped for the best, and one morning, I saw a little bit of light."

His vision slowly returned, but Parent was left with permanent damage to his depth perception and his ability to focus. He was forced to retire from hockey at the age of 34. The Flyers retired his No. 1 sweater in the first game of the following season, and he entered the Hockey Hall of Fame in 1984. As Philadelphia's goaltending coach, Parent helped Pelle Lindbergh to a Vezina Trophy–winning season in 1984–85 and Ron Hextall to the same in 1986–87.

ROGIE VACHON

1967–1982

A Puck Stopping King

ROGATIEN "ROGIE" VACHON BURST UPON THE NHL SCENE WITH THE MONTREAL CANADIENS LATE IN THE 1966–67 SEASON. Called up from the Houston Apollos of the Central Pro Hockey League while Gump Worsley was hurt and backup Charlie Hodge was slumping, Vachon went 11-3-5 in 18 starts and posted a 2.48 goals-against average. In the playoffs, he posted four straight wins to eliminate the New York Rangers and set up a Stanley Cup Final match against the Toronto Maple Leafs. With Toronto's Punch Imlach ridiculing him as a Junior B goaltender, Vachon finally faltered in game five of the final and the Leafs defeated Worsley in game six to win the Stanley Cup. But Rogie was just getting started.

Over the next two seasons, Vachon split the Montreal net with Worsley. The two shared the Vezina Trophy in 1967–68 and 1968–69 while leading the Canadiens to two straight post-expansion Stanley Cup titles. Vachon was Montreal's No. 1 goaltender in 1969–70 and 1970–71, but lost the starting job to Ken Dryden just before the 1971 playoffs and was traded to the Los Angeles Kings on November 4.

After a solid debut season as a 1967 NHL expansion team, the Kings struggled over the next few years. Even the acquisition of Vachon didn't help much at first — mostly because the team in front of him wasn't nearly as talented as he was.

"On most nights, when we would win close games, 3–1 or 2–1," recalled former Los Angeles teammate Bob Berry, "it was usually him who bailed us out and made big stops. He would keep the ship afloat and we'd finally understand that we'd better get going. It didn't happen every night, but it happened enough. He taught us how to win."

The Kings finally seemed to put all the pieces together during the 1974–75 season, when they finished fourth in the NHL's overall standings with 105 points on a record of 42-17-21 during an 80-game season. Vachon had 27 of those wins (27-14-13) and posted a 2.24 goals-against average as he and partner Gary Edwards finished second behind Bernie Parent of the Stanley Cup–champion Philadelphia Flyers for the Vezina Trophy. In September of 1976, Vachon played every game for Canada's championship team at the inaugural Canada Cup tournament,

going 6-1-0 with a 1.39 goals-against average and two shutouts.

With the Kings through the 1977–78 season, Vachon set franchise records for most career games by a goaltender (389), most career wins (171), most career shutouts (32), lowest single-season goals-against average (2.24) and most shutouts in a season (8) — although all these marks have since been surpassed by Jonathan Quick. Vachon finished his playing career in 1981–82 after two seasons in Detroit and two more in Boston, but returned to Los Angeles and became general manager of the Kings in 1983–84. He served in that role through 1991–92 and also spent three short stints behind the bench as interim coach.

On February 14, 1985, Rogie Vachon's No. 30 became the first number retired by the Los Angeles Kings.

TONY ESPOSITO

1969–1984
Shutouts, Chicago-Style

AS ONE HALF OF PERHAPS THE MOST COLORFUL BROTHER ACT IN NHL HISTORY, TONY ESPOSITO WAS AS SENSATIONAL at keeping pucks out of the net as his older brother Phil was at scoring goals. When Phil joined the Chicago Black Hawks in 1963–64, Tony took the academic route to NHL hockey by attending Michigan Tech. He graduated four years later, with three All-American seasons and an NCAA championship under his belt. But he had also been keeping close tabs on Phil's teammate Glenn Hall.

"I'd go down and visit," he said. "I'd spend hours with Glenn Hall. We would go out and have a sociable beer, and he would talk goaltending and stuff with me." The tips from the well-seasoned Hall were not wasted on the college boy. "I tried to copy his style," admitted Esposito, who refined Hall's butterfly with an even wider stance and helped make it a critical component of his game. "I went down a lot," he said. "For me, if I'm screened or I can't see the shot, my instinct is to cover the lower half of the net. I stopped a lot of pucks without seeing them."

Although stocky in build — he was a successful halfback in high school football — he had quick reflexes and a lightning-fast glove hand, made all the more effective by the glove being on his right hand, an unusual look that confounded more than a few shooters. Esposito also had a strong

competitive streak, barking instructions to his teammates and in his later years unafraid to complain to management when he was dissatisfied with the team in front of him.

The Montreal Canadiens first signed Esposito in 1967 and, after some minor-pro seasoning, he made his NHL debut on December 5, 1968, facing the Boston Bruins, the club his brother had joined the previous season. Although Phil put two pucks past him into the net, Tony acquitted himself admirably in a 2–2 draw. In spite of posting two shutouts in the next dozen games he played for Montreal, he was sent back to the minors when Rogie Vachon and Gump Worsley recovered from their injuries. When Worsley got hurt again in the playoffs, Esposito suited up as backup again and earned what would prove to be his only Stanley Cup ring.

"He makes fundamental errors one minute and a miraculous save the next," observed Montreal

coach Claude Ruel who, along with the rest of Montreal's brain trust, had dismissed Esposito as a valuable asset. They soon looked foolishly shortsighted.

The Habs left Esposito unprotected in the intra-league draft and he was scooped up by Chicago, where he spent the next 15 seasons. The standard goalie numbers — 1 and 30 — were already assigned, but Esposito, who had worn the unconventional 29 in Montreal (Ken Dryden later made it famous there) made the unusual request for No. 35, which had never been worn by an NHL goalie. "I wanted something different," he later explained, "something to make me stand out and for people to notice." He quickly had his wish fulfilled.

By then age 26, Esposito was still officially a rookie in 1969–70 when he won the Calder Trophy, the Vezina and a First All-Star Team berth. Additionally, he was runner-up for the Hart Trophy as the NHL's

Most Valuable Player, an award that his brother Phil had won the previous season. Esposito took charge of the Black Hawks' net in training camp and played 63 games of the 70-game schedule. His 15 shutouts that season remain the modern record, the only goalie to have posted more was George Hainsworth with 22 in 1928–29.

"Tony O" was the Vezina Trophy runner-up the following season (1970–71), and then shared it with teammate Gary Smith in 1971–72 with a league- and career-best 1.77 goals-against average. The following season, Esposito notched 10 more shutouts and shared the Vezina with Philadelphia's Bernie Parent. He backstopped the Hawks to the 1971 and 1973 Stanley Cup Final and joined Team Canada for the 1972 Summit Series against the Soviet Union, posting two wins, a tie and one loss. He made the First All-Star Team again in 1972 and 1980, joining the Second Team in 1973 and 1974.

While Esposito's style was considered radical early in his career, he was even more innovative when it came to his equipment. In 1969, he fitted an elastic mesh between his pant legs, making a considerable impediment to pucks going through the five hole with a 12-inch by 6-inch web. The league quickly wrote a rule to ban his device, so Esposito added 2- to 3-inch rolls of foam inside each leg instead.

He designed a protective neckpiece to cover a spot often left bare by goalie armor in 1971 after taking a shot in the throat. Esposito was the first to add a cheater to his catching glove, effectively making the cuff of the glove as wide as the mitt on top — the prototype of the modern catcher. After he suffered a number of eye injuries from pucks and wayward sticks, he made significant improvements to mask design in 1974–75. He fitted a wire cage over the eyeholes of his mask and added a fiberglass extension to protect the top of his head, both important steps toward the standard mask of today.

For all his success, and obvious dedication to his profession, Esposito claimed he didn't truly enjoy the game. "It's a job," he said in 1972. "I have to do it. But it's tough. I don't like it. To be playing well as a goalkeeper, you have to be afraid. Not afraid that you'll get hurt, but afraid that they're going to score on you. Every time they come down the ice with that puck, I'm afraid the puck is going to go in." But Esposito's fear didn't prevent him from wanting to play as many games as possible. Although the two-goalie system was well entrenched around the league, in Chicago Esposito averaged more than 60 games a year until his final two seasons.

After residing in Chicago for over a decade, Esposito took out American citizenship in 1981 and received some grief from Canadians for backstopping the United States team in the Canada Cup tournament that fall. Esposito had begun serving as president of the NHL Players' Association (NHLPA) after Ken Dryden retired in 1979, and he continued to work for the NHLPA as a consultant after he retired. Esposito helped negotiate a new collective bargaining agreement that prevented a labor disruption in 1982.

At 41, and the oldest player in the league, Esposito hung up his pads after the 1983–84 season. Despite not winning a Cup in Chicago, his teams never failed to make the playoffs, and his 76 career regular season shutouts were sixth highest at the time of his retirement; he remains tied at ninth spot today. Esposito entered the Hall of Fame in 1988, the same year the Hawks retired his No. 35, which had long become a favorite number for young and aspiring goalies everywhere.

KEN DRYDEN

1971–1979
The Thinker

N HIS DAY, KEN DRYDEN WAS CONSIDERED BY SOME TO BE TOO BIG TO BE AN NHL GOALIE. AT 6-FOOT-4 AND OVER 200 POUNDS, he was certainly above average in size, and conventional wisdom would have seen him turned into a defenseman. Yet, Dryden's cerebral approach and remarkable athleticism combined to make him a netminder truly larger than life. His brief but spectacular NHL career was richly studded with both individual and team accomplishments, and his early retirement was almost as surprising as his NHL debut.

Boston drafted Dryden in 1964, but the Montreal Canadiens quickly acquired the 17-year-old's rights in a four-player trade. Perhaps it was Dryden's pedigree that caught their attention, as the other players in the swap were never heard of again. Dryden's brother Dave, six years older and also a goaltender, had already made one appearance in an NHL game for the New York Rangers and had posted the lowest goals-against average the previous season in the Ontario Hockey Association's senior league. Regardless, the deal would prove to be one of Montreal's most astute.

Ken Dryden made an unusual move in the 1960s and, rather than join a quasi-professional junior team, he attended Cornell University. He had to sit out his freshman year, but over the next three All-American seasons, he went 76-4-1 while getting a history degree as a step to becoming a lawyer. His

brother Dave, meanwhile, had secured a backup goaltending position with the Chicago Black Hawks, but Ken always followed his own path, playing for Canada's national team in order to continue his studies over the 1969–70 season. When the team was disbanded, he finally stepped into Montreal's farm system, where he proved that his apprenticeship had served him well.

Dryden made a strong impression with the AHL's Montreal Voyageurs in 1970–71 and was rewarded with a six-game callup to the parent club late in the season. History was made when he faced his brother Dave, then with the Buffalo Sabres in their inaugural season, on March 20, 1971, the first time the brothers had ever played goal against each other in the NHL. The two shook hands at center ice after the game, a ritual they repeated over the handful of times they met over the remainder of their careers. Ken won that first game, as well as the other five games he played for Montreal that campaign, allowing only nine goals in total, yet it was still a shocking decision when the Habs decided to start their rookie against the powerhouse Boston Bruins in the 1971 playoffs.

With Bobby Orr in his prime, Boston was the defending Stanley Cup champion and had scored a record 399 goals that season to establish themselves as one of the most powerful offensive clubs of all time. Dryden, however, seemed totally unfazed.

After most whistles, he stood with his arms crossed and gloves stacked on the butt end of his stick, with the blade tip spearing the ice, looking completely calm and collected. In truth, the ritual served to stretch out his spine, a relief from his constant crouch in game action, but his unique pose served as further proof that here was someone very different, and Dryden managed to get into the heads of the opposition.

"That was the greatest save that's ever been made off me in my life," said sniper Phil Esposito after Game 4, who'd set a new record that season with 76 goals and 76 assists. "My God, he's got arms like a giraffe." Dryden got all the credit when his team defeated the Bruins in seven games, an enormous upset. He then backed Montreal to a six-game victory over the Minnesota North Stars, to face the heavily favored Chicago Black Hawks in the Stanley Cup Final. Montreal once again prevailed in a seven-game series, and Dryden was presented with the Conn Smythe Trophy as the league's most valuable playoff performer.

Dryden dispelled any notion of a sophomore jinx when he won the 1972 Calder Trophy as top rookie

Ken Dryden's unique resting pose added to his mystique during his rookie season.

and made the Second All-Star Team, leading the league with 64 appearances and 39 wins. He played in the famous 1972 Summit Series for Canada against the Soviets the following September, and then earned his first Vezina Trophy (with a 2.26 goals-against average) and a First All-Star Team berth while backstopping Montreal to another Cup victory over Chicago. Understanding his role on the team, Dryden grew disenchanted with his contract. When the Canadiens refused to renegotiate it, Dryden joined a law firm as an articling student and sat out the 1973–74 season, during which the Habs faltered. Dryden got the new contract he wanted, with his salary quadrupled in accordance with the going rate for the league's top talent.

From the 1975–76 season, up until the end of his career in 1979, Dryden performed impeccably. He never posted worse than a goals-against mark of 2.30 per game and his team won the Stanley Cup four times in a row, giving him six rings in eight seasons. Dryden was awarded the Vezina Trophy and was on the First All-Star Team four more times. He blanked the opposition 46 times over his career, peaking with 10 shutouts in 1976–77, compiling a stellar 2.14 goals-against average during the regular season and lowering it to 1.56 in the playoffs. His powerhouse club had no real weakness, but Dryden was inarguably a key to Montreal's success.

Dryden always had back problems, but they flared up more dramatically in 1979. So, too, did the awareness that he had little new to accomplish in the game. Although physically sound enough to continue to play, Dryden quit the game to pursue other interests. He launched what proved to be a successful writing and broadcasting career, penning *The Game* (one of hockey's most insightful books) and several other bestsellers on various topics. In 1997, he was lured back into NHL hockey as an executive with the Toronto Maple Leafs, and in 2004 he entered the political arena, where he has served as a Toronto Member of Parliament and a Liberal cabinet minister.

BILLY SMITH

1972–1989

Battlin' Billy

BILLY SMITH'S COMPETITIVE STREAK WAS A MILE WIDE. HE WAS KNOWN TO FORSAKE THE RITUAL OF SHAKING HANDS with the opposition after a playoff defeat and he regularly lambasted the referee and even his own teammates at times. But Smith picked up his nickname "Battlin' Billy" for more than verbal assaults. He frequently demonstrated his willingness to wield his stick like a scythe to rid his crease of encroaching forwards, and once received a six-game suspension for breaking an opponent's jaw and cheekbone.

"I just try to give myself a little working room," he once explained. "But if a guy bothers me, then I retaliate." As a rookie, Smith set a record for penalty minutes in a season (42) by a goalie, and once broke three of his sticks on the ankles of Buffalo players in one period. He also fought some of the league's toughest forwards and, by the time he retired, he had accumulated 489 penalty minutes in the regular season and 78 in the playoffs.

The Islanders experienced several difficult years but, primarily through judicious drafting, eventually assembled a team for the ages. Smith, who got his first NHL starts for Los Angeles — playing five games for the Kings in 1971–72 — was drafted to Long Island for the 1972–73 season when the NHL expanded to 16 teams. He started sharing duties with Glenn "Chico" Resch in 1974–75, when they back-stopped the Isles into the playoffs for the first time. The partnership lasted for seven seasons, and Smith was content to watch half the games from the bench. "You can't do your job and keep an eye on the other guy," noted Smith, "so the most help you can give another goalie is to get along as partners." Resch, gregarious and colorful, seemed to outsiders more the leader than the terse, gruff Smith, but when the playoffs rolled around, New York coach Al Arbour increasingly leaned on Smith.

Smith played in only one All-Star Game, in 1978, and was voted Most Valuable Player, an unusual feat in what is usually a high-scoring goal-fest. In later years, Smith identified this time period, in his late twenties, as when he hit his peak. "I was comfortable and had my game under control," he said. "When I was younger, I was feistier and tried to do too much. A lot of times when I was poking guys or trying to push them out of my crease, I'd be scored on. I couldn't take control of my opponent and stop the puck at the same time."

Smith made history on November 28, 1979, when he became the first NHL netminder to be credited with a goal. The Colorado Rockies pulled their goalie during a delayed penalty call, and when a pass between two Rockies went astray and inadvertently landed in the Colorado net, Smith's name was put on the score sheet as the last Islander to touch the puck — he had taken a shot off his chest.

The 1979–80 season became even more memorable when the Islanders won their first of four consecutive Stanley Cups. "Just to get out of our own division was always a battle," recalled Smith. "Many

series went to seven games. The first and the fourth Stanley Cups were probably the most satisfying. The first was special because we didn't know yet if we were capable of winning." The Islanders beat the Philadelphia Flyers in the final, although the Flyers had finished the regular season 25 points ahead of them in the standings.

"I think we lost a couple of Stanley Cups before we won the first one because we just didn't know what it took," said Smith. "We caught a couple of teams sleeping right at the beginning and then in the end against Philly, we scored in overtime in the sixth game. I'll predict today that if we had lost that game on Long Island, we would have had our hands more than full in Philadelphia. We would have been pretty shaken. But we had a good team, we had a good system, and we stuck with it even in overtime, and we got a break at the right time."

Smith and the Isles finished atop the league in 1980–81 and successfully defended the Cup, but the team was at its most powerful in the 1981–82 season. Led by forwards Mike Bossy and Bryan Trottier and defenseman Denis Potvin, and backed by Smith (Resch was traded in March 1981), the team finished high atop the league with 118 points. Bossy and Trottier were among the top five scorers, and Smith was named to the First All-Star Team and won the Vezina Trophy, awarded for the first time to the league's best goalie as determined by the NHL's general managers. They swept the Vancouver Canucks in the Stanley Cup Final, and Smith had his third ring.

In 1982–83, Smith shared the Jennings Trophy with his new partner Roland Melanson for the league's lowest goals-against average. For Smith, the Islanders' fourth consecutive Cup win was all the sweeter for the "hype" over the high-flying Wayne Gretzky and the Edmonton Oilers, their opponent in the Stanley Cup Final. "The Islanders were three-time champions but got little respect," said Smith, who managed to stop Gretzky from scoring in four straight games, and allowed only six goals in total in the final. "We won the first game against Edmonton 2–0, probably the finest game I ever played. Even though the series ended in four games, it was far from a sweep. Every game was do-or-die, and it was great hockey. To top things off for me personally, I also won the Conn Smythe award."

In 1983–84, the Islanders finished tied for first in their conference, and Smith had the satisfaction of becoming the league's all-time playoff-win leader with 81 victories, passing Ken Dryden on April 28, 1984 (Patrick Roy is the current holder of the record with 151 wins). The Islanders' dynastic reign came to an end three weeks later, however, when the Oilers beat them in the final.

Billy Smith retired after the 1988–89 season, the last of the original Islanders. He turned to coaching goalies, first for the Islanders and later for the Florida Panthers. Smith's No. 31 was retired on Long Island in 1993, the same year he entered the Hall of Fame.

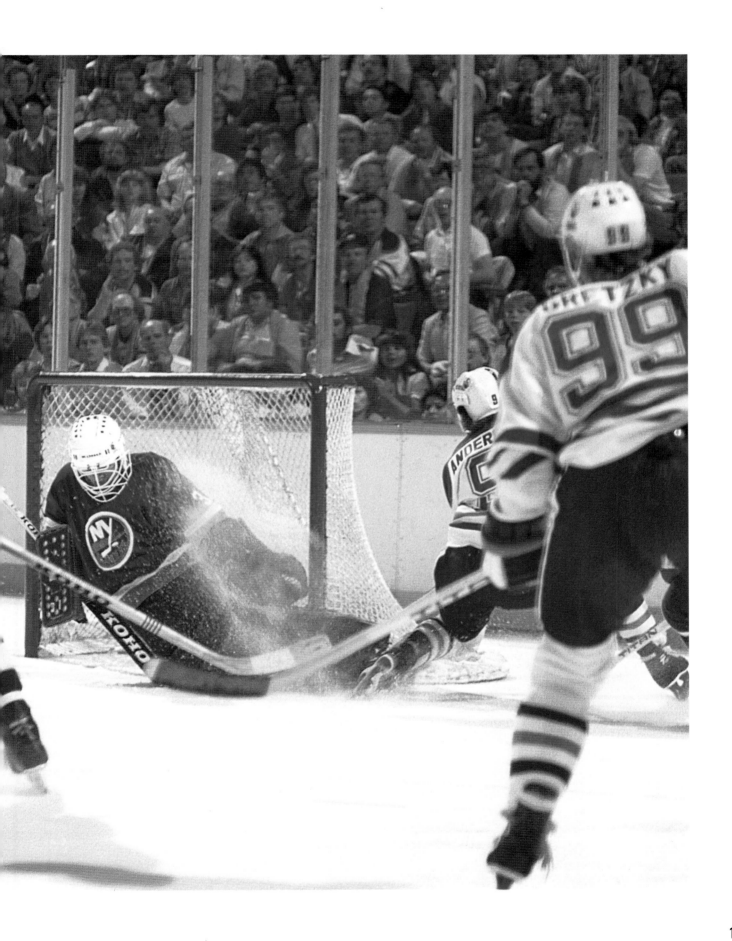

GRANT FUHR

1982–2000

Fuhr-ious Goaltending

GRANT FUHR HAD THE RARE EXPERIENCE OF HITTING HOCK-EY'S HIGHEST HEIGHTS AS A HOMETOWN HERO. BORN IN Spruce Grove, Alberta, located just outside the city of Edmonton, he had the good fortune to be coached as a peewee by the legendary Glenn Hall, whose farm was only five miles away. Fuhr picked up Hall's butterfly style, which helped him get drafted in the first round by the Edmonton Oilers in the 1981 NHL entry draft after an auspicious two years of junior hockey with the Victoria Cougars.

Still a teenager, Fuhr played 48 games for the 1981–82 Oilers, posting a 28-5-14 record, finishing second to Billy Smith for the Vezina Trophy, and making the Second All-Star Team. Midseason, he became the youngest goalie to play in the NHL All-Star Game. Before the decade was out, he had earned five Stanley Cup rings with a star-laden but predominantly offensive-minded Edmonton club.

"We all knew he was great from the first day of camp," recalled Ron Low, a former Oiler goalie and coach. "A natural. Yet he had no style. Or, rather, his style was all styles. He would come out 15 feet to challenge the shot on one offensive rush. The next time he would be back in his crease. He could read the game so well. He anticipated the game. Grant was just … different. Different from anyone I'd ever seen."

"I rate him right up there among [the best] goalies of any era," said Glenn Hall, years after Fuhr had starred in the NHL. "He gave [Edmonton] the opportunity to play that run-and-gun style. Without a goalie like Fuhr, none of it works." Fuhr shared regular season duties with goaltender Andy Moog, but in 1983–84, he became the Oilers' go-to goalie in the playoffs. He tallied a record for netminders with 14 points in the regular season (all assists), then backstopped the Oilers to their first Cup win. The Oilers defended their crown the following season, were upset in the 1986 playoffs, but then won two more consecutive Stanley Cups (1987, 1988).

The 1987–88 campaign was undoubtedly Fuhr's personal best. He was a workhorse, guiding Canada to victory in the preseason Canada Cup tournament, most notably against the last great team from the Soviet Union in a closely fought three-game final, then setting an NHL regular-season record by starting 75 games. Fuhr made the First All-Star Team, earned the Vezina Trophy as top goaltender and finished runner-up to Mario Lemieux for the Hart Trophy as the league's Most Valuable Player.

Things began to unravel in Edmonton when team owner Peter Pocklington sold Wayne Gretzky to the Los Angeles Kings in the summer of 1988, the start of a fire sale. "Grant never gets excited," Gretzky had said in 1985. "He never gets mad. He never gets happy. His attitude to anything is just, 'Oh well.' He's like a relief pitcher. Nothing gets him down. Nothing

gets him up. He's a hard guy to describe." But Fuhr was not himself by 1989, his play slipping due to what he later admitted was a longstanding drug problem. He was relegated to being a backup for Bill Ranford when the Oilers won a fifth Cup in 1990 and was suspended for 60 games in 1990–91 when his drug use became public. He successfully underwent treatment but was traded to Toronto in September 1991.

Fuhr seemed back on track with the Maple Leafs, and he was the league's highest paid netminder with a salary of $1.6 million, but he mentored young goalie Felix Potvin so successfully that, midway through the 1992–93 season, Toronto traded Fuhr to Buffalo. Again, an up-and-coming NHL star — Dominik Hasek — usurped his starting role. The two shared the 1994 Jennings Trophy for the lowest team goals-against average, but the Sabres traded Fuhr to Los Angeles early in the 1994–95 campaign.

Fuhr's goals-against average was never his strong suit. "The only statistic that matters is winning," he said. Yet when his average ballooned to over four goals a game, and the wins were no longer coming, it appeared he was just playing out the string. Fuhr signed with the St. Louis Blues as a free agent in July 1995, but when he was sent home from training camp after arriving almost 25 pounds over-weight, many thought his career was over. Fuhr, however, had more great hockey in him. He quickly took off much of the excess weight, returned to St. Louis, and went on to set a new NHL record with 79 starts — 76 in succession — in 1995–96. Unfortunately, a knee injury suffered in the playoffs against Toronto ended his season, and he was never quite the same again.

During his four-year stop in St. Louis (1995–96 to 1998–99) Fuhr's goals-against average had consistently stayed below 3.00 for the first time in his career, but he still looked back fondly on his days with the firewagon Oilers. "The style of hockey we played was a lot of fun," he said. "A 7–4 or 7–3 game is a lot of fun to play in and it's exciting for the fans. When I got to St. Louis, the game had changed and I was putting up much better stats, but we weren't as successful a team as we should have been. I would much rather have the team success."

At 37, age and injuries started to take their toll. "You hear a lot of talk about the goalie who flops or goes down too much," Fuhr once said. "The problem is not going down; it's returning to your feet too slowly." Fuhr returned to Alberta in a trade, but this time joined the Calgary Flames for his last NHL season. In 1999–2000, he notched his 400th career victory, becoming only the sixth NHL goalie to hit that milestone. His final game was against

the Oilers, in Edmonton, and although he lost the game, the Edmonton fans chanted his name throughout the game and gave him a number of standing ovations.

In 2003, in his first year of eligibility, Fuhr was inducted to the Hockey Hall of Fame. "Being a black athlete going into the Hall of Fame is obviously a special honor," he told the *Philadelphia Enquirer*, "especially in hockey, being the first one — but the reason you get into the Hall of Fame is for what you have accomplished on the ice, and I probably take the most pride in that." That same year Oiler fans got to cheer for their acrobatic netminder one last time as his No. 31 was raised to the rafters.

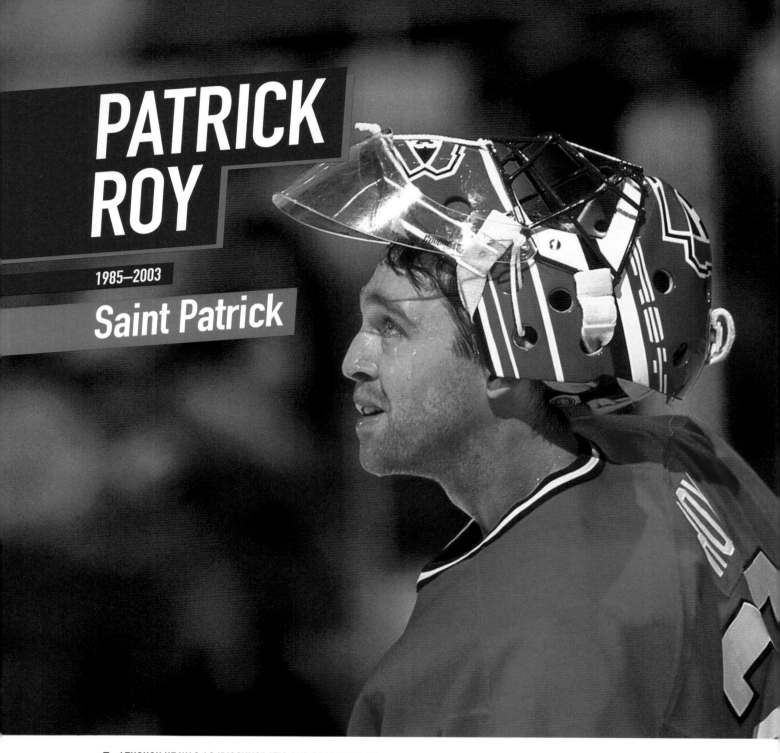

PATRICK ROY

1985–2003

Saint Patrick

ALTHOUGH HE WAS AS IDIOSYNCRATIC AND ECCENTRIC AS ANY MAN WHO HAS DONNED THE PADS IN THE NATIONAL Hockey League, Patrick Roy developed a style that gave rise to a new breed of goaltender emerging from the province of Quebec — and copied around the world.

Refining the butterfly style and blending it with standup-style elements proved wonderfully effective and Roy hung up his skates as the NHL's goaltending record holder in a multitude of categories, including

games (1,029), wins (551) and playoff wins (151). "I was extremely comfortable when I retired," said Roy. "I emptied the tank." Although Martin Brodeur bettered some of Roy's achievements, "St. Patrick" made an indelible mark on goaltending history.

Roy played his junior hockey for the Granby Bisons in Quebec, and was drafted 51st overall by the Montreal Canadiens in the 1984 NHL entry draft. Ironically, Roy had grown up hating the Habs, as he was a fan of Montreal's provincial rival, the

Quebec Nordiques. Roy was called up to Montreal to serve as backup for one game midway through his last junior season (1984–85), and notched his first NHL win when he entered a tied game in the third period and held the fort for the remaining time as Montreal took the lead. He returned to his junior team, but when Granby missed the playoffs, he got called up to Montreal's AHL club. Roy starred in helping the Sherbrooke Canadiens win the 1985 Calder Cup. Playoff successes would prove to be the highlights of his career.

With only 20 minutes of NHL experience, Roy was the unlikely, but successful, candidate to win a full-time NHL job when he attended his first professional training camp. Goaltending coach François Allaire found Roy to be the perfect pupil. He cured Roy's tendency to dive for the puck (head coach Jacques Lemaire told him he "needed a mattress and a pillow" for all the time he spent lying on the ice, recalled Roy), and soon had the young puckstopper moving side-to-side on his knees by pushing off on his toes, adding a two-pad slide and working on reducing rebounds and using his blocker more effectively. With Roy still rather ungainly in net, yet stopping most of the pucks, Montreal made an improbable run to Stanley Cup victory in 1985–86. Roy, only 20 years old, was awarded the Conn Smythe Trophy.

Although the Canadiens struggled at times over the next six seasons, Roy was firmly entrenched as one of the league's elite goalies. With Brian Hayward as his partner, Roy shared the Jennings Trophy (for lowest goals-against) for the next three seasons, and won it solo for his work in 1991–92. He was named to the NHL First All-Star Team in 1989, 1990 and 1992, and the Second Team in 1988 and 1991, and won the Vezina Trophy as the league's top netminder in 1989, 1990 and 1992.

Roy superstitiously never skated on the blue lines, hopping over them carefully, and his frequent craning of his neck and "talking to his goal posts" looked to some like nervous habits. He was, in truth, meticulous in preparing himself mentally for the challenge at hand. "I really like to look back on goals I gave up against that team in past games," he explained in 1996. "In reviewing the goal, I try

Roy celebrates his second Stanely Cup championship in 1993.

to understand what I could have done to stop the puck. If there is a question about my positioning or how I reacted, I imagine the situation changed and I'm making the save. In my visualizations, I'm focusing mostly on myself and what I'm going to do, but sometimes, I focus on specific players on the other team. Players like Mario Lemieux and Wayne Gretzky usually have an impact on the game, so I'll see myself facing them and making some saves. Just before the game, I like to look at the net and imagine the goal posts shrinking, the net grown smaller."

By 1993, only Roy and captain Guy Carbonneau remained from Montreal's 1986 Cup-winning team. The Canadiens finished fourth in their conference over the regular season, but Roy became almost unbeatable in the playoffs. He lost only four times against 16 wins, including 10 consecutive overtime victories. Roy was in such a "zone" in the Stanley Cup Final against Wayne Gretzky's Los Angeles Kings, he even gave a cocky wink to L.A.'s Tomas Sandstrom after continually thwarting the Finnish sniper. "I knew he wasn't going to beat me," said Roy, and the moment, caught by a TV camera, became a defining one for Roy. He won his second Conn Smythe Trophy when the Habs defeated the Kings in five games.

Roy's career took a shocking turn on December 2, 1995. At home facing the Detroit Red Wings, Montreal played its worst home game in franchise history, losing 12–1. The crowd jeered Roy, who was kept in by coach Mario Tremblay for nine of the goals. When he was pulled midway through the second period, Roy stormed over to team president Ronald Corey and publicly announced he had played his final game for the club. General Manager Réjean Houle was forced to trade Roy and dealt him to the Colorado Avalanche (the newly transplanted Quebec Nordiques).

A new Roy era began immediately. "I felt that with the offense that was on that team that we had a good chance to win the Stanley Cup," said Roy. "I knew the talent that was on that team and I was excited about the challenge. It was a perfect situation for me." The Avalanche were a team on the rise, and with Roy backstopping the high-powered offense,

they swept the Florida Panthers in the 1996 Stanley Cup Final.

Roy won the 2000–01 Jennings Trophy on his way to another Stanley Cup ring and a third Conn Smythe Trophy. He was named to the 2002 First All-Star Team, but left the game on his own terms while still in top form after the 2002–03 season. The Avalanche retired his No. 33 the following season, and he entered the Hall of Fame in 2006, the first year he was eligible.

Proving "time heals all wounds," the Montreal Canadiens retired his number in 2008. "Looking back, I know I had great years with the Canadiens," said Roy. "I think we brought joy to Habs' fans and even probably surprised them somewhat with the two Cups we won. That's what I want people in Montreal to remember."

ED BELFOUR

1989–2007

The Eagle

I N THE SUMMER OF 1997, ED BELFOUR WAS A FREE AGENT FOR THE SECOND TIME IN HIS CAREER. THE FIRST TIME WAS 10 years prior, when the Chicago Blackhawks took a chance on a 22-year-old goalie just looking for an opportunity to prove he could play in the NHL. In 1997, the Dallas Stars signed Belfour to a big-money contract believing he was the final piece to a championship puzzle. Not bad for a guy who was never drafted and didn't establish himself as a No. 1 goalie in the NHL until he was 25 years old.

Both the Hawks and Stars were rewarded for their faith in "Eddie the Eagle," though in different ways. The hot-tempered puckstopper soared in Chicago, racking up individual honors for a franchise that hadn't had a bona fide All-Star goalie since Tony Esposito in the 1970s. Belfour made Chicago a legitimate contender, but, for as good as he was, the Blackhawks never quite got over the hump. It was in Dallas, however, that Belfour finally became the man to push a talented squad all the way up the mountain.

Belfour grew up about an hour's drive from Winnipeg in Carman, Manitoba. He played Junior A hockey in his native province for the Winkler Flyers before joining the University of North Dakota Fighting Sioux for the 1986–87 NCAA campaign. After signing with the Hawks in the fall of 1987, Belfour spent another year honing his craft in the International Hockey League before finally getting his NHL shot in 1988–89.

Yet things didn't work out exactly as Belfour had envisioned, as he scuffled to a 4-12-3 mark on a struggling team. He then spent the next season with the Canadian national program and arrived at the Blackhawks training camp for the 1990–91 campaign ready to stand his ground. It was to be a superb year for Belfour, during which he led all goalies with 74 games played, 43 wins, a 2.47 goals-against average and .910 save percentage. Chicago also topped the NHL with 106 points thanks largely to Belfour, who won both the Calder Trophy as rookie of the year and the Vezina Trophy as the NHL's best puckstopper.

Despite their stellar season, Belfour and the Hawks were shocked in the first round of the playoffs, losing in six games to a Minnesota North Stars team that finished with 38 fewer points than Chicago. But that upset made what happened the next year all the

sweeter, as the Blackhawks tore through the 1992 playoffs, dropping just two games in three series wins en route to a Stanley Cup Final appearance. It seemed like Chicago was going to completely atone for its flop a year earlier, but Mario Lemieux and the powerhouse Pittsburgh Penguins had other ideas, sweeping the Hawks in four straight games to claim their second of back-to-back titles.

After losing to the Pens, Chicago fired head coach Mike Keenan. Belfour may have flourished while Keenan was behind the bench, but the relationship between the two men was rocky at times, with Keenan being notoriously quick to yank his goalies from the crease. For Belfour, a player who fell somewhere between spirited and crazy, getting the hook wasn't always easy to take. With more assuredness under new coach Darryl Sutter in 1992–93, life was good for Belfour, and he once again won the Vezina

Trophy. But, just as they had done two years prior, the Hawks squandered a first-overall finish by being upset in the first round of the playoffs.

Belfour's strong regular season play largely continued over the next few years, but the Blackhawks started to lose their status as a league power. By the 1996–97 season, Chicago was going nowhere and it was clear Belfour didn't intend to sign a long-term deal with the club. He was traded to San Jose in January of 1997, before becoming an unrestricted free agent that summer. Though he had a sparkling résumé, Belfour never really seemed to get the same amount of credit around the league as some of his goaltending brethren. When it came to debates about the best-masked men in the game, names like Patrick Roy, Martin Brodeur and Dominik Hasek would often come up before Belfour's. Whether it was because he hadn't won a Cup, or because his

Belfour was known for playing outside the crease.

sometimes prickly personality rubbed people the wrong way, Belfour didn't quite get his proper due.

If he was motivated to prove the naysayers wrong, Belfour found the perfect match when he signed on to join the Dallas Stars. Like the Blackhawks teams from the early 1990s, Dallas had become a club that perennially shone in the regular season, but couldn't finish the job in the playoffs. All that was about to change.

In his first season, playing alongside stars like Mike Modano and Derian Hatcher, Belfour helped lead Dallas to the Western Conference final, where the Stars succumbed to a Detroit Red Wings team that was on its way to winning a second consecutive Stanley Cup. The following year, Dallas was back in the NHL's final four, but this time the Stars refused to go down, knocking off the Colorado Avalanche in a thrilling seven-game series. That win set up an all-time great goalie match up in the final, as Belfour squared off against Hasek and the Sabres.

After dropping game one 3–2 in overtime, Belfour and the Stars defense got seriously stingy, never allowing more than 2 goals in any of the remaining five games. Dallas famously — or infamously, depending on your perspective — won the championship in overtime of Game 6, when Brett Hull scored with Hasek down and out and Hull's foot just inside the blue ice of the crease. At the time, if any part of a player was in the crease when the puck crossed the goal line, the

goal was disallowed. But Dallas, which was clearly the superior team, got away with one, and both Belfour and the Stars finally had their Cup.

Dallas went all the way back to the final the following year, making it three consecutive campaigns of deep playoff hockey. This time, however, they lost in six games to the New Jersey Devils and Martin Brodeur. Despite the setback, Belfour had definitely established himself as a money goalie. His playoff record in Dallas' back-to-back trips to the Stanley Cup Final was 30-16, and his save percentage was .930 or above each spring.

Terrific as his time with the Stars was, age and aches were beginning to catch up with Belfour and, at 37 years old, he signed with the Toronto Maple Leafs. The cagey netminder showed he still had some gas left in the tank in 2003–04 as he posted a .929 save percentage and 2.09 goals-against average before the Leafs bowed out in round two of that season's playoffs. After one more year in Toronto and a swan song with the Florida Panthers, Belfour's NHL career ended in 2007. His body of work is staggering, most notably the 484 career wins that represent a higher total than any-body in hockey history other than Brodeur and Roy.

And today, if Belfour feels he's not getting the respect he deserves, he can simply direct his naysayers toward his plaque in the Hockey Hall of Fame.

DOMINIK HASEK

1991–2008

Czech-mate

CANADIAN HOCKEY FANS ARE FAIRLY UNITED IN THEIR STANCE THAT SHOOTOUTS ARE AN AWFUL WAY TO DECIDE HIGH- stakes international games. And if there's one scar on the collective Canadian psyche that solidified that opinion, it was etched by Dominik Hasek's joint-twisting brilliance at the 1998 Olympics in Japan.

With a berth in the gold medal game on the line, Canada sent five players to the center-ice dot, asking each to figure out a way to beat a goalie who was, quite possibly, playing his position better than anyone had ever played it — before or since. One by one, the first four Canadians made their best attempt, and four times they failed to score on Hasek. By the time the fifth shooter, Brendan Shanahan, touched the puck, he may as well have been puckhandling a basketball. "We had the best goalie," Czech star Jaromir Jagr beamed after his team's 2–1 win.

Hasek's performance at the 1998 Games highlighted a stretch in which his nickname, "the Dominator," stood up as one of the most appropriate monikers in sports. After disposing of the Canadians, Hasek blanked Team Russia in the final, as the Czechs took gold with a 1–0 victory. That same season, Hasek won the Hart Trophy as the NHL's Most Valuable Player for the second straight time. The season prior, he'd become the first goalie to win the league's signature trophy since Jacques Plante in 1962. All these achievements came after a seemingly

minor trade between the Chicago Blackhawks and Buffalo Sabres launched the career of a man whose unorthodox and stunningly effective moves were always set to a different beat.

Hasek's status in his homeland was essentially elevated to that of a deity upon delivering Olympic gold in 1998, but he was already a mega-star in the Czech Republic long before he joined the NHL. The Blackhawks drafted Hasek 207th overall in 1983. But given that he was in Czechoslovakia, which was still buried behind the Iron Curtain, the odds Hasek — who didn't learn about his being drafted until months after the fact — was going to land in North America any time soon weren't good. Instead, he starred for his national team at the World Championships, the Olympics and the Canada Cup.

It wasn't until the 1990–91 NHL season, when he was already 26 years old, that Hasek saw his first action with the Hawks. Regardless of how well he played, though, it was going to be tough for Hasek trying to supplant Chicago star Ed Belfour, who was racking up individual accolades and leading the Blackhawks to a Cup Final appearance. So, in a move that barely registered on the NHL radar, the Buffalo Sabres scooped up Hasek from the Hawks for goalie Stephane Beauregard and a fourth-round draft pick in the summer of 1992.

The trade didn't pay immediate dividends for

Buffalo, but by Hasek's second season in Western New York, he was starting to sizzle. He paced all goalies with a .930 save percentage, 1.95 goals-against average and seven shutouts in 1993–94. Not surprisingly, he claimed the Vezina Trophy as the league's top goalie. But good as Hasek was, there were no shortage of detractors ready to tear apart his game. Goaltending was becoming an increasingly refined art at that time, with reflex-reliant stoppers viewed as less dependable than those who had a defined technique. Hasek had no discernible style and often did unconventional things like dropping his stick so he could pluck the puck with his blocking hand. Pundits who couldn't categorize his approach defaulted to calling it luck.

"They say I am unorthodox, I flop around like some kind of fish," Hasek once said. "I say, 'Who cares as long as I stop the puck?'"

Those who wished to call Hasek's breakout season an anomaly soon had no choice but to acknowledge

his jaw-dropping ability. From 1994 through 2001, Hasek won six of the eight Vezina Trophies handed out by the league. More tellingly, his 1997 Hart Trophy spelled out, in no uncertain terms, what his heroics meant to the Sabres. The team finished first in its division despite a very modest talent level, evidenced by the fact that Derek Plante led Buffalo with just 53 points. When Hasek got hurt in the first round of the playoffs, the Sabres were on borrowed time and got bounced in the second round. The following year, when Hasek claimed his second MVP nod, Buffalo made it to the Eastern Conference final despite having an offense that ranked 17th in the league. Hasek nearly led Buffalo all the way to a championship in the spring of 1999, posting a .939 save percentage in 19 postseason games as the Sabres fell in the Cup Final to the Dallas Stars thanks to Brett Hull's notorious foot-in-the-crease overtime winner in Game 6.

Though Hasek keyed the Sabres to some playoff

success, Buffalo management wasn't in a position to support his stellar play by shelling out top dollar to bring in big offensive stars. Never one to bite his tongue, the aging keeper requested a trade that resulted in him joining the Detroit Red Wings in the summer of 2001.

In terms of talent, the perennially dominant Wings were at the other end of the spectrum from the Sabres, icing what amounted to an all-star team after adding Hasek, Brett Hull and former Los Angeles Kings sniper Luc Robitaille to a club that already boasted Steve Yzerman, Sergei Fedorov and Nicklas Lidstrom. At 37, Hasek no longer had to be the sole savior for his team, though he was still an integral part of the equation. Detroit cruised to a league-best 51 wins in the regular season, but quickly found itself in an 0-2 hole in its first-round, best-of-seven series versus the Vancouver Canucks. Hasek certainly had his struggles in the initial contests, coughing up eight goals on a combined 45 shots. However, he tightened up his play, allowing just three goals over the next three games as Detroit stormed back to win the series. Stirring as that comeback was, it paled in comparison to what happened in the Western Conference final. Facing the Colorado Avalanche, Detroit's hated rival, the Wings fell behind 3-2 in the series. But Hasek rose to the challenge and blanked Colorado in both Game 6 and Game 7 to win the series and move onto the final, during which Detroit brushed aside an overmatched Carolina Hurricanes team in five games.

Though Hasek announced his retirement after the Wings' triumph, he couldn't stay away from the game and was back in the NHL for the 2003–04 campaign. Injuries dramatically hampered the final act of his career; even the man many people considered the goaltending equivalent of Gumby had his limits.

Hasek's résumé doesn't stack up to some of the other great goalies of his generation in terms of career wins and Cups victories. But whenever a hockey debate turns to the matter of the best goaltending stretch of all-time, Hasek's almost 10-year run from 1994 to 2002 is as good as anything the game has ever seen.

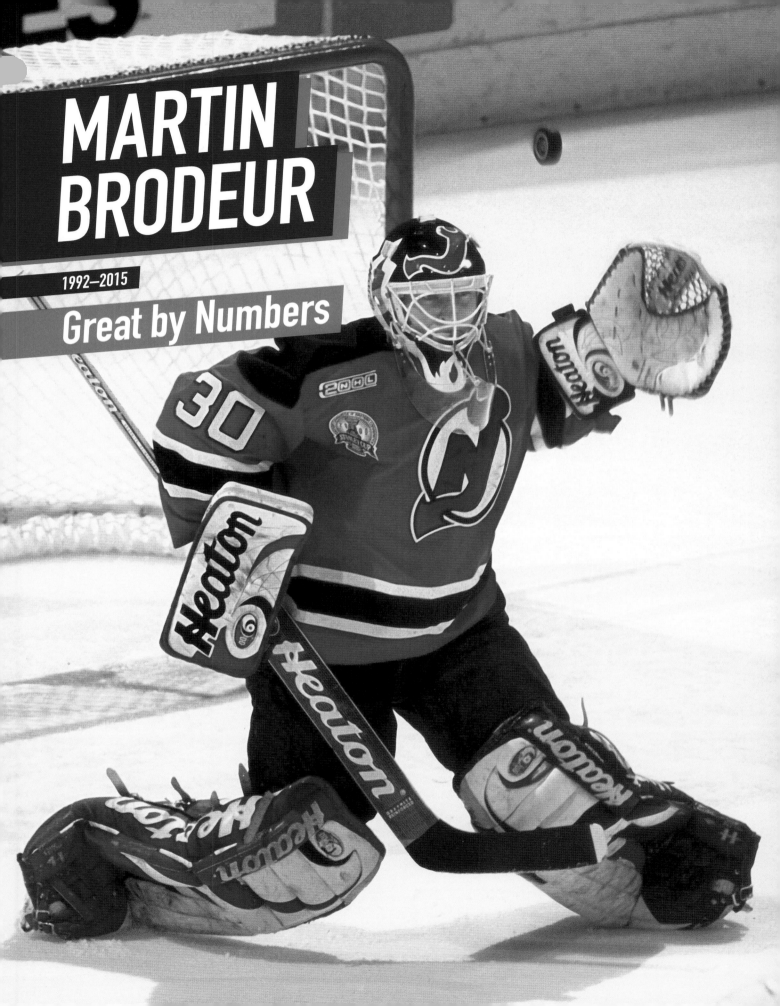

MARTIN BRODEUR

1992–2015

Great by Numbers

THE NUMBERS SPEAK FOR THEMSELVES. MARTIN BRODEUR PLAYED 22 SEASONS IN THE NHL BETWEEN 1991 AND 2015: more than any goalie in league history. His 1,266 games played are also the most for any goalie in the NHL. His 691 wins are not just the most ever, but are 140 wins more than anyone else. He is also the career leader with 125 shutouts. His 48 wins in 2006–07 broke Bernie Parent's 23-year-old record of 47 wins (although Brodeur did have the advantage of overtime and shootouts) and is one of a record eight seasons of 40-or-more wins. No one else has done it more than three times. His 14 seasons with

30-or-more wins is a record, too. Still, in playing 21 of his 22 years with the New Jersey Devils — a team that emphasized defense above all others — Brodeur didn't earn the recognition he deserved until his numbers became too big to overlook.

No one ignored Brodeur completely. After making a brief four-game appearance with the Devils in 1991–92, he won the Calder Trophy as rookie of the year in his first full NHL season in 1993–94. Firmly established as New Jersey's No. 1 goaltender the following year, he helped the Devils win the Stanley Cup for the first of three times over a nine-season span. In 1995–96, Brodeur played in 77 of 82 games (second in the NHL behind Grant Fuhr's record 79 that year). It was the first of a record 12 times that he'd play in 70 games or more, including a streak of 10 years in a row. In 1996–97, Brodeur won the Jennings Trophy (a team accomplishment for the fewest goals against) for the first of five times. And yet the individual acclaim was slow to come. Someone else — often Patrick Roy or Dominik Hasek — was, as his biography on NHL.com states, "more charismatic, more quotable, more colorful, more physical, more acrobatic or more technically exacting" than Brodeur was.

In the age of butterfly goalies, Brodeur was something of a throwback to the standup era, combining elements of the old and the new for his own, unique hybrid style. "I needed to be able to poke-check," he would write, "to stack the pads and be able to play the puck behind the net." Handling the puck was something else he did better than any other goalie of his time, scoring three goals in his career, including one in a playoff game. His skill with the puck is a big reason why the NHL introduced the trapezoid behind the goal line to limit where a goalie can play the puck. Over his first nine NHL seasons, Brodeur finished second in voting for the Vezina Trophy as the NHL's best goalie twice. He finished third once and fourth two other times. He finally won the award in 2002–03 when he received 24 of 30 first-place votes, and he would receive the Vezina three more times in the next four years. That's when the big numbers truly began to accumulate.

On March 17, 2009, the Devils defeated the Chicago Blackhawks 3–2 to give Brodeur his 552nd victory, breaking Patrick Roy's career mark of 551. On December 18, 2009, he made his 1,030th career appearance in net to move past Roy's previous record of 1,029. Three days and two games later, Brodeur set a new record that once seemed unbreakable. On December 21, 2009, he blanked the Pittsburgh Penguins 4–0 for his 104th shutout, surpassing Terry Sawchuk's record of 103 that had stood for 39 years. Following a serious injury that had limited him to just 31 games in 2008–09, Brodeur's record-breaking season of 2009–10 was a year of redemption and his last truly great season. He led the NHL in wins (45),

shutouts (9) and games played (77); earned his fifth and final Jennings Trophy; and led the Devils to a divisional championship.

After years of giving the Devils a so-called hometown discount on his contracts, Martin Brodeur became a free agent after the 2013–14 season. In November of 2014, he signed with the St. Louis Blues. Brodeur played just seven games with St. Louis before announcing his retirement on January 29, 2015. Not to be ignored, he finished his playing career in style with a 3–0 shutout.

PART 3

VERSUS

By Eric Zweig

IF YOU'RE A HOCKEY FAN OLD ENOUGH TO REMEMBER IT, THE TERM "SHOWDOWN" BRINGS TO MIND JUST ONE THING: a classic battle of one-on-one hockey skills!

Showdown was a between-periods feature on televised hockey broadcasts from 1973–74 through 1979–80, pitting some of the best players (but not all of them) against some of the top goalies in penalty shot competitions. Over the years, *Showdown* evolved to include an oldtimers segment and expanded to feature target shooting and agility races similar to what's been seen in the NHL All-Star Skills Competition since the 1990s. Then as now, these neatly packaged skills competitions may have been fun to watch, but they're not really hockey. (Opponents of the shootout to break ties after overtime are constantly reminding us of that.)

It's long been a part of hockey to hype the greatest one-on-one matchups, be it Gordie Howe vs. Maurice Richard, Wayne Gretzky vs. Mario Lemieux, Sidney Crosby vs. Alex Ovechkin or Connor McDavid vs. Auston Matthews. Still, those debates are usually more about analyzing the skills of one player versus another, and less about their head-to-head results. And while there's always excitement whenever a pitcher with a blazing fastball faces a top slugger (be it Sandy Koufax vs. Willie Mays, Nolan Ryan vs. Reggie Jackson or Gerrit Cole vs. Mike

Trout), you don't often hear much about Brett Hull vs. Patrick Roy or Jaromir Jagr vs. Martin Brodeur.

That's because hockey is truly a team game. One big star just isn't enough to win. *Showdown* may have proven that as well as anything ever did. The first winner in 1974 was Rangers goalie Gilles Villemure over Chicago's Jim Pappin. Decent stars, for sure, but not superstars and certainly not Hall of Famers. And over the seven seasons that it aired, the only two-time *Showdown* winner was Danny Grant, who had a few good seasons and even scored 50 goals in 1974–75, but probably isn't on anyone's list of all-time greats.

That being said, the purpose of this section in this book is to make head-to-head comparisons between the NHL's greatest goal-scorers of all time (defined for these purposes as Hockey Hall of Famers with 500 NHL goals or more) and the NHL goaltenders who've joined them in the hockey shrine.

No one is claiming that this exercise will actually determine who's the best player or the best goalie in NHL history … but some fun and interesting things do emerge. For instance, when Phil Esposito scored 76 goals for the Boston Bruins in 1970–71, he scored 15 times against fellow future Hall of Famers. When Teemu Selanne scored 76 for the Winnipeg Jets in 1992–93, he scored none. He did it again in 1997–98, when he led the NHL with 52 goals.

SPORT REVUE
Le magazine sportif des Canadiens-Français

Novembre 1957   25 cents
Comment Ivan
a dérobé un
plan au Détroit

Jarome Iginla did the same thing when he won the scoring title in 2003–04. Selanne and Iginla are the only single-season goal-scoring leaders among the 500-goal Hall of Fame players not to score a single goal against a Hall of Fame goalie. Does that mean anything? Probably not, but it's a strange statistic.

One thing that becomes abundantly clear is that the star players of the so-called "Original Six" era scored a much higher percentage of their goals against Hall of Fame netminders than any player since then. Maurice Richard, Gordie Howe, Jean Beliveau and Bobby Hull scored between 25 percent and 82 percent of their goals against Hall of Fame goalies in their league-leading scoring seasons between 1942–43 and 1966–67. Most scoring stars since the 1980s have rarely scored at a rate as high as 10 percent.

Where the old guys better players? Probably not … but in an era where six NHL teams mainly carried just one goaltender a piece, the star scorers of this era faced all-time greats such as Turk Broda, Terry Sawchuk, Jacques Plante, Glenn Hall and Johnny Bower far more times each year than the players in the years since then have had to face the best goalies of their era.

So, enjoy the numbers but be sure to keep it all in perspective. We're not out to prove anything; we're just having some fun.

Scorers Stats

■ Career NHL Games Played   ■ Total Career NHL Assists

■ Total Career NHL Goals   ■ Total Career NHL Points

■ Games Played VS HHOF Goalies   ■ Goals VS HHOF Goalies

MAURICE RICHARD (1943–1960)

NHL GP 978   NHL ASSISTS 422

NHL GOALS 544   NHL POINTS 966

GP VS HHOF Goalies 592   GOALS VS HHOF Goalies 308

GORDIE HOWE (1947–1980)

NHL GP 1767   NHL ASSISTS 1049

NHL GOALS 801   NHL POINTS 1850

GP VS HHOF Goalies 986   GOALS VS HHOF Goalies 424

JEAN BELIVEAU (1951–1971)

NHL GP 1125   NHL ASSISTS 712

NHL GOALS 507   NHL POINTS 1219

GP VS HHOF Goalies 342   GOALS VS HHOF Goalies 263

JOHNNY BUCYK (1956–1978)

NHL GP 1540   NHL ASSISTS 813

NHL GOALS 556   NHL POINTS 1369

GP VS HHOF Goalies 753   GOALS VS HHOF Goalies 228

FRANK MAHOVLICH (1957–1978)

NHL GP 1181   NHL ASSISTS 570

NHL GOALS 533   NHL POINTS 1103

GP VS HHOF Goalies 530   GOALS VS HHOF Goalies 216

Scorers Stats

BOBBY HULL (1958–1980)

NHL GP 1063   NHL ASSISTS 560

NHL GOALS 610   NHL POINTS 1170

GP VS HHOF Goalies 535   GOALS VS HHOF Goalies 271

STAN MIKITA (1959–1980)

NHL GP 1396   NHL ASSISTS 926

NHL GOALS 541   NHL POINTS 1467

GP VS HHOF Goalies 545   GOALS VS HHOF Goalies 166

PHIL ESPOSITO (1964–1981)

NHL GP 1282   NHL ASSISTS 873

NHL GOALS 717   NHL POINTS 1590

G VS HHOF Goalies P 386   GOALS VS HHOF Goalies 158

GILBERT PERREAULT (1971–1987)

NHL GP 1191   NHL ASSISTS 814

NHL GOALS 512   NHL POINTS 1326

GP VS HHOF Goalies 199   GOALS VS HHOF Goalies 68

MARCEL DIONNE (1972–1989)

NHL GP 1348   NHL ASSISTS 1040

NHL GOALS 731   NHL POINTS 1771

GP VS HHOF Goalies 193   GOALS VS HHOF Goalies 74

GUY LAFLEUR (1972–1991)

NHL GP 1126   NHL ASSISTS 793

NHL GOALS 560   NHL POINTS 1353

GP VS HHOF Goalies 172   GOALS VS HHOF Goalies 82

Scorers Stats

LANNY MCDONALD (1974–1989)

NHL GP 1111 — NHL ASSISTS 506

NHL GOALS 500 — NHL POINTS 1006

GP VS HHOF Goalies 178 — GOALS VS HHOF Goalies 83

BRYAN TROTTIER (1976–1994)

NHL GP 1279 — NHL ASSISTS 901

NHL GOALS 524 — NHL POINTS 1425

GP VS HHOF Goalies 128 — GOALS VS HHOF Goalies 42

MIKE BOSSY (1978–1987)

NHL GP 752 — NHL ASSISTS 553

NHL GOALS 573 — NHL POINTS 1126

GP VS HHOF Goalies 66 — GOALS VS HHOF Goalies 55

MIKE GARTNER (1979–1998)

NHL GP 1432 — NHL ASSISTS 627

NHL GOALS 708 — NHL POINTS 1335

GP VS HHOF Goalies 137 — GOALS VS HHOF Goalies 53

MICHEL GOULET (1979–1994)

NHL GP 1089 — NHL ASSISTS 605

NHL GOALS 548 — NHL POINTS 1153

GP VS HHOF Goalies 79 — GOALS VS HHOF Goalies 34

WAYNE GRETZKY (1979–1999)

NHL GP 1487 — NHL ASSISTS 1963

NHL GOALS 894 — NHL POINTS 2857

GP VS HHOF Goalies 120 — GOALS VS HHOF Goalies 40

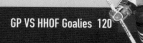

Scorers Stats

MARK MESSIER (1979–2004)

NHL GP 1756
NHL GOALS 694
NHL ASSISTS 1193
NHL POINTS 1887
GP VS HHOF Goalies 149
GOALS VS HHOF Goalies 31

JARI KURRI (1980–1998)

NHL GP 1251
NHL GOALS 601
NHL ASSISTS 797
NHL POINTS 1398
GP VS HHOF Goalies 83
GOALS VS HHOF Goalies 25

DINO CICCARELLI (1981–1999)

NHL GP 1232
NHL GOALS 608
NHL ASSISTS 592
NHL POINTS 1200
GP VS HHOF Goalies 116
GOALS VS HHOF Goalies 37

RON FRANCIS (1982–2004)

NHL GP 1731
NHL GOALS 549
NHL ASSISTS 1249
NHL POINTS 1798
GP VS HHOF Goalies 169
GOALS VS HHOF Goalies 35

DALE HAWERCHUK (1982–1997)

NHL GP 1188
NHL GOALS 518
NHL ASSISTS 891
NHL POINTS 1409
GP VS HHOF Goalies 118
GOALS VS HHOF Goalies 44

JOE MULLEN (1982–1997)

NHL GP 1062
NHL GOALS 502
NHL ASSISTS 561
NHL POINTS 1063
GP VS HHOF Goalies 99
GOALS VS HHOF Goalies 39

Scorers Stats

DAVE ANDREYCHUK (1983–2006)

NHL GP 1639 — NHL ASSISTS 698
NHL GOALS 640 — NHL POINTS 1338
GP VS HHOF Goalies 151 — GOALS VS HHOF Goalies 49

STEVE YZERMAN (1984–2006)

NHL GP 1514 — NHL ASSISTS 1063
NHL GOALS 692 — NHL POINTS 1755
GP VS HHOF Goalies 153 — GOALS VS HHOF Goalies 51

MARIO LEMIEUX (1985–2006)

NHL GP 915 — NHL ASSISTS 1033
NHL GOALS 690 — NHL POINTS 1723
GP VS HHOF Goalies 82 — GOALS VS HHOF Goalies 41

BRETT HULL (1987–2006)

NHL GP 1269 — NHL ASSISTS 650
NHL GOALS 741 — NHL POINTS 1391
GP VS HHOF Goalies 137 — GOALS VS HHOF Goalies 59

JOE NIEUWENDYK (1987–2007)

NHL GP 1257 — NHL ASSISTS 562
NHL GOALS 564 — NHL POINTS 1126
GP VS HHOF Goalies 107 — GOALS VS HHOF Goalies 38

LUC ROBITAILLE (1987–2006)

NHL GP 1431 — NHL ASSISTS 726
NHL GOALS 668 — NHL POINTS 1394
GP VS HHOF Goalies 145 — GOALS VS HHOF Goalies 51

BRENDAN SHANAHAN (1988–2009)

NHL GP 1524 — NHL ASSISTS 698
NHL GOALS 656 — NHL POINTS 1354
GP VS HHOF Goalies 172 — GOALS VS HHOF Goalies 62

Scorers Stats

MARK RECCHI (1989–2011)

NHL GP 1652   NHL ASSISTS 956

NHL GOALS 577   NHL POINTS 1533

GP VS HHOF Goalies 133   GOALS VS HHOF Goalies 26

JOE SAKIC (1989–2009)

NHL GP 1378   NHL ASSISTS 1016

NHL GOALS 625   NHL POINTS 1641

GP VS HHOF Goalies 119   GOALS VS HHOF Goalies 40

MIKE MODANO (1990–2011)

HL GP 1499   NHL ASSISTS 813

NHL GOALS 561   NHL POINTS 1374

GP VS HHOF Goalies 129   GOALS VS HHOF Goalies 44

MATS SUNDIN (1991–2009)

NHL GP 1346   NHL ASSISTS 785

NHL GOALS 564   NHL POINTS 1349

GP VS HHOF Goalies 135   GOALS VS HHOF Goalies 51

TEEMU SELANNE (1993–2014)

NHL GP 1451   NHL ASSISTS 773

NHL GOALS 684   NHL POINTS 1457

GP VS HHOF Goalies 127   GOALS VS HHOF Goalies 39

JAROME IGINLA (1996-2017)

NHL GP 1554   NHL ASSISTS 675

NHL GOALS 625   NHL POINTS 1300

GP VS HHOF Goalies 73   GOALS VS HHOF Goalies 22

MARIAN HOSSA (1997-2017)

NHL GP 1309   NHL ASSISTS 609

NHL GOALS 525   NHL POINTS 1134

GP VS HHOF Goalies 79   GOALS VS HHOF Goalies 25

Goalies Stats

- Career NHL Games Played
- Total Career NHL Goals Against
- Games Played VS HHOF 500 Scorers

- Career NHL Save Percentage*
- Total Career NHL Wins
- Goals VS by HHOF 500 Scorers

NHL began calculating save percentage in 1955–56

- SV% VS HHOF 500 Scorers*

TURK BRODA (1937–1952)

NHL GP 629

NHL GA 1608

GP VS HHOF 500 Scorers 110

NHL SV% NA

NHL WINS 304

GA by HHOF 500 Scorers 54

SV% VS HHOF 500 Scorers NA

FRANK BRIMSEK (1939–1950)

NHL GP 514

NHL GA 1403

GP VS HHOF 500 Scorers 103

NHL SV% NA

NHL WINS 252

GA by HHOF 500 Scorers 42

SV% VS HHOF 500 Scorers NA

CHUCK RAYNER (1941–1953)

NHL GP 425

NHL GA 1291

GP VS HHOF 500 Scorers 133

NHL SV% NA

NHL WINS 138

GA by HHOF 500 Scorers 63

SV% VS HHOF 500 Scorers NA

BILL DURNAN (1944–1950)

NHL GP 383

NHL GA 901

GP VS HHOF 500 Scorers 44

NHL SV% NA

NHL WINS 208

GA by HHOF 500 Scorers 15

SV% VS HHOF 500 Scorers NA

HARRY LUMLEY (1944–1960)

NHL GP 803

NHL GA 2196

GP VS HHOF 500 Scorers 336

NHL SV% .905*

NHL WINS 330

GA by HHOF 500 Scorers 184

SV% VS HHOF 500 Scorers .877*

Goalies Stats

TERRY SAWCHUK (1950–1970)

NHL GP 971
NHL SV% .907*
NHL GA 2385
NHL WINS 445
GA by HHOF 500 Scorers 144
GP VS HHOF 500 Scorers 666
SV% VS HHOF 500 Scorers .903*

GLENN HALL (1953–1971)

NHL GP 906
NHL SV% .918*
NHL GA 2223
NHL WINS 407
GA by HHOF 500 Scorers 144
GP VS HHOF 500 Scorers 594
SV% VS HHOF 500 Scorers .903*

JACQUES PLANTE (1953–1975)

NHL GP 837
NHL SV% .920*
NHL GA 1960
NHL WINS 437
GA by HHOF 500 Scorers 156
GP VS HHOF 500 Scorers 579
SV% VS HHOF 500 Scorers .896*

GUMP WORSLEY (1953–1974)

NHL GP 860
NHL SV% .914*
NHL GA 2398
NHL WINS 333
GA by HHOF 500 Scorers 204
GP VS HHOF 500 Scorers 756
SV% VS HHOF 500 Scorers .894*

JOHNNY BOWER (1954–1970)

NHL GP 552
NHL SV% .922*
NHL GA 1336
NHL WINS 250
GA by HHOF 500 Scorers 131
GP VS HHOF 500 Scorers 476
SV% VS HHOF 500 Scorers .915*

GERRY CHEEVERS (1962–1980)

NHL GP 418
NHL SV% .901
NHL GA 1174
NHL WINS 227
GA by HHOF 500 Scorers 92
GP VS HHOF 500 Scorers 223
SV% VS HHOF 500 Scorers .877

Goalies Stats

EDDIE GIACOMIN (1966–1977)

NHL GP 610
NHL SV% .902
NHL GA 1672
NHL WINS 290
GA by HHOF 500 Scorers 184
GP VS HHOF 500 Scorers 442
SV% VS HHOF 500 Scorers .878

BERNIE PARENT (1966–1979)

NHL GP 608
NHL SV% .915
NHL GA 1493
NHL WINS 271
GA by HHOF 500 Scorers 140
GP VS HHOF 500 Scorers 343
SV% VS HHOF 500 Scorers .881

ROGIE VACHON (1967–1982)

NHL GP 795
NHL SV% .896
NHL GA 2310
NHL WINS 353
GA by HHOF 500 Scorers 189
GP VS HHOF 500 Scorers 371
SV% VS HHOF 500 Scorers .856

TONY ESPOSITO (1969–1984)

NHL GP 886
NHL SV% .906
NHL GA 2563
NHL WINS 423
GA by HHOF 500 Scorers 182
GP VS HHOF 500 Scorers 367
SV% VS HHOF 500 Scorers .938

KEN DRYDEN (1971–1979)

NHL GP 397
NHL SV% .922
NHL GA 870
NHL WINS 258
GA by HHOF 500 Scorers 52
GP VS HHOF 500 Scorers 149
SV% VS HHOF 500 Scorers .878

BILLY SMITH (1972–1989)

NHL GP 679
NHL SV% .895
NHL GA 2031
NHL WINS 305
GA by HHOF 500 Scorers 178
GP VS HHOF 500 Scorers 335
SV% VS HHOF 500 Scorers .874

Goalies Stats

GRANT FUHR (1982–2000)

NHL GP 868

NHL SV% .887

NHL GA 2756

NHL WINS 403

GA by HHOF 500 Scorers 266

GP VS HHOF 500 Scorers 626

SV% VS HHOF 500 Scorers .859

PATRICK ROY (1985–2003)

NHL GP 1029

NHL SV% .910

NHL GA 2546

NHL WINS 484

GA by HHOF 500 Scorers 231

GP VS HHOF 500 Scorers 705

SV% VS HHOF 500 Scorers .888

ED BELFOUR (1989–2007)

NHL GP 963

NHL SV% .906

NHL GA 2317

NHL WINS 551

GA by HHOF 500 Scorers 148

GP VS HHOF 500 Scorers 559

SV% VS HHOF 500 Scorers .902

DOMINIK HASEK (1991–2008)

NHL GP 735

NHL SV% .922

NHL GA 1572

NHL WINS 389

GA by HHOF 500 Scorers 88

GP VS HHOF 500 Scorers 334

SV% VS HHOF 500 Scorers .910

MARTIN BRODEUR (1992–2015)

NHL GP 1266

NHL SV% .912

NHL GA 2781

NHL WINS 691

GA by HHOF 500 Scorers 109

GP VS HHOF 500 Scorers 453

SV% VS HHOF 500 Scorers .904

TURK BRODA
(1937–1952)

Maurice Richard (34 G in 60 GP)
Gordie Howe (20 G in 50 GP)

FRANK BRIMSEK
(1939–1950)

Maurice Richard (30 G in 56 GP)
Gordie Howe (12 G in 47 GP)

CHUCK RAYNER
(1941–1953)

Maurice Richard (42 G in 70 GP)
Gordie Howe (18 G in 61 GP)
Jean Beliveau (3 G in 2 GP)

WHO FACED WHOM?

BILL DURNAN
(1944–1950)

Gordie Howe (15 G in 44 GP)

HARRY LUMLEY
(1944–1960)

Maurice Richard (88 G in 150 GP)
Gordie Howe (58 G in 96 GP)
Jean Beliveau (25 G in 50 GP)
Johnny Bucyk (0 G in 8 GP)
Bobby Hull (11 G in 11 GP)
Frank Mahovlich (2 G in 15 GP)
Stan Mikita (0 G in 6 GP)

TERRY SAWCHUK
(1950–1970)

Maurice Richard (38 G in 103 GP)
Gordie Howe (23 G in 43 GP)
Jean Beliveau (68 G in 136 GP)
Johnny Bucyk (27 G in 98 GP)
Bobby Hull (48 G in 104 GP)
Frank Mahovlich (21 G in 76 GP)
Stan Mikita (18 G in 79 GP)
Phil Esposito (7 G in 27 GP)

Who Faced Whom?

GERRY CHEEVERS
(1962–1980)

Gordie Howe (17 G in 33 GP)
Jean Beliveau (7 G in 21 GP)
Bobby Hull (23 G in 26 GP)
Frank Mahovlich (13 G in 30 GP)
Stan Mikita (12 G in 33 GP)
Phil Esposito (1 Goal in 9 GP)
Gilbert Perreault (4 G in 13 GP)
Marcel Dionne (1 Goal in 11 GP)

Guy Lafleur (3 G in 14 GP)
Lanny McDonald (4 G in 14 GP)
Bryan Trottier (1 Goal in 7 GP)
Mike Bossy (5 G in 5 GP)
Mike Gartner (1 Goal in 3 GP)
Michel Goulet (0 G in 2 GP)
Wayne Gretzky (0 G in 1 Game)
Mark Messier (0 G in 1 Game)

EDDIE GIACOMIN
(1966–1977)

Gordie Howe (19 G in 48 GP)
Jean Beliveau (16 G in 43 GP)
Johnny Bucyk (21 G in 64 GP)
Bobby Hull (37 G in 44 GP)
Frank Mahovlich (21 G in 57 GP)
Stan Mikita (22 G in 58 GP)
Phil Esposito (24 G in 63 GP)

Gilbert Perreault (4 G in 13 GP)
Marcel Dionne (12 G in 19 GP)
Guy Lafleur (6 G in 20 GP)
Lanny McDonald (1 Goal in 8 GP)
Bryan Trottier (1 Goal in 4 GP)
Mike Bossy (0 G in 1 Game)

JOHNNY BOWER
(1954–1970)

Maurice Richard (19 G in 31 GP)
Gordie Howe (51 G in 99 GP)
Jean Beliveau (23 G in 88 GP)
Johnny Bucyk (18 G in 88 GP)

Bobby Hull (35 G in 77 GP)
Stan Mikita (17 G in 68 GP)
Phil Esposito (4 G in 25 GP)

GUMP WORSLEY
(1953–1974)

Maurice Richard (40 G in 71 GP)
Gordie Howe (69 G in 142 GP)
Jean Beliveau (54 G in 96 GP)
Johnny Bucyk (32 G in 111 GP)
Bobby Hull (50 G in 103 GP)
Frank Mahovlich (45 G in 99 GP)

Stan Mikita (25 G in 82 GP)
Phil Esposito (11 G in 35 GP)
Gilbert Perreault (3 G in 9 GP)
Marcel Dionne (3 G in 3 GP)
Guy Lafleur (0 G in 3 GP)
Lanny McDonald (0 G in 2 GP)

GLENN HALL
(1953–1971)

Maurice Richard (17 G in 51 GP)
Gordie Howe (44 G in 120 GP)
Jean Beliveau (68 G in 145 GP)
Johnny Bucyk (39 G in 126 GP)
Bobby Hull (5 G in 34 GP)
Frank Mahovlich (52 G in 127 GP)
Stan Mikita (4 G in 5 GP)
Phil Esposito (3 G in 12 GP)
Gilbert Perreault (0 G in 3 GP)

JACQUES PLANTE
(1953–1975)

Gordie Howe (54 G in 136 GP)
Jean Beliveau (10 G in 24 GP)
Johnny Bucyk (27 G in 110 GP)
Bobby Hull (37 G in 98 GP)
Frank Mahovlich (31 G in 98 GP)

Stan Mikita (28 G in 79 GP)
Phil Esposito (10 G in 17 GP)
Gilbert Perreault (2 G in 7 GP)
Marcel Dionne (1 Goal in 6 GP)
Guy Lafleur (1 Goal in 4 GP)

Who Faced Whom?

BERNIE PARENT
(1966–1979)

Gordie Howe (7 G in 22 GP)	Gilbert Perreault (7 G in 22 GP)
Jean Beliveau (3 G in 26 GP)	Marcel Dionne (5 G in 13 GP)
Johnny Bucyk (15 G in 35 GP)	Guy Lafleur (11 G in 22 GP)
Bobby Hull (14 G in 33 GP)	Lanny McDonald (4 G in 12 GP)
Frank Mahovlich (11 G in 26 GP)	Bryan Trottier (5 G in 13 GP)
Stan Mikita (15 G in 50 GP)	Mike Bossy (6 G in 9 GP)
Phil Esposito (37 G in 60 GP)	

ROGIE VACHON
(1967–1982)

Gordie Howe (8 G in 28 GP)	Marcel Dionne (13 G in 23 GP)	Wayne Gretzky (4 G in 6 GP)
Johnny Bucyk (11 G in 38 GP)	Guy Lafleur (29 G in 42 GP)	Mark Messier (2 G in 6 GP)
Bobby Hull (10 G in 26 GP)	Lanny McDonald (17 G in 32 GP)	Jari Kurri (1 Goal in 3 GP)
Frank Mahovlich (13 G in 28 GP)	Bryan Trottier (11 G in 22 GP)	Dino Ciccarelli (2 G in 3 GP)
Stan Mikita (13 G in 46 GP)	Mike Bossy (11 G in 13 GP)	Ron Francis (0 G in 1 Game)
Phil Esposito (21 G in 47 GP)	Mike Gartner (2 G in 7 GP)	Dale Hawerchuk (2 G in 2 GP)
Gilbert Perreault (17 G in 31 GP)	Michel Goulet (2 G in 8 GP)	Joe Mullen (1 Goal in 1 Game)

KEN DRYDEN
(1971–1979)

Johnny Bucyk (9 G in 22 GP)	Marcel Dionne (8 G in 24 GP)
Bobby Hull (0 G in 15 GP)	Lanny McDonald (6 G in 18 GP)
Stan Mikita (3 G in 17 GP)	Bryan Trottier (5 G in 12 GP)
Phil Esposito (8 G in 24 GP)	Mike Bossy (4 G in 7 GP)
Gilbert Perreault (6 G in 20 GP)	

TONY ESPOSITO
(1969–1984)

Gordie Howe (9 G in 17 GP)	Marcel Dionne (13 G in 38 GP)	Mark Messier (5 G in 14 GP)
Jean Beliveau (2 G in 12 GP)	Guy Lafleur (21 G in 27 GP)	Jari Kurri (2 G in 2 GP)
Johnny Bucyk (14 G in 34 GP)	Lanny McDonald (9 G in 26 GP)	Dino Ciccarelli (8 G in 10 GP)
Bobby Hull (0 G in 1 Game)	Bryan Trottier (12 G in 27 GP)	Ron Francis (1 G in 4 GP)
Frank Mahovlich (6 G in 18 GP)	Mike Bossy (20 G in 17 GP)	Dale Hawerchuk (4 G in 7 GP)
Stan Mikita (1 Goal in 1 Game)	Mike Gartner (4 G in 11 GP)	Joe Mullen (2 G in 3 GP)
Phil Esposito (24 G in 41 GP)	Michel Goulet (4 G in 8 GP)	
Gilbert Perreault (11 G in 33 GP)	Wayne Gretzky (6 G in 14 GP)	

BILLY SMITH
(1972–1989)

Johnny Bucyk (15 G in 19 GP)	Dino Ciccarelli (5 G in 10 GP)
Frank Mahovlich (1 Goal in 5 GP)	Ron Francis (0 G in 6 GP)
Stan Mikita (8 G in 21 GP)	Dale Hawerchuk (7 G in 12 GP)
Phil Esposito (8 G in 26 GP)	Joe Mullen (7 G in 11 GP)
Gilbert Perreault (7 G in 35 GP)	Dave Andreychuk (7 G in 14 GP)
Marcel Dionne (5 G in 25 GP)	Steven Yzerman (1 Goal in 3 GP)
Guy Lafleur (7 G in 26 GP)	Mario Lemieux (7 G in 10 GP)
Lanny McDonald (7 G in 25 GP)	Brett Hull (3 G in 4 GP)
Mike Gartner (15 G in 24 GP)	Joe Nieuwendyk (1 Goal in 4 GP)
Michel Goulet (7 G in 45 GP)	Luc Robitaille (3 G in 3 GP)
Wayne Gretzky (10 G in 13 GP)	Brendan Shanahan (0 G in 3 GP)
Mark Messier (4 G in 27 GP)	Joe Sakic (3 G in 1 Game)
Jari Kurri (7 G in 10 GP)	

GRANT FUHR
(1982–2000)

Gilbert Perreault (6 G in 6 GP)	Jari Kurri (1 Goal in 13 GP)	Luc Robitaille (16 G in 36 GP)
Marcel Dionne (12 G in 27 GP)	Dino Ciccarelli (10 G in 30 GP)	Brendan Shanahan (14 G in 37 GP)
Guy Lafleur (1 Goal in 8 GP)	Ron Francis (9 G in 20 GP)	Mark Recchi (5 G in 13 GP)
Lanny McDonald (17 G in 36 GP)	Dale Hawerchuk (20 G in 41 GP)	Joe Sakic (7 G in 18 GP)
Bryan Trottier (5 G in 16 GP)	Joe Mullen (17 G in 37 GP)	Mike Modano (13 G in 24 GP)
Mike Bossy (8 G in 11 GP)	Dave Andreychuk (9 G in 25 GP)	Mats Sundin (9 G in 18 GP)
Mike Gartner (11 G in 26 GP)	Steven Yzerman (15 G in 43 GP)	Teemu Selanne (7 G in 19 GP)
Michel Goulet (6 G in 18 GP)	Mario Lemieux (9 G in 15 GP)	Jarome Iginla (3 G in 7 GP)
Wayne Gretzky (6 G in 15 GP)	Brett Hull (9 G in 17 GP)	Marian Hossa (0 G in 2 GP)
Mark Messier (0 G in 12 GP)	Joe Nieuwendyk (21 G in 36 GP)	

Who Faced Whom?

MARTIN BRODEUR
(1992–2015)

Mike Gartner (1 Goal in 7 GP)
Michel Goulet (0 G in 2 GP)
Wayne Gretzky (5 G in 18 GP)
Mark Messier (4 G in 30 GP)
Jari Kurri (0 G in 5 GP)
Dino Ciccarelli (2 G in 10 GP)
Ron Francis (4 G in 37 GP)
Dale Hawerchuk (0 G in 7 GP)
Joe Mullen (1 Goal in 10 GP)
Dave Andreychuk (6 G in 20 GP)
Steven Yzerman (0 G in 10 GP)
Mario Lemieux (10 G in 19 GP)

Brett Hull (7 G in 16 GP)
Joe Nieuwendyk (1 Goal in 14 GP)
Luc Robitaille (2 G in 21 GP)
Brendan Shanahan (6 G in 30 GP)
Mark Recchi (10 G in 49 GP)
Joe Sakic (10 G in 21 GP)
Mike Modano (4 G in 18 GP)
Mats Sundin (9 G in 32 GP)
Teemu Selanne (4 G in 24 GP)
Jarome Iginla (7 G in 14 GP)
Marian Hossa (16 G in 39 GP)

DOMINIK HASEK
(1991–2008)

Bryan Trottier (0 G in 5 GP)
Mike Gartner (3 G in 9 GP)
Michel Goulet (1 Goal in 2 GP)
Wayne Gretzky (2 G in 12 GP)
Mark Messier (1 Goal in 16 GP)
Jari Kurri (1 Goal in 8 GP)
Dino Ciccarelli (4 G in 13 GP)
Ron Francis (3 G in 32 GP)
Dale Hawerchuk (1 Goal in 6 GP)
Dave Andreychuk (4 G in 16 GP)
Steven Yzerman (2 G in 7 GP)
Mario Lemieux (3 G in 11 GP)

Brett Hull (2 G in 12 GP)
Joe Nieuwendyk (4 G in 7 GP)
Luc Robitaille (4 G in 14 GP)
Brendan Shanahan (6 G in 13 GP)
Mark Recchi (6 G in 29 GP)
Joe Sakic (7 G in 26 GP)
Mike Modano (10 G in 19 GP)
Mats Sundin (10 G in 31 GP)
Teemu Selanne (7 G in 20 GP)
Jarome Iginla (4 G in 12 GP)
Marian Hossa (3 G in 14 GP)

PATRICK ROY
(1985–2003)

Gilbert Perreault (1 Goal in 7 GP)
Marcel Dionne (1 Goal in 3 GP)
Lanny McDonald (1 Goal in 5 GP)
Bryan Trottier (2 G in 16 GP)
Mike Bossy (1 G in 3 GP)
Mike Gartner (10 G in 28 GP)
Michel Goulet (14 G in 24 GP)
Wayne Gretzky (6 G in 22 GP)
Mark Messier (9 G in 35 GP)
Jari Kurri (5 G in 19 GP)
Dino Ciccarelli (2 G in 22 GP)
Ron Francis (15 G in 50 GP)
Dale Hawerchuk (8 G in 31 GP)
Joe Mullen (7 G in 22 GP)

Dave Andreychuk (17 G in 46 GP)
Steven Yzerman (14 G in 35 GP)
Mario Lemieux (8 G in 20 GP)
Brett Hull (16 G in 38 GP)
Joe Nieuwendyk (7 G in 30 GP)
Luc Robitaille (16 G in 36 GP)
Brendan Shanahan (17 G in 37 GP)
Mark Recchi (4 G in 23 GP)
Joe Sakic (7 G in 29 GP)
Mike Modano (12 G in 39 GP)
Mats Sundin (14 G in 30 GP)
Teemu Selanne (10 G in 28 GP)
Jarome Iginla (7 G in 23 GP)
Marian Hossa (0 G in 4 GP)

ED BELFOUR
(1989–2007)

Marcel Dionne (0 G in 1 Game)
Guy Lafleur (0 G in 2 GP)
Bryan Trottier (0 G in 6 GP)
Mike Gartner (6 G in 22 GP)
Wayne Gretzky (1 G in 19 GP)
Mark Messier (6 G in 25 GP)
Jari Kurri (3 G in 18 GP)
Dino Ciccarelli (4 G in 18 GP)
Ron Francis (3 G in 19 GP)
Dale Hawerchuk (2 G in 12 GP)
Joe Mullen (0 G in 4 GP)
Dave Andreychuk (6 G in 30 GP)
Steven Yzerman (19 G in 54 GP)

Mario Lemieux (4 G in 7 GP)
Brett Hull (22 G in 50 GP)
Joe Nieuwendyk (4 G in 16 GP)
Luc Robitaille (10 G in 35 GP)
Brendan Shanahan (19 G in 52 GP)
Mark Recchi (1 Goal in 19 GP)
Joe Sakic (6 G in 24 GP)
Mike Modano (5 G in 29 GP)
Mats Sundin (9 G in 24 GP)
Teemu Selanne (11 G in 36 GP)
Jarome Iginla (1 G in 17 GP)
Marian Hossa (6 G in 20 GP)

Scoring against Hall of Famers
Richard vs. Howe: Goal 1 to 544

During their days together in the NHL, hockey
fans debated which one was the greatest player.
Who fared better against the best goalies?

Bill Durnan

▶ Howe: 15 (44 GP)
Richard: 0 (0 GP)

Glenn Hall

▶ Howe: 34 (82 GP)
Richard: 17 (51 GP)

Gump Worsley

▶ Howe: 58 (115 GP)
Richard: 40 (71 GP)

Jacques Plante

▶ Howe: 41 (108 GP)
Richard: 0 (0 GP)

HOWE
309 / 544 GOALS

VS.

RICHARD
308 / 544 GOALS

Johnny Bower

▶ Howe: 41 (72 GP)
Richard: 19 (31 GP)

Chuck Rayner

▶ Richard: 42 (70 GP)
Howe: 18 (61 GP)

Frank Brimsek

▶ Richard: 30 (56 GP)
Howe: 12 (47 GP)

Turk Broda

▶ Richard: 34 (60 GP)
Howe: 20 (50 GP)

▶ Richard: 88 (150 GP)
Howe: 58 (96 GP)

▶ Richard: 38 (103 GP)
Howe: 12 (21 GP)

Scoring against Hall of Famers
Hull vs. Mikita as Black Hawks (1958—72)

Bobby Hull was the greatest goal-scorer
of his day. Teammate **Stan Mikita** was a
record playmaker with a knack for the net.

▶ Hull: 37 (98 GP)
  Mikita: 28 (79 GP)

Jacques Plante

▶ Hull: 50 (103 GP)
  Mikita: 25 (81 GP)

Gump Worsley

▶ Hull: 37 (44 GP)
  Mikita: 22 (50 GP)

Eddie Giacomin

▶ Hull: 23 (26 GP)
  Mikita: 10 (27 GP)

Gerry Cheevers

▶ Hull: 1 (1 GP)
  Mikita: 0 (1 GP)

Billy Smith

▶ Hull: 11 (11 GP)
  Mikita: 0 (6 GP)

Harry Lumley

▶ Hull: 5 (5 GP)
  Mikita: 4 (5 GP)

Glenn Hall

▶ Hull: 48 (104 GP)
  Mikita: 18 (79 GP)

Terry Sawchuk

▶ Hull: 9 (24 GP)
  Mikita: 8 (29 GP)

Rogie Vachon

▶ Hull: 35 (77 GP)
  Mikita: 17 (68 GP)

Johnny Bower

Hull: 14 (33 GP)
Mikita: 14 (35 GP)

Bernie Parent

▶ Mikita: 1 (1 GP)
  Hull: 0 (1 GP)

Tony Esposito

HULL
270 / 591 GOALS

VS.

MIKITA
147 / 374 GOALS

Bossy vs. Trottier as Islanders (1977—87)

Mike Bossy seemed born to be a goal scorer. Bryan
Trottier helped set him up, but he could score too.

Bernie Parent

▶ Bossy: 6 (9 GP)
Trottier: 5 (13 GP)

▶ Bossy: 8 (11 GP)
Trottier: 5 (12 GP)

Grant Fuhr

Gerry Cheevers

▶ Bossy: 5 (5 GP)
Trottier: 1 (7 GP)

▶ Bossy: 20 (17 GP)
Trottier: 12 (27 GP)

Tony Esposito

BOSSY
55 / 573 GOALS

VS.

TROTTIER
40 / 440 GOALS

Patrick Roy

▶ Bossy: 1 (3 GP)
Trottier: 0 (5 GP)

Bossy: 11 (13 GP)
Trottier: 11 (22 GP)

Rogie Vachon

▶ Trottier: 1 (4 GP)
Bossy: 0 (1 GP)

▶ Trottier: 5 (12 GP)
Bossy: 4 (7 GP)

Scoring against Hall of Famers
Lafleur vs. Dionne: The French Connection

As French Canadian superstars and the top two picks in the 1971 NHL Draft, Guy Lafleur and Marcel Dionne will always be linked.

Lafleur as a Rookie (4/29 goals)   ### Dionne as a Rookie (9/28 goals)

| Bernie Parent | Billy Smith | Jacques Plante | Rogie Vachon | Eddie Giacomin | Gerry Cheevers | Gump Worsley | Ken Dryden |
| 1 Goal | 1 Goal | 1 Goal | 1 Goal Each | 3 Goals | 1 Goal | 1 Goal | 3 Goals |

▶ Lafleur: 11 (22 GP)
Dionne: 5 (13 GP)

Bernie Parent

▶ Lafleur: 3 (4 GP)
Dionne: 1 (3 GP)

Patrick Roy

▶ Lafleur: 7 (26 GP)
Dionne: 5 (25 GP)

Billy Smith

▶ Lafleur: 21 (27 GP)
Dionne: 13 (38 GP)

Tony Esposito

▶ Lafleur: 3 (14 GP)
Dionne: 1 (11 GP)

Gerry Cheevers

LAFLEUR
82 / 560 GOALS

VS.

DIONNE
74 / 731 GOALS

▶ Lafleur: 29 (42 GP)
Dionne: 13 (23 GP)

Rogie Vachon

Lafleur: 1 (4 GP)
Dionne: 1 (6 GP)

Jacques Plante

▶ Dionne: 12 (19 GP)
Lafleur: 6 (20 GP)

Eddie Giacomin

▶ Dionne: 3 (3 GP)
Lafleur: 0 (3 GP)

Gump Worsley

▶ Dionne: 12 (27 GP)
Lafleur: 1 (8 GP)

▶ Dionne: 8 (24 GP)
Lafleur: 0 (0 GP)

Scoring against Hall of Famers
Hull Sr. vs. Hull Jr.

They say, "Like father, like son." Is that true when it comes
to the Hulls facing Hockey Hall of Fame goalies?

BERNIE PARENT
14 goals
(33 GP)

BILLY SMITH
1 goals
(2 GP)

HARRY LUMLEY
1 goals
(11 GP)

JACQUES PLANTE
37 goals
(98 GP)

EDDIE GIACOMIN
37 goals
(44 GP)

GERRY CHEEVERS
23 goals
(26 GP)

JOHNNY BOWER
35 goals
(77 GP)

ROGIE VACHON
10 goals
(26 GP)

GLENN HALL
5 goals
(5 GP)

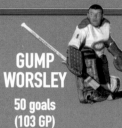

GUMP WORSLEY
50 goals
(103 GP)

BOBBY HULL
44% OF GOALS VS HHOF
(270/610)

VS.

BRETT HULL
8% OF GOALS VS HHOF
(59/741)

TERRY SAWCHUK
48 goals
(104 GP)

BILLY SMITH
3 goals (4 GP)

GRANT FUHR
9 goals (17 GP)

DOMINIK HASEK
2 goals (12 GP)

MARTIN BRODEUR
7 goals (16 GP)

ED BELFOUR
22 goals (50 GP)

PATRICK ROY
16 goals (38 GP)

Scoring against Hall of Famers
The Espositos: Tony vs. Phil (1968–81)

Two brothers. Two Hall of Famers.
How did Tony and Phil do head-to-head?

VS.

PHIL ESPOSITO

CAREER HEAD-TO-HEAD (41 GAMES)
BROTHER G/S%: 24 /13.8
TOTAL G/S%: 608 /14.1

TONY ESPOSITO

CAREER HEAD-TO-HEAD (41 GAMES)
BROTHER SV%: .861
TOTAL SV%: .911

1968–69 (3 GAMES)

> PHIL <
BROTHER G/S%: 4/15.3
TOTAL G/S%: 49/14.0

TONY
BROTHER SV%: .733
TOTAL SV%: .919

1969–70 (8 GAMES)

PHIL
BROTHER G/S%: 2/6.2
TOTAL G/S%: 43/10.6

> TONY <
BROTHER SV%: .953
TOTAL SV%: .932

1970–71 (4 GAMES)

> PHIL <
BROTHER G/S%: 4/17.4
TOTAL G/S%: 76/13.8

TONY
BROTHER SV%: .826
TOTAL SV%: .919

1971–72 (3 GAMES)

> PHIL <
BROTHER G/S%: 4/28.5
TOTAL G/S%: 66/15.5

TONY
BROTHER SV%: .714
TOTAL SV%: .934

1972–73 (3 GAMES)

PHIL
BROTHER G/S%: 1/6.3
TOTAL G/S%: 55/13.4

> TONY <
BROTHER SV%: .938
TOTAL SV%: .917

1973–74 (5 GAMES)

PHIL
BROTHER G/S%: 2/10.0
TOTAL G/S%: 68/17.3

TONY
BROTHER SV%: .900
TOTAL SV%: .929

1974–75 (3 GAMES)

PHIL
BROTHER G/S%: 0/0
TOTAL G/S%: 61/17.6

> TONY <
BROTHER SV%: 1.000
TOTAL SV%: .906

1975–76 (1 GAME)

> PHIL <
BROTHER G/S%: 1/33.3
TOTAL G/S%: 35/12.8

TONY
BROTHER SV%: .667
TOTAL SV%: .905

1976–77 (2 GAMES)

> PHIL <
BROTHER G/S%: 2/20.0
TOTAL G/S%: 34/9.9

TONY
BROTHER SV%: .800
TOTAL SV%: .901

1977–78 (2 GAMES)

PHIL
BROTHER G/S%: 1/8.4
TOTAL G/S%: 38/14.6

> TONY <
BROTHER SV%: .917
TOTAL SV%: .914

1978–79 (1 GAME)

> PHIL <
BROTHER G/S%: 1/50.0
TOTAL G/S%: 42/19.5

TONY
BROTHER SV%: .500
TOTAL SV%: .902

1979–80 (4 GAMES)

> PHIL <
BROTHER G/S%: 1/11.1
TOTAL G/S%: 34/13.9

TONY
BROTHER SV%: .889
TOTAL SV%: .903

1980–81 (2 GAMES)

> PHIL <
BROTHER G/S%: 1/1.00
TOTAL G/S%: 7/7.1

TONY
BROTHER SV%: 0
TOTAL SV%: .890

Scoring against Hall of Famers
The Oilers: Gretzky, Kurri and Messier (1980—88)

Wayne Gretzky made the Oilers go, but Mark Messier and Jari Kurri were superstars too. How did these HHOF 500-goal scorers do against the best goalies?

WAYNE GRETZKY

Billy Smith

9
GOALS
(11 GP)

Patrick Roy

4
GOALS
(6 GP)

Tony Esposito

6
GOALS
(12 GP)

> **19 / 586** GOALS

> **1000** ASSISTS

JARI KURRI

Billy Smith
7 GOALS (10 GP)

Tony Esposito
7 GOALS (7 GP)

Patrick Roy
2 GOALS (9 GP)

Rogie Vachon
1 GOALS (3 GP)

> 17 / 397 GOALS   > 451 ASSISTS

MARK MESSIER

Billy Smith
4 GOALS (8 GP)

Tony Esposito
5 GOALS (12 GP)

Patrick Roy
1 GOALS (8 GP)

Rogie Vachon
1 GOALS (4 GP)

> 11 / 290 GOALS   > 424 ASSISTS

Best 50 in 50

Whether it's 50 goals in 50 games (or in a record 39), how many of those goals were scored against future Hall-of-Fame goalies.

50 Goals in 50 Games >>> March 18, 1945

Maurice RICHARD

Goals	Date	Goalie	
5	December 28, 1944	Harry Lumley	
1	January 12, 1945	Harry Lumley	
3	January 21, 1945	Harry Lumley	
1	February 3, 1945	Harry Lumley	
1	February 4, 1945	Harry Lumley	
2	February 4, 1945	Harry Lumley	
1	March 10, 1945	Harry Lumley	

50 Goals in 50 Games >>> January 24, 1981

Mike BOSSY

Goals	Date	Goalie	
3	November 8, 1980	Tony Esposito	

50 Goals in 39 Games >>> December 30, 1981

Wayne GRETZKY

Goals	Date	Goalie	
1	October 18, 1981	Tony Esposito	
1	December 23, 1981	Billy Smith	

January 7, 1984 ◀◀◀ **50 Goals in 42 Games**

Wayne GRETZKY

Goals	Date	Goalie	
1	December 13, 1983	Billy Smith	

January 26, 1985 ◀◀◀ **50 Goals in 49 Games**

Wayne GRETZKY

Goals	Date	Goalie	
1	December 5, 1984	Billy Smith	

January 20, 1989 ◀◀◀ **50 Goals in 46 Games**

Mario LEMIEUX

Goals	Date	Goalie	
0	–	–	

January 25, 1991 ◀◀◀ **50 Goals in 49 Games**

Brett HULL

Goals	Date	Goalie	
1	October 27, 1990	Patrick Roy	
1	December 2, 1990	Ed Belfour	
1	December 26, 1990	Ed Belfour	

January 28, 1992 ◀◀◀ **50 Goals in 50 Games**

Brett HULL

Goals	Date	Goalie	
2	November 20, 1991	Grant Fuhr	
1	December 22, 1991	Ed Belfour	
1	December 26, 1991	Ed Belfour	
1	January 6, 1992	Grant Fuhr	
3	January 16, 1992	Patrick Roy	

Scoring against Hall of Famers
Original 6

Between 1942 and 1967, which HHOF 500 goal scorers
come out on top against Hall of Fame Goalies?

MAURICE RICHARD
(1943–60 | 592 GP)

308

Goalie	Goals
Turk Broda	34
Frank Brimsek	30
Chuck Rayner	42
Harry Lumley	88
Terry Sawchuk	38
Glenn Hall	17
Gump Worsley	40
Johnny Bower	19
Total:	308

GORDIE HOWE
(1947–67 | 863 GP)

385

Goalie	Goals
Turk Broda	20
Frank Brimsek	12
Chuck Rayner	18
Bill Durnan	15
Harry Lumley	58
Terry Sawchuk	23
Glenn Hall	43
Jacques Plante	53
Gump Worsley	66
Johnny Bower	49
Gerry Cheevers	13
Eddie Giacomin	10
Rogie Vachon	3
Bernie Parent	2
Total:	385

JEAN BELIVEAU
(1951–67 | 569 GP)

259

Goalie	Goals
Chuck Rayner	3
Harry Lumley	25
Terry Sawchuk	67
Glenn Hall	66
Jacques Plante	8
Gump Worsley	54
Johnny Bower	23
Gerry Cheevers	2
Eddie Giacomin	9
Bernie Parent	2
Total:	259

JOHNNY BUCYK
(1956–67 | 561 GP)

151

Goalie	Goals
Harry Lumley	0
Terry Sawchuk	27
Glenn Hall	39
Jacques Plante	27
Gump Worsley	29
Johnny Bower	18
Eddie Giacomin	8
Bernie Parent	1
Rogie Vachon	2
Total:	151

FRANK MAHOVLICH
(1957–67 | 427 GP)

160

Goalie	Goals
Harry Lumley	2
Terry Sawchuk	21
Glenn Hall	50
Jacques Plante	25
Gump Worsley	40
Gerry Cheevers	8
Eddie Giacomin	9
Bernie Parent	4
Rogie Vachon	1
Total:	160

BOBBY HULL
(1958–67 | 423 GP)

217

Goalie	Goals
Harry Lumley	11
Terry Sawchuk	47
Glenn Hall	4
Jacques Plante	32
Gump Worsley	47
Johnny Bower	35
Eddie Giacomin	23
Gerry Cheevers	10
Bernie Parent	6
Rogie Vachon	2
Total:	217

STAN MIKITA
(1959–67 | 351 GP)

102

Goalie	Goals
Harry Lumley	0
Terry Sawchuk	17
Glenn Hall	0
Jacques Plante	24
Gump Worsley	20
Johnny Bower	15
Eddie Giacomin	12
Gerry Cheevers	5
Bernie Parent	8
Rogie Vachon	1
Total:	102

PHIL ESPOSITO
(1964–67 | 142 GP)

45

Goalie	Goals
Terry Sawchuk	7
Glenn Hall	2
Jacques Plante	3
Gump Worsley	5
Johnny Bower	4
Eddie Giacomin	7
Gerry Cheevers	0
Bernie Parent	11
Rogie Vachon	6
Total:	45

How did these Hall of Famers fare against each other on the biggest stage?

Total NHL playoff games played
Total NHL playoff goals
NHL playoff goals against HHOF
HHOF goalies faced in the NHL playoffs
NHL playoff games played against HHOF

MAURICE RICHARD (1943–1960)

NHL GP 132
NHL GOALS 82
HHOF FACED 8
NHL GP VS HHOF 74
NHL GOALS VS HHOF 38

GORDIE HOWE (1947–1980)

NHL GP 157
NHL GOALS 68
HHOF FACED 9
NHL GP VS HHOF 125
NHL GOALS VS HHOF 55

JEAN BELIVEAU (1951–1971)

NHL GP 162
NHL GOALS 79
HHOF FACED 8
NHL GP VS HHOF 122
NHL GOALS VS HHOF 52

JOHNNY BUCYK (1956–1978)

NHL GP 124
NHL GOALS 41
HHOF FACED 10
NHL GP VS HHOF 99
NHL GOALS VS HHOF 22

FRANK MAHOVLICH (1957–1978)

NHL GP 137
NHL GOALS 51
HHOF FACED 9
NHL GP VS HHOF 88
NHL GOALS VS HHOF 33

BOBBY HULL (1958–1980)

NHL GP 119
NHL GOALS 62
HHOF FACED 8
NHL GP VS HHOF 76
NHL GOALS VS HHOF 35

STAN MIKITA (1959–1980)

NHL GP 155
NHL GOALS 59
HHOF FACED 9
NHL GP VS HHOF 98
NHL GOALS VS HHOF 37

PHIL ESPOSITO (1964–1981)

NHL GP 130
NHL GOALS 61
HHOF FACED 11
NHL GP VS HHOF 81
NHL GOALS VS HHOF 37

GILBERT PERREAULT (1971–1987)

NHL GP 90
NHL GOALS 33
HHOF FACED 4
NHL GP VS HHOF 46
NHL GOALS VS HHOF 20

MARCEL DIONNE (1972–1989)

NHL GP 49
NHL GOALS 21
HHOF FACED 3
NHL GP VS HHOF 22
NHL GOALS VS HHOF 10

GUY LAFLEUR (1972–1991)

NHL GP 128
NHL GOALS 58
HHOF FACED 4
NHL GP VS HHOF 45
NHL GOALS VS HHOF 13

Playoffs Stats: Scorers

LANNY MCDONALD (1974–1989)
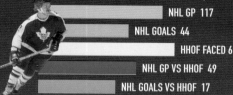
- NHL GP 117
- NHL GOALS 44
- HHOF FACED 6
- NHL GP VS HHOF 49
- NHL GOALS VS HHOF 17

BRYAN TROTTIER (1976–1994)
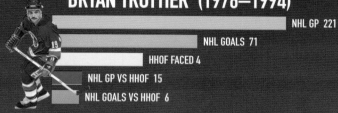
- NHL GP 221
- NHL GOALS 71
- HHOF FACED 4
- NHL GP VS HHOF 15
- NHL GOALS VS HHOF 6

MIKE BOSSY (1978–1987)
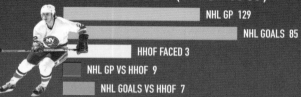
- NHL GP 129
- NHL GOALS 85
- HHOF FACED 3
- NHL GP VS HHOF 9
- NHL GOALS VS HHOF 7

MIKE GARTNER (1979–1998)

- NHL GP 122
- NHL GOALS 43
- HHOF FACED 3
- NHL GP VS HHOF 24
- NHL GOALS VS HHOF 6

MICHEL GOULET (1979–1994)

- NHL GP 92
- NHL GOALS 39
- HHOF FACED 3
- NHL GP VS HHOF 6
- NHL GOALS VS HHOF 2

WAYNE GRETZKY (1979–1999)
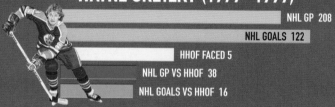
- NHL GP 208
- NHL GOALS 122
- HHOF FACED 5
- NHL GP VS HHOF 38
- NHL GOALS VS HHOF 16

MARK MESSIER (1979–2004)
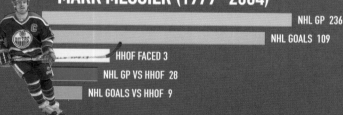
- NHL GP 236
- NHL GOALS 109
- HHOF FACED 3
- NHL GP VS HHOF 28
- NHL GOALS VS HHOF 9

JARI KURRI (1980–1998)
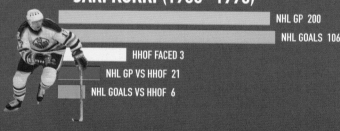
- NHL GP 200
- NHL GOALS 106
- HHOF FACED 3
- NHL GP VS HHOF 21
- NHL GOALS VS HHOF 6

DINO CICCARELLI (1981–1999)
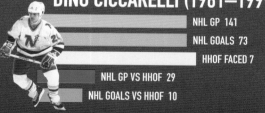
- NHL GP 141
- NHL GOALS 73
- HHOF FACED 7
- NHL GP VS HHOF 29
- NHL GOALS VS HHOF 10

RON FRANCIS (1982–2004)
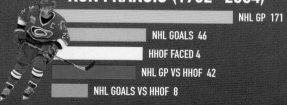
- NHL GP 171
- NHL GOALS 46
- HHOF FACED 4
- NHL GP VS HHOF 42
- NHL GOALS VS HHOF 8

DALE HAWERCHUK (1982–1997)

- NHL GP 97
- NHL GOALS 30
- HHOF FACED 3
- NHL GP VS HHOF 23
- NHL GOALS VS HHOF 6

JOE MULLEN (1982–1997)
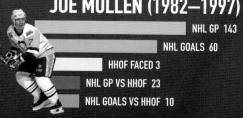
- NHL GP 143
- NHL GOALS 60
- HHOF FACED 3
- NHL GP VS HHOF 23
- NHL GOALS VS HHOF 10

DAVE ANDREYCHUK (1983–2006)
- NHL GP 162
- NHL GOALS 43
- HHOF FACED 3
- NHL GP VS HHOF 37
- NHL GOALS VS HHOF 10

STEVE YZERMAN (1984–2006)
- NHL GP 196
- NHL GOALS 70
- HHOF FACED 4
- NHL GP VS HHOF 62
- NHL GOALS VS HHOF 15

MARIO LEMIEUX (1985–2006)
- NHL GP 107
- NHL GOALS 76
- HHOF FACED 3
- NHL GP VS HHOF 17
- NHL GOALS VS HHOF 7

BRETT HULL (1987–2006)
- NHL GP 202
- NHL GOALS 103
- HHOF FACED 5
- NHL GP VS HHOF 50
- NHL GOALS VS HHOF 27

JOE NIEUWENDYK (1987–2007)
- NHL GP 158
- NHL GOALS 66
- HHOF FACED 4
- NHL GP VS HHOF 45
- NHL GOALS VS HHOF 15

LUC ROBITAILLE (1987–2006)
- NHL GP 159
- NHL GOALS 58
- HHOF FACED 3
- NHL GP VS HHOF 48
- NHL GOALS VS HHOF 17

BRENDAN SHANAHAN (1988–2009)
- NHL GP 184
- NHL GOALS 60
- HHOF FACED 5
- NHL GP VS HHOF 59
- NHL GOALS VS HHOF 13

MARK RECCHI (1989–2011)
- NHL GP 189
- NHL GOALS 61
- HHOF FACED 3
- NHL GP VS HHOF 50
- NHL GOALS VS HHOF 20

JOE SAKIC (1989–2009)
- NHL GP 172
- NHL GOALS 84
- HHOF FACED 4
- NHL GP VS HHOF 39
- NHL GOALS VS HHOF 16

MIKE MODANO (1990–2011)
- NHL GP 176
- NHL GOALS 58
- HHOF FACED 5
- NHL GP VS HHOF 49
- NHL GOALS VS HHOF 10

MATS SUNDIN (1991–2009)
- NHL GP 91
- NHL GOALS 38
- HHOF FACED 5
- NHL GP VS HHOF 31
- NHL GOALS VS HHOF 14

TEEMU SELANNE (1993–2014)
- NHL GP 130
- NHL GOALS 44
- HHOF FACED 2
- NHL GP VS HHOF 13
- NHL GOALS VS HHOF 7

JAROME IGINLA (1996–2017)
- NHL GP 81
- NHL GOALS 37
- HHOF FACED 1
- NHL GP VS HHOF 5
- NHL GOALS VS HHOF 2

MARIAN HOSSA (1997–2017)
- NHL GP 205
- NHL GOALS 52
- HHOF FACED 2
- NHL GP VS HHOF 14
- NHL GOALS VS HHOF 6

Playoffs Stats: Goalies

How did these Hall of Famers fare against each other on the biggest stage?

TURK BRODA (1937–1952)

- NHL GP 101
- NHL GA 211
- NHL SV% NA
- HHOF 500 Scorer: 2
- NHL GP VS HHOF 500 Scorer 23
- NHL GA VS HHOF 500 Scorer 5
- NHL SV% VS HHOF 500 Scorer NA

FRANK BRIMSEK (1939–1950)

- NHL GP 68
- NHL GA 186
- NHL SV% NA
- HHOF 500 Scorer: 1
- NHL GP VS HHOF 500 Scorer 10
- NHL GA VS HHOF 500 Scorer 6
- NHL SV% VS HHOF 500 Scorer NA

CHUCK RAYNER (1941–1953)

- NHL GP 18
- NHL GA 46
- NHL SV% NA
- HHOF 500 Scorer: 2
- NHL GP VS HHOF 500 Scorer 11
- NHL GA VS HHOF 500 Scorer 2
- NHL SV% VS HHOF 500 Scorer NA

BILL DURNAN (1944–1950)

- NHL GP 45
- NHL GA 99
- NHL SV% NA
- HHOF 500 Scorer: 1
- NHL GP VS HHOF 500 Scorer 7
- NHL GA VS HHOF 500 Scorer 8
- NHL SV% VS HHOF 500 Scorer NA

HARRY LUMLEY (1944–1960)

- NHL GP 76
- NHL GA 196
- NHL SV% NA
- HHOF 500 Scorer: 4
- NHL GP VS HHOF 500 Scorer 33
- NHL GA VS HHOF 500 Scorer 16
- NHL SV% VS HHOF 500 Scorer NA

TERRY SAWCHUK (1950–1970)

- NHL GP 106
- NHL GA 265
- NHL SV% .894*
- HHOF 500 Scorer: 6
- NHL GP VS HHOF 500 Scorer 118
- NHL GA VS HHOF 500 Scorer 52
- NHL SV% VS HHOF 500 Scorer .887*

GLENN HALL (1953–1971)

- NHL GP 115
- NHL GA 320
- NHL SV% .909
- HHOF 500 Scorer: 6
- NHL GP VS HHOF 500 Scorer 86
- NHL GA VS HHOF 500 Scorer 40
- NHL SV% VS HHOF 500 Scorer .866

JACQUES PLANTE (1953–1975)

- NHL GP 112
- NHL GA 235
- NHL SV% .920
- HHOF 500 Scorer: 7
- NHL GP VS HHOF 500 Scorer 87
- NHL GA VS HHOF 500 Scorer 27
- NHL SV% VS HHOF 500 Scorer .833*

GUMP WORSLEY (1953–1974)

- NHL GP 70
- NHL GA 189
- NHL SV% .909
- HHOF 500 Scorer: 9
- NHL GP VS HHOF 500 Scorer 59
- NHL GA VS HHOF 500 Scorer 22
- NHL SV% VS HHOF 500 Scorer .833

JOHNNY BOWER (1954–1970)

- NHL GP 74
- NHL GA 180
- NHL SV% .921
- HHOF 500 Scorer: 7
- NHL GP VS HHOF 500 Scorer 78
- NHL GA VS HHOF 500 Scorer 33
- NHL SV% VS HHOF 500 Scorer .893

GERRY CHEEVERS (1962–1980)

NHL GP 88
NHL GA 242
NHL SV% .902
HHOF 500 Scorer: 6
NHL GP VS HHOF 500 Scorer 53
NHL GA VS HHOF 500 Scorer 26
NHL SV% VS HHOF 500 Scorer .844

EDDIE GIACOMIN (1966–1977)

NHL GP 65
NHL GA 180
NHL SV% .897
HHOF 500 Scorer: 7
NHL GP VS HHOF 500 Scorer 80
NHL GA VS HHOF 500 Scorer 26
NHL SV% VS HHOF 500 Scorer .901

BERNIE PARENT (1966–1979)

NHL GP 71
NHL GA 174
NHL SV% .916
HHOF 500 Scorer: 4
NHL GP VS HHOF 500 Scorer 45
NHL GA VS HHOF 500 Scorer 11
NHL SV% VS HHOF 500 Scorer .924

ROGIE VACHON (1967–1982)

NHL GP 48
NHL GA 133
NHL SV% .907
HHOF 500 Scorer: 7
NHL GP VS HHOF 500 Scorer 32
NHL GA VS HHOF 500 Scorer 6
NHL SV% VS HHOF 500 Scorer .931

TONY ESPOSITO (1969–1984)

NHL GP 48
NHL GA 133
NHL SV% .907
HHOF 500 Scorer: 12
NHL GP VS HHOF 500 Scorer 87
NHL GA VS HHOF 500 Scorer 51
NHL SV% VS HHOF 500 Scorer .830

KEN DRYDEN (1971–1979)

NHL GP 112
NHL GA 274
NHL SV% .915
HHOF 500 Scorer: 6
NHL GP VS HHOF 500 Scorer 64
NHL GA VS HHOF 500 Scorer 23
NHL SV% VS HHOF 500 Scorer .894

BILLY SMITH (1972–1989)

NHL GP 132
NHL GA 346
NHL SV% .905
HHOF 500 Scorer: 9
NHL GP VS HHOF 500 Scorer 106
NHL GA VS HHOF 500 Scorer 36
NHL SV% VS HHOF 500 Scorer .887

GRANT FUHR (1982–2000)

NHL GP 150
NHL GA 430
NHL SV% .898
HHOF 500 Scorer: 14
NHL GP VS HHOF 500 Scorer 131
NHL GA VS HHOF 500 Scorer 54
NHL SV% VS HHOF 500 Scorer .868

PATRICK ROY (1985–2003)

NHL GP 247
NHL GA 584
NHL SV% .918
HHOF 500 Scorer: 18
NHL GP VS HHOF 500 Scorer 216
NHL GA VS HHOF 500 Scorer 72
NHL SV% VS HHOF 500 Scorer .887

ED BELFOUR (1989–2007)

NHL GP 161
NHL GA 359
NHL SV% .920
HHOF 500 Scorer: 13
NHL GP VS HHOF 500 Scorer 134
NHL GA VS HHOF 500 Scorer 47
NHL SV% VS HHOF 500 Scorer .889

DOMINIK HASEK (1991–2008)

NHL GP 119
NHL GA 246
NHL SV% .925
HHOF 500 Scorer: 10
NHL GP VS HHOF 500 Scorer 69
NHL GA VS HHOF 500 Scorer 17
NHL SV% VS HHOF 500 Scorer .918

MARTIN BRODEUR (1992–2015)

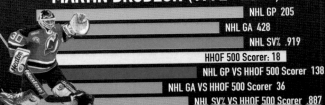

NHL GP 205
NHL GA 428
NHL SV% .919
HHOF 500 Scorer: 18
NHL GP VS HHOF 500 Scorer 138
NHL GA VS HHOF 500 Scorer 36
NHL SV% VS HHOF 500 Scorer .887

Calder Season
Scorers

How do these standout rookie seasons
look up against Hall of Famers?

FRANK MAHOVLICH
1957–58
Goals **20**

14
Goals against
HHOFers

 GLENN HALL 5 goals
 JACQUES PLANTE 5 goals
 GUMP WORSLEY 3 goals
  TERRY SAWCHUK 1 goals

BRYAN TROTTIER
1975–76
Goals **32**

5
Goals against
HHOFers

 KEN DRYDEN 1 goals
 ROGIE VACHON 4 goals

MIKE BOSSY
1977–78
Goals **53**

13
Goals against
HHOFers

 BERNIE PARENT 6 goals
GERRY CHEEVERS 1 goals
 KEN DRYDEN 2 goals
 ROGIE VACHON 1 goals
 TONY ESPOSITO 3 goals

DALE HAWERCHUK
1981–82
Goals **45**

6
Goals against
HHOFers

 TONY ESPOSITO 4 goals
 ROGIE VACHON 2 goals

MARIO LEMIEUX
1984–85
Goals **43**

3
Goals against
HHOFers

 BILLY SMITH 2 goals
 GRANT FUHR 1 goals

JOE NIEUWENDYK
1987–88
Goals **51**

5
Goals against
HHOFers

 GRANT FUHR 4 goals
 PATRICK ROY 1 goals

TEEMU SELANNE
1992–93
Goals **76**

0
Goals against
HHOFers

Calder Season
Goalies

How do these standout rookie seasons
look up against Hall of Famers?

FRANK BRIMSEK
1938–39

HHOF GA **0**
TOTAL GA **68**

TERRY SAWCHUK
1950–51

HHOF GA **7**
TOTAL GA **138**

> MAURICE
RICHARD
7 goals

GUMP WORSLEY
1952–53

HHOF GA **14**
TOTAL GA **151**

GORDIE
HOWE
7 goals

MAURICE
RICHARD
7 goals

GLENN HALL
1955–56

HHOF GA **11**
TOTAL GA **147**

JEAN
BELIVEAU
11 goals

TONY ESPOSITO
1969–70

HHOF GA **17** | HHOF SV% **.864**
TOTAL GA **136** | TOTAL SV% **.932**

FRANK
MAHOVLICH
4 goals

GORDIE
HOWE
4 goals

PHIL
ESPOSITO
2 goals

JOHNNY
BUCYK
6 goals

JEAN
BELIVEAU
1 goals

KEN DRYDEN
1971–72

HHOF GA **6** | HHOF SV% **.928**
TOTAL GA **142** | TOTAL SV% **.930**

JOHNNY
BUCYK
1 goals

MARCEL
DIONNE
3 goals

PHIL
ESPOSITO
2 goals

ED BELFOUR
1990–91

HHOF GA **12** | HHOF SV% **.930**
TOTAL GA **170** | TOTAL SV% **.910**

BRETT
HULL
4 goals

DALE
HAWERCHUK
1 goals

MATS
SUNDIN
1 goals

JOE
NIEUWENDYK
1 goals

JOE
SAKIC
1 goals

LUC
ROBITAILLE
1 goals

MIKE
MODANO
1 goals

STEVE
YZERMAN
2 goals

Scoring Title

Which scoring-title winners had to go through the most Hall of Famers?

■ Non-HHOF goals　　■ HHOF goals

MAURICE RICHARD

1944–45	15/50 goals
1946–47	25/45 goals
1949–50	31/43 goals
1953–54	19/37 goals
1954–55	21/38 goals

GORDIE HOWE

1950–51	22/43 goals
1951–52	17/47 goals
1952–53	21/49 goals
1956–57	18/44 goals
1962–63	23/38 goals

JEAN BELIVEAU

1955–56	39/47 goals
1958–59	30/45 goals

BOBBY HULL

1959–60	32/39 goals
1961–62	30/50 goals
1963–64	17/43 goals
1965–66	29/54 goals
1966–67	21/52 goals
1967–68	24/44 goals
1968–69	16/58 goals

PHIL ESPOSITO

1969–70	14/43 goals
1970–71	15/76 goals
1971–72	15/66 goals
1972–73	8/55 goals
1973–74	10/68 goals
1974–75	11/61 goals

1977—78   6/60 goals

MIKE BOSSY

1978—79   9/69 goals
1980—81   10/68 goals

WAYNE GRETZKY

1981—82   3/92 goals
1982—83   3/71 goals
1983—84   1/87 goals
1984—85   1/73 goals
1986—87   2/62 goals

JARI KURRI

1985—86   1/68 goals

MARIO LEMIEUX

1987—88   6/70 goals
1988—89   2/85 goals
1995—96   8/69 goals

BRETT HULL

1989—90   4/72 goals
1990—91   5/86 goals
1991—92   9/70 goals

TEEMU SELANNE

1992—93   0/76 goals
1997—98   0/52 goals
1998—99   9/47 goals

JAROME IGINLA

2001—02   5/52 goals
2003—04   0/41 goals

TURK BRODA

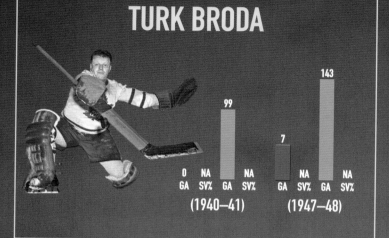

99
0 NA NA
GA SV% GA SV%
(1940–41)

7   143
NA   NA
SV%   SV%
(1947–48)

FRANK BRIMSEK

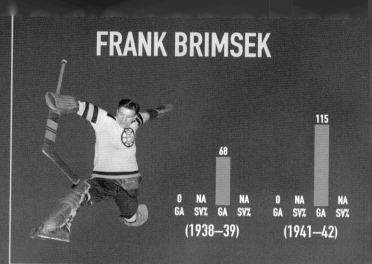

68
0 NA NA
GA SV% GA SV%
(1938–39)

115
0 NA NA
GA SV% GA SV%
(1941–42)

BILL DURNAN

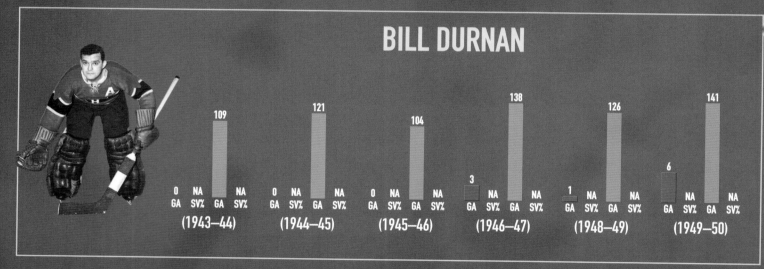

109
0 NA NA
GA SV% GA SV%
(1943–44)

121
0 NA NA
GA SV% GA SV%
(1944–45)

104
0 NA NA
GA SV% GA SV%
(1945–46)

138
3 NA NA
GA SV% GA SV%
(1946–47)

126
1 NA NA
GA SV% GA SV%
(1948–49)

141
6 NA NA
GA SV% GA SV%
(1949–50)

HARRY LUMLEY

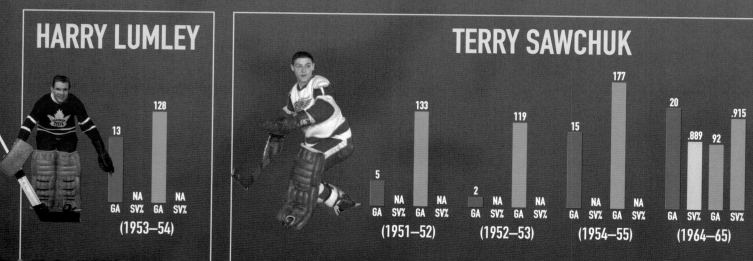

128
13 NA NA
GA SV% GA SV%
(1953–54)

TERRY SAWCHUK

133
5 NA NA
GA SV% GA SV%
(1951–52)

119
2 NA NA
GA SV% GA SV%
(1952–53)

177
15 NA NA
GA SV% GA SV%
(1954–55)

20 .889 92 .915
GA SV% GA SV%
(1964–65)

Vezina

Legend: ■ HHOF 500 Goal GA ■ HHOF 500 Goal SV% ■ Total season GA ■ Total season SV%

GLENN HALL

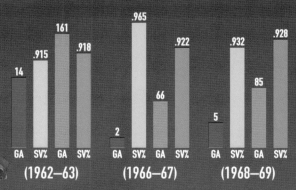

- (1962–63): GA 14, SV% .915, GA 161, SV% .918
- (1966–67): GA 2, SV% .965, GA 66, SV% .922
- (1968–69): GA 5, SV% .932, GA 85, SV% .928

GUMP WORSLEY

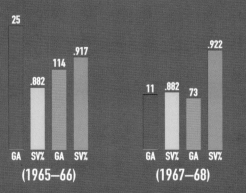

- (1965–66): GA 25, SV% .882, GA 114, SV% .917
- (1967–68): GA 11, SV% .882, GA 73, SV% .922

JOHNNY BOWER

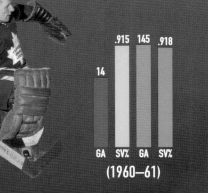
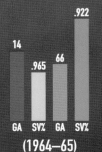

- (1960–61): GA 14, SV% .915, GA 145, SV% .918
- (1964–65): GA 14, SV% .965, GA 66, SV% .922

JACQUES PLANTE

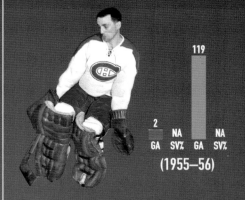
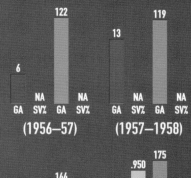
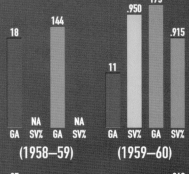
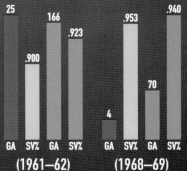

- (1955–56): GA 2, SV% NA, GA 119, SV% NA
- (1956–57): GA 6, SV% NA, GA 122, SV% NA
- (1957–1958): GA 13, SV% NA, GA 119, SV% NA
- (1958–59): GA 18, SV% NA, GA 144, SV% NA
- (1959–60): GA 11, SV% .950, GA 175, SV% .915
- (1961–62): GA 25, SV% .900, GA 166, SV% .923
- (1968–69): GA 4, SV% .953, GA 70, SV% .940

Vezina

EDDIE GIACOMIN

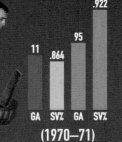

11 .864 95 .922

GA SV% GA SV%

(1970–71)

BERNIE PARENT

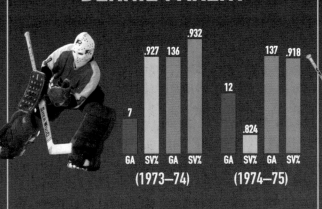

7 .927 136 .932 12 .824 137 .918

GA SV% GA SV% GA SV% GA SV%

(1973–74) (1974–75)

ROGIE VACHON

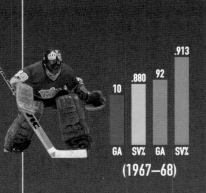

10 .880 92 .913

GA SV% GA SV%

(1967–68)

KEN DRYDEN

7 .885 119 .926 | 8 .875 121 .927 | 7 .870 117 .920 | 8 .826 105 .922 | 5 .915 108 .909

GA SV% GA SV% GA SV% GA SV% GA SV% GA SV% GA SV% GA SV% GA SV% GA SV%

(1972–73) (1975–76) (1976–77) (1977–78) (1978–79)

BILLY SMITH

9 .855 133 .898

GA SV% GA SV%

(1981–82)

TONY ESPOSITO

16 .877 136 .932 | 3 .909 82 .934 | 8 .887 141 .929

GA SV% GA SV% GA SV% GA SV% GA SV% GA SV%

(1969–70) (1971–72) (1973–74)